TEENAGE
GIRLS

TEENAGE GIRLS

A Parent's Survival Manual

LAUREN K. AYERS, Ph.D.

CROSSROAD • NEW YORK

1994

The Crossroad Publishing Company
370 Lexington Avenue, New York, NY 10017

Copyright © 1994 by Lauren Ayers

Printed in the United States of America

Library of Congress Cataloging-in-Publication Data

Ayers, Lauren K.
    Teenage girls : a parent's survival manual / Lauren K. Ayers.
    p. cm.
    ISBN 0-8245-1356-8
    1. Teenage girls. 2. Teenage girls—Psychology. 3. Parent and
teenager.   I. Title.
HQ798.A82 1994
649'.125—dc20
                          93-48386
                             CIP

To
Florida Wilford, Bertha Hinkel,
and Johanna deHaan

Contents

Four
CRISES _____ 185

PREFACE

YOU'RE PROBABLY doing a better job with your daughter than you think, but if this is a bad day, it won't seem so. This book comes from a wide range of experiences with teenage girls, some at their best and some at their worst, but all of them struggling to be women.

I have seen teenage girls stay up all night baking to raise money for homeless families and girls who would fight their own shyness to make a handicapped veteran laugh. I have seen young heroines, girls who cook, clean, raise younger brothers and sisters, go to school and hold a job, all the while with unbounded hope for the future.

I have also seen girls who sold drugs, or themselves, or both, girls who hated everyone and seemed intent on destroying everything good and beautiful in and around themselves, girls who wanted nothing more than for life to be over and done with. I have puzzled at the difference between the heroines and the defeated, but learned from Melissa, who at fifteen was indicted for arson and attempted murder and who said, when asked how she would raise her children: "I'll teach them about life."

I have seen my own daughters struggle with challenge and complexity, sometimes defeated, sometimes triumphant, and I have wondered how we can help them all to be their best, to reach all that they dream, because we love them as parents, and because as a society, we cannot afford to lose them.

Raising daughters isn't much different from raising a garden; it is slow, steady work and requires attention every day, with respect for the givens of the situation. There are no secrets, no magic words, and you can never be completely sure of the outcome. Sunshine, cultivation, weeding, over the long course of a growing season usually produce a result, and so it is with girls.

The main elements in parenting are kindness, which is love

demonstrated, nurturing or caring for a girl's need, and teaching, which weeds out her unproductive behaviors. It takes a long time for these things to have an effect, so if you must measure your success as a parent, it is best done when your daughter reaches thirty; measures before then are apt to be misleading.

But I would encourage you to avoid measuring yourself as a parent, to enjoy the ride and do the best that you can. For if you care about a teenage girl, and how she grows up, you have already offered her more than the rest of the human race can provide. For far too many girls, there is no one at all who cares. When you love a teenage girl, the rest is footnotes on technique.

There is no guaranteed way to raise a teenage girl successfully, and this book does not offer the final answer. It does provide many ideas when you are stuck in trying to solve a problem that doesn't yield to your efforts. We are all test pilots when we try to raise human beings, and rather than looking for answers, we need to expand our creative repertoires so that we have many tricks in our bags.

There are so many problems that come up during a girl's adolescence that a parent can quickly feel besieged and inadequate, and it is easy to forget our long-term goals as we try to patch through problems, crises, and sometimes an emergency. The objective is to help a girl to become a capable, reasonably happy woman, one who can use her talents and values to create a life for herself. It is parents who do this, in alliance with a girl, and the result is an adult companion and relative who enriches our lives and hers. The path to adulthood is through problems, crises, and perhaps an emergency, and these are the opportunities for shaping and molding and for changing our relationship with a daughter. To survive the experience of a daughter's adolescence requires that we change as parents, that we see ourselves and our offspring differently, for when we do, we grow as much as she does.

ACKNOWLEDGMENTS

S INCERE THANKS to the faculty and students of Voorheesville High School, St. Anne's Institute for Girls, Guilder-
land High School, Andrew Jackson High School, Emma
Willard School for Girls, Albany Academy for Girls, Academy
of the Holy Names, Hebrew Academy, Troy High School, and
others.

Deep appreciation is due the staff at the Voorheesville Public
Library, particularly Gail Alter Sacco, and the Bethlehem Public Library, for their help. The Bethlehem Writers Group was a
wonderful source of support.

The technical wizardry of Steve Ayers and the research skills
of Andrew Ayers were invaluable in producing this book. Eliza-
beth and Philip Roberts were of great help and support at many
points.

The encouragement, support, and practical help offered by
Michael Leach and his staff at the Crossroad Publishing Co.
made this book a joy to write. Bill Van Ornum was a fine person
to work with, and John Eagleson was thorough and skilled.

Finally, a few of the many girls who helped with this book
need to be thanked: Jennifer, JaNine, Emily, Jessie, Florelle,
Jessie, Precious, Chrystal, Carmina, Margaret, Anne, Denise,
Rita, LaVerne, Huan, Deena, Gayle, Annabelle, Lisa, Aleysha,
Shilie, Sandy, Julie, Angela, Karen, Debbie, Maud, Kidane,
Romi, Janice, Kathleen, Nancy, Maribel, and many others.

INTRODUCTION

T HINK OF TWO YOUNG TEENAGERS, both pretty and healthy, with the lovely youthful sparkle that comes from energy and optimism. The first is working hard in a science laboratory on a project aiming to discover the effect of pollution on grain harvesting. The second is working hard to try to support herself and her two small children.

The life potential for each of these young women is sharply different: the one is constricted and hemmed in by responsibilities, while the other has all of life's options open. The value of the two to the culture is a clear contrast as well; the one is an asset, the other a liability. All adolescent girls have dreams and hopes, but for many, life's options will begin to narrow early.

This book is about raising teenage girls in such a way that all of life's opportunities remain open to them, allowing them to create rather than accept their futures. It presents a view of females as indispensable to American society, their perspective, talents, and creativity essential to the healthy evolution of American culture.

What do we raise teenage girls toward?

Most of our childrearing with girls teaches them to be obedient and respectful, and we see teenage girls as most difficult when they violate these norms. When a girl is surly, sassy, belligerent, defiant, rebellious, uncooperative, insensitive, argumentative, or hostile, she is not the "good little girl" we like, and she seems most out of character. It is difficult to see how a troublesome teenage girl can become a healthy, strong woman. It is easy to yearn for the return of the sweet, submissive child.

But something important happens to a girl at puberty, a constriction of her world and future, so that she sees her possibilities as more limited and less contingent on her choices. She sees herself as taking second place to boys and may prefer to do so as a way to be taken care of by a theoretically stronger person. It is at this point that girls begin to minimize their own talents and to avoid selecting high-prestige occupations as goals. As in the 1950s, a girl begins to foresee her life as determined by the man she marries.

In adolescent competitions during puberty, girls begin to drop back, slow down, and avoid showing their best efforts, as though this were a sort of sacrifice to placate fate. By seventh grade, girls have learned that the bright, high-achieving girl is vulnerable to social ostracism. Do girls need to see boys as stronger and wiser? Boys do not seem to be excessively driven by the need to be stronger and wiser and in several studies have shown a tendency to choose bright, high-achieving girls as partners. Do girls create this difference in order to make boys something they need them to be?

What is the future for girls who do not conform to the society's expectations that they be obedient and sweet? It may be that resistant and defiant girls have more promising futures, since in their determination to shape their own view of the world they are least interested in conforming to the wishes of others.

Underneath the problematical behaviors that we see so frequently with teenage girls are drives that a youngster tries to satisfy with whatever resources she has available. Her need to be important, respected, and powerful are all positive motivations. If we can help her to meet these needs in a way that fits her, not only will we avoid problems, but we will more fully utilize her talents, raising her self-esteem and providing a great resource for the society at large.

A girl's first priority cannot be getting along with parents or behaving properly in order not to embarrass the family. Instead, it must be learning to speak her truth clearly and kindly and to persevere in her efforts until she satisfies herself. To develop qualities for a productive life, such as courage, perseverance, and independent judgment, she will need a great deal of teaching and practice.

Women are important to the culture beyond the development of their unique talents. Even with all of the changes of recent years, it is still women who raise children, and the future of the society takes shape in the exchanges between mother and child. Along with the new approaches and thinking that females will bring to government, industry, the arts, and education, girls will set the tone for families and children.

Given the central role of females in American culture, what do we offer them in their growing-up years? A large set of discouraging predictions, if the statistics are to be believed. The suicide rate for teen girls has tripled in the past three decades, and the years from fifteen to nineteen are a peak time for serious depression. Twenty percent of teenage girls report attempting suicide. Phobia disorders, panic disorder, and obsessive compulsive disorder all typically begin in these years, and mostly afflict women. One teenage girl in ten gets pregnant every year, which is twice the rate of other industrialized countries. There are about 1.5 million homeless adolescents, including runaways, street youths, throwaways, and system kids, and about sixty thousand of them are afflicted with AIDS. Police in New York City report that there are twenty thousand runaways in the city at any given time. Prostitution to keep oneself fed while on the streets generally begins by age fourteen, but can start younger.

What is the cost to the individual and the culture of this human waste? In terms of corrective and supportive services, lost girls represent an entire industry, and an expensive one as well. The price in lost talents, wasted ability, burned-out energy, and hopelessness is immeasurable.

Some of the difficulty in raising competent adult females originates in underestimating the skills needed to be a capable and effective woman in whatever course of life one chooses. Girls often have to find their own way, learning by trial and error, because there is little guidance in how to be an effective and productive woman. And the larger culture is unsure about a woman's place. There is ambivalence about women who work outside the home and use child care, a restless sense that perhaps the children are not getting what they need. But there is also doubt about whether women can be truly satisfied with remaining at home as homemakers, mothers, and wives.

In the 1950s, 80 percent of college students were men, as compared to 46 percent in 1989. In those days, two-thirds of

women did not complete college, opting for marriage instead.*
In the 1960s surveys showed that women judged themselves as
successful if their children were accomplished and their husbands were prominent. But women have increasingly sought
to make their own independent and unique contributions, as
shown in the increase of women in the various professions:

	1960	1990
% women who work	34.8	57.8
lawyers & judges	7,500	180,000
doctors	15,672	108,200
engineers	7,404	174,000[†]

But the role of woman as mother has changed very little
in the intervening years, except perhaps to become more demanding, since men have taken less of a role in the culture in
childrearing. Far from being more involved, the number of men
who desert their children or who fail to support them financially has increased dramatically, and if a woman is divorced,
there is only a 10 percent chance that her children's father will
support them.

What does this mean for women raising children, a job that
usually takes up about one-quarter of a woman's life? It means
that the sole responsibility for nurturing and financing children
often lies with her, with little help from a partner. There are
certainly exceptions, and many of them, but the general trend is
for women to carry the job of childraiser and provider. It would
seem that the stretching of women's competence would raise
their self-esteem, but this is not necessarily the case.

Women's confidence levels seem to follow cultural values,
and so women often have a limited view of their own abilities.
This begins early when, for example, in middle school, girls rate
their math ability as lower than their actual aptitude, a prejudice also shown by their mothers in assessing a girl's talents.
For women supporting children, or contemplating doing so, the
result can be a search for a fantasy spouse who will assume the
burden of parent and provider. Some women will marry men

---

*Claudia Wallis, "Women Face the '90's, *Time,* December 4, 1989, 80.
†Wallis, "Women Face the '90's," 82.

who are chronically underachieving and unsupportive, but the fantasy of the good provider will be projected onto them, while a woman does the work of supporting the household.

Parenthood is a time-limited occupation, and a woman's vista can change radically as her children become independent adults. Eighty percent of married women can expect to be widowed at some point in their lives, surviving their husbands by an average of sixteen years. If a woman has developed her own abilities, this can be a rewarding time.

Without realizing it, women have entered a new era where the old choices no longer exist in the same form. Marriage is far less available as a choice, with many men choosing not to marry or become involved in traditional family relationships. Homosexuality in males and females has changed the form of American families as well. In most of these transitions, women have continued to be responsible for the care of children.

Across these conflicts cuts a different consideration, the economic and market changes of past decades. For many families, to provide what children seem to require demands that both adults be income producers; single mothers are rarely supported by fathers or anyone else and therefore are forced to depend on themselves, or the state, to care for their children financially.

Children are dependent, but women are not intrinsically so, although whoever takes care of children assumes some of their dependent status. Raising children requires full-time child care *and* full-time income-producing, and often these two jobs fall to one person. This is most often a woman, and often a single one with no help. Most girls simply don't envision their lives this way when they are younger and are not prepared for life's eventualities. Boys are clearer about their future and the need to become income producers. Among girls, one-quarter will become unmarried mothers, with many more becoming single as their children grow up.* Child support payments to women are extremely low, averaging $2460 annually, and even under court order one-third of all support is never paid.†

---

*Robert Pear, "Bigger Number of Newer Mothers Are Unmarried," *New York Times*, December 4, 1991, A20.

†U.S.Bureau of the Census, Child Support and Alimony, 1983, Current Population Reports, Series P-23, no. 148 (Washington, D.C.: U.S. Government Printing Office, 1986).

In the last years of this millennium, Western culture appears to use its youth poorly, expecting little significant contribution to the society and seeing youth as followers rather than as leaders. This is a change in the culture; in earlier days young people were seen to have greater value, for example, in the great movement westward, when pioneers were often teenagers and their energy, courage, and creativity were well utilized for themselves and for the benefit of the larger society. There were far fewer problems of low self-esteem in that period; teenagers were an integral part of the community.

Have we any use for our teenage girls, or must we make work for them to convince them that they are valuable to the society? Have they nothing to offer that is essential or that can make them genuinely important? And if we have not, how can it be that a country with so many problems can afford to waste the skills and creativity of so many of its members or to ask them to sit still until they are adults?

As we raise teenage girls, it is important to convey that they are necessary to our communities and our nation, a message quite different from telling them that we love them. But we can communicate their value only by using their talents, demanding their energy and creativity and courage, and letting them draw the obvious conclusion about themselves from the difference they make.

Why parents struggle with raising teenage girls

Adolescence is a time of interesting and occasionally frightening problems, all of which offer the chance for a girl to learn more and to become a stronger and more capable person. One-third of girls will experience problems and difficulties during this period, enough to concern their parents, while another one-third will have smooth sailing, with little upset in the household. Another third will have severe difficulties of the sort that interfere with the normal course of growth.

Most of our efforts with teenage girls in educational programs seem to be geared toward preventing trouble and solving the problems they've created. Raising a teenage girl can seem like a test of survival for a parent, with a bewildering array of demands and difficulties and a not-too-friendly youngster as a partner.

The result for many parents is a choice between endless battles or withdrawal, with the latter resulting in girls raising themselves. Much current parental anguish may be the result of the eclipsing of parental wisdom in the 1960s and 1970s, a period of great turbulence, where generations were in conflict and traditional ways of raising children became suspect. Unfortunately, old ways of teaching skills have not been replaced by new ways of doing so. Instead, much of the endeavor seems to have been abandoned.

If girls fail to become competent in the years before womanhood, then their need for help will be transferred from parents to others, perhaps a boyfriend or a peer group. Becoming a mother herself might seem to a girl like a shortcut to adult competence.

Parents teach a girl three things: how to care for herself, how to get along with others, and how to set a course for life. Problems with teen girls usually represent a difficulty in one or all of these areas.

When parents love and care for us, they give us a sense of value and teach us those habits that guard our health and open our future. A loving relationship with parents offers an opportunity to learn how to get along lovingly with others. Perhaps the current generation of parents, needy themselves and alienated from the culture during their own adolescence, has lost the faith to raise another generation. Or perhaps this generation of parents accepts that a girl's adolescence will be as turbulent as its own.

How much do parents, and the culture in general, know about girls in the years ten to twenty? Relatively little, since this has not been an area of great research or clinical practice. Teen girls' problems or abilities have generated little interest, and instead academic theories dominate childrearing practice with little direct examination of girls in this period of transition, the most noteworthy exception being Carol Gilligan and her colleagues at Harvard.

Rarely does anybody ask teen girls about their opinions or their needs, even though most girls can reason, observe, and generate useful solutions. If teen girls were asked to work seriously at the problems of the society, perhaps their solutions would open new possibilities in areas like racism, unemployment, and crime.

There is little systematic observation of teenage girls, in the manner of the great Swiss psychologist Jean Piaget. Instead, adults assume that they know a girl's thoughts, feelings, and needs, and rarely do they verify their assumptions. Teenage girls just don't seem important enough to merit much attention, unless they cause trouble. We would do far better to adopt the stance of anthropologists in raising daughters, treating them as interesting aliens requiring close observation. It would also help to ask them what they think and then to listen to what they say.

Have the feminist movement and changes associated with it given us a better understanding of teenage girls? Generally not, for this movement has focused on women, female adults with a very different set of life contingencies. Teenage girls generally feel that they have more in common with teen boys than with women, for the power differential of child/adult overrides the gender difference. Women have more power than boy children, who have more power than girl children.

Learning about teenage girls requires an adult to cognitively and emotionally move over and allow room for another person, and this may be far more difficult to do with a girl than with a boy. Somehow, it seems legitimate for a boy to need more power, more independence, and more respect since we expect him to have these in his life. But to offer these to a girl seems to take her beyond her place, and so we limit our offerings and thus our receptiveness to her. To take a girl too seriously may seem like pandering to her and demeaning ourselves.

But it is really in this way that we come to know a girl and to begin to help her develop as a woman. For many years, psychology has looked for the origins of women in early childhood, a psychoanalytic orientation, and has sought for gender biases and restrictive parenting in the early years as an explanation for sexist differences: Did she play with dolls or trucks? Did she have to wear dresses? But these are the years when an organism is made human, and it is in adolescence that a girl becomes a woman. This is the period where her future as a woman takes shapes and form, and it is to this period that attention must be paid.

As teenage girls go, so go women

For a mother raising a daughter, adolescence is a period in which the mother is likely to reflect a great deal on her own upbringing, particularly her own adolescence, and the effect it has had on her life. Parenting is a powerful experience, and one that shapes a woman's later life as she begins to reevaluate her early choices.

A girl's relationship with a mother, however, must take second place to her development as a person, and it may be that she and her mother become very far apart in these years. How else can they come together as two women later in their lives? A mother's job is to make herself increasingly *less* necessary to a girl and more and more peripheral. A teenage girl needs to become far more than her parents' daughter.

For a parent, there may be sadness and anger or delight and confidence in raising a teenage girl, and often there are all of these. Along with the sense that time has been lost in living our lives comes the satisfaction in being able to help another from our own struggles. To approach this challenge fearlessly and with an open mind rewards us with a mature period of life transition for our daughters and for ourselves.

But as we look at teenage girls and try to help them to grow up better, it is wise to consider that there is nothing intrinsically more valuable in one life than in another. Parents need to pay as much attention to themselves as to a daughter.

This is a good time to throw out the guilt/inadequacy approach to childrearing. Even if we have raised ten teenage girls, we have not raised *this* teenage girl, and what works with her will be unique. Perhaps the most important lessons parents learn from raising many children are flexibility, creativity, and a sense of humor.

With the great number of books written about raising children, although there are relatively few written about raising teenage girls, there is not much good, practical advice available to parents. Most parents struggle to find solutions that will give their daughter help and themselves peace.

Raising a teenage daughter becomes easier if we get into the habit of changing ourselves to meet new challenges and opportunities in life. This need not be a threat to our confidence, but rather a chance to get closer to the life we had in mind.

It is the aim of this book to help parents and girls to do far more than to survive adolescence. Rather, what is wanted is a full utilization of all of the opportunities for growth and change that the stage of adolescence encompasses, which is also incidentally a parent's best strategy for surviving a teenage girl's adolescence and helping her to deal with its problems.

To be able to do this requires some understanding of the stranger in the house who used to be a little girl. Although it is always necessary to *listen* to a girl's thoughts, just as you would have her listen to yours, there are some basics that adults would benefit from keeping in mind.

Changing behavior, which initially sounds like a violation of a child's personality and uniqueness, is, after all, the point of raising children. If we do not change their behavior, they will not naturally evolve into civilized human beings, and instead will remain forever imprisoned by childish ways. Changing behavior is easier if we consider the task of teachers, who are employed for the specific purpose of changing childish behavior to adult behavior. But it is to parents that the primary responsibility falls, and there are many places where a parent needs to teach.

There are three levels of problems that develop in female adolescence, and all of them can be seen either as trials of endurance or as opportunities for promoting growth and accumulating wisdom and experience. At a moderate level are those difficulties that routinely turn up and cause us concern, but do not interrupt the course of growth, even though they may limit a youngster's learnings. When girls are sloppy or have nervous tics, when they fight with brothers or sisters or hog the bathroom, parents must intervene, if only to keep peace in the household.

But these are the first encounters with problems that will turn up again and again in life, and to a great extent our life's happiness depends on how good we are at teaching a girl competence in dealing in these areas. Problems in this period are the raw material that we work on to produce adult habits and behaviors.

Crises are those problems that interrupt a parent's routines and activities and force us to take action and offer help. They are usually sudden, causing parental anxiety and demanding that parents act. Crises can frighten a girl, or they may stimulate her as she enjoys the excitement and the attention of the moment. In either case, there is a need for action, usually a change in the course of things to a more promising course and a decision to intervene actively in a girl's life.

Emergencies take adults to a different level of concern, and they generally move a girl to an adult level of risk, with lifelong consequences. When there is an emergency, there is often little emotion and, instead, a drive to move a girl out of danger quickly. Following the emergency, there can be a full range of human feeling, as well as an emotional crisis.

Solving teenage problems as a way to prepare for a competent adulthood

Although it is difficult to be optimistic about the many problems in a teenage girl's life, they nonetheless present many opportunities for developing her judgment, increasing her confidence, refining her values, and helping her to learn from mistakes. They present opportunities that will not arise again as she goes off on her own after age eighteen.

Achievement and independence cannot be acquired readymade at her eighteenth birthday; they develop gradually, in small pieces, at an uneven pace. When we think of developing mental habits and behavioral practices that will stay with her for the next six decades of her life, we are more apt to take our time and give each exercise the attention it deserves. Teenage problems serve as the object lessons of maturity for a girl.

Furthermore, we need to aim to develop habits that will carry a girl through the typical range of adult female experiences, including holding a job and advancing and supporting herself and perhaps her family, forming an intimate partnership, raising children, being widowed, aging. Although the media have made a great distinction between women who work and women who stay home as caretakers, most women experience a combination of these in the course of their lives and so need a set of skills to cover all contingencies.

The types of skills needed include habits of thought, attitude, and behavior, done so often that they become automatic, like brushing our teeth, or eating with a fork. It is an economy to teach a girl a whole stack of competencies so that she can then use her time creatively to do those things that are uniquely hers rather than struggling lifelong with basic habits of self-care and personal organization. To be regular and orderly in dealing with life and its problems frees one for more adventurous pursuits.

One

INSIDE HER HEAD: TEEN GIRLS' THINKING

T HROUGHOUT HISTORY, in all cultures, it has generally been the young who have carried the civilization forward and insured its advances with their courage and creativity, and so youth has been seen as mystical, treasured, and a source of endless reward. In contrast, our culture, although valuing the physical appearance and vitality of youth, has little use for its energy and boldness.

Most of the teen years are spent in education and in preparation for jobs and adult life, leaving few options for other adolescent drives: adventure, pioneering, experimenting, and self-testing. And so, when young people are discussed by their elders, it is often with frustration and annoyance that they present so many problems.

It would be more useful to see our young people for what they are, an enormous resource for a society that is often tired and sterile. Adolescence is a time of creativity and energy, and if more of this resource were treasured and employed to deal with the many problems that the society faces, there would be far fewer places for young people to create problems.

Although youthful needs for valor are sometimes encouraged in boys, rarely is this the case with girls. Instead, female children are rewarded for being good rather than being courageous, for being agreeable rather than being independent, and for conforming rather than being creative. In return, girls can feel loved, cherished, and protected.

But in adolescence, the girl's bargain begins to come undone, for no matter how good and kind and strong her parents

13

are, they cannot get her what she wants. This can only occur through her own efforts, which set in motion a fundamental conflict between depending on parents and an old set of understandings or plunging into the limbo of self-reliance. It will take many years to resolve this conflict, and sometimes it is merely transferred to new relationships: a teacher, boyfriend, or husband.

In sorting out her stance, a teenage girl does most of the sorting inside her head, using recently developed mental abilities to turn over a variety of problems. Certain themes and dilemmas present themselves repeatedly, and they seem to capture the essence of a girl's conflicts.

Because of the growth spurt of puberty, a teenage girl looks and talks much more like a woman than a girl, and her thinking is more like that of an adult, although still markedly limited. She becomes aware that her childhood powerlessness is not a life condition and there are places where she can be quite powerful. Along with this comes the realization that adulthood is not as easy as it looks and that many simple things, like driving a car, are hard to learn.

In all of her learnings there is a critical audience of other youngsters dealing with the same issues, and the fear of humiliation, real or projected, is potent. Strong emotions, the combined result of physical maturation, cognitive broadening, and changed circumstances, are a hallmark of adolescence, and teen girls struggle with understanding and utilizing their feelings. Exploring the inner self takes up a great deal of mental time in these years. The sense of splendid isolation and lonely uniqueness mark the personality separation from family and the beginning awareness of a singular and distinct self. But this is not a completely reliable self, and it often proves rather fickle as a leader. The indecision and procrastination that seem common in these years are the consequence of an unsure hand at the helm.

Excessive criticism of parents seems to be the common language of young teenage girls, but it disappears in the late teens, for by then it is no longer necessary for most girls. It helps younger girls to escape the all-too-familiar stance of dependent girl children and to build a stronger feminine adult image inside. Along with the internal view of a girl who is more than she seems comes a good deal of concern with how one looks on the outside.

A teenage girl's thinking, always simmering under her behavior, is the laboratory for experimenting with thousands of possibilities. It is a valuable crucible, for the more creative and productive her thinking, the more she is likely to construct a satisfying life for herself.

The following sections explore the major themes of female adolescent thinking.

Abilities: All of a sudden, I can do things I could never do before!

Recent research has shown that early human development does not occur evenly, with well-paced sequences, but is instead characterized by sudden spurts of growth.

A teenage girl may suddenly be able to do things she was unable to do before, or she may be surprised at her ease at doing things that six months ago were impossible. Since she now has to upwardly revise her estimates of herself, she may adopt this approach as a rule and consistently overestimate her abilities, thinking, "I am much more capable than I thought I was."

This overestimation may show up in the form of assurance in her own ability in things that she has not yet experienced, a generalization from one previous incident. She may say, with complete confidence, "I can handle the mail order tape club, there won't be any problem," while a parent can imagine the unwanted tapes arriving, not being returned, bills accumulating, and collection letters arriving. To point all this out to a young teenage girl is futile, however, for she will know herself differently and with a certainty adults rarely possess, for this is a confidence based on wishful thinking.

A young teen girl will also believe that she is a better judge of her capabilities than you are and will argue strongly for the right to have the last word here. It is not so much a matter of believing that she is invincible, which both teens and adults sometimes do, as believing that she knows herself better than you know her. Because she feels like a child when she is with her parents, she assumes that they must see her like a child and cannot see her newly developing abilities.

It is an amazing experience to go from a stupid state to a competent state, and a girl may feel at times that she has secret capacities, or capacities as yet unimagined, of limitless potential. Her capacities, further, seem unique and mysterious, produced and generated by herself, without any help at all from parents or anybody else. Although teen girls often blame others for their failures, rarely do they give others credit for their achievements.

Adults seem a poor substitute for teen creativity and expansiveness, and generally dull by comparison. When there are young female heroines in books or movies, admittedly a rarity, they are uniquely clever, achieving solutions to problems that adults could never produce

There is also an awareness of contrast: as a girl becomes more capable, her parents appear to become less so, and also quite tedious, offering the same observations and advice that she has heard from childhood, while she is brimming with new perceptions, observations, and possibilities. Is it any wonder that conversation between them is sometimes strained?

What's more, a girl becomes aware that parents, not infrequently, are mistaken about things. Awareness comes gradually, for example, when a parent is sure that a television program is on, but it isn't, or when a mother says to wear her boots or she'll catch cold, and she doesn't. The realization of adult fallibility develops from small and undramatic events, but they are events that carry great significance for a girl, for they change her estimates of her parents' reliability and wisdom.

Parental ideas for solutions to teenage problems, necessarily an arm's-length exercise, are similarly fallible. Parents seem quite assured of the success of their solutions ("If you would only try..."), but teen girls find that if they try a parent's suggestions, they often produce either no resolution or more problems. If a fifteen-year-old is concerned about her friend's using marijuana, a parent might well suggest that she talk to the girl's parents to alert them to the problem and get the girl some help. This might be a good solution for the smoker, since it involves her in fruitful discussion with her parents and gets her to reevaluate her behavior, but for our girl it is apt to be a disaster. She will be heartily resented by the smoker, ostracized by anyone else who has ever smoked, and seen as a tattler by most of her tenth-grade acquaintances. Most girls dodge a parent's advice of this sort, hopefully with some tact, and come up with other solutions, which may be more or less successful.

Much of adult error in this department is the result of adults being outside the teen group, with little direct information about teen norms or exposure to the adolescent subculture. The problems and difficulties that confront girls are real and usually accurately perceived, whereas adults are likely to insist that a girl's world is as they prefer to conceptualize it or remember it as from their own adolescence.

Girls also begin to notice that in many ways parents fail to meet their own standards. This cool observation includes the recognition that parents are not always fair or kindly, that they are not distinguishably admirable among other parents, and that they often do not practice all of the advice that they give their daughters. Sometimes they are truly horrible; they may drink, violate the law, or endanger a daughter's welfare. When adults truly fail as adults, it sets a limit on adult hypocrisy, and it gives a girl a standard that she can easily surpass.

Adolescence is an exciting period for a girl and may often involve matching wits with adults to test her own skill. She may not seem very deflated when she is shown to be wrong, but may be surprised and smug when she is right. Parents will no longer receive automatic deference or obedience, and orders and directions will increasingly be questioned. Arbitrary rules will be a real problem, and telling a girl, "Do it because I say so" will provoke a strong reaction.

Girls often get into the habit of discounting parental advice, ("You're just saying that because you're my mother"), rather than critically examining what is being said. A girl underestimates her parents' judgment because she generalizes from a few instances to the whole picture, and she assumes that her parents have value only as parents and are not otherwise competent adults.

There is a great range of adult wisdom, as anyone who lives in the society can observe, and there are plenty of instances where teen girls are more capable than their parents, although as a general rule this is not the case. The daughter of two parents dealing drugs comes to mind: her maturity and judgment at fourteen were far above theirs, putting her in an untenable position. Of greater importance, however, is the more common problem of getting a teenage girl to set aside her prejudice against her parents long enough to take seriously their advice.

Power: The escape from childhood and being treated like a child

For human beings at all stages of the life process, resistance is usually a sign of self-direction. When we see a teenage girl being mischievous, sneaky, or oppositional, we may attribute it to adolescent rebellion, but this is a trivialization of her behavior. She is more than "just rebellious," and to categorize a whole realm of human response in this way belittles it and robs it of significance.

The underground mentality, the strategy of subversion and opposition, that is observed in teens usually represents a first awareness of power differences in society and an attempt to achieve some power for themselves. This is a major change from childhood, when a girl might have been content to be a "good little girl" and accept the nurturing and protection of her betters. The rebellion and defiance we see in teen girls is often the only alternative to being owned by adults, but unfortunately, if pushed too far, it leads them to be more controlled by others.

But how does a female become powerful in this society? Girls register their awareness that some creatures are indeed powerless (e.g., puppies), and they relate with so much compassion that we can sense they identify with the position. This does not mean, of course, that a teenage girl will offer any real help to those who are powerless, even though she may have very strong feelings. The helpless, the poor, the disadvantaged may all stir her emotions, but not necessarily her efforts.

From an early age girls are aware of the power differentials in the larger culture: that older people are generally more powerful than children, that bigger people are more powerful than smaller, richer than poorer, and male than female. Girls also notice the characteristics of those who appear to have power in society, and they are most often white males. When girls think about the things they would like to have as adults and then are asked how to get them, their first response is usually, "marry a rich man."

This is not support for Freud's theories of women, which say that girls suffer from penis envy, castration anxiety, and the Electra complex, and that they are invariably inferior to males and resent that inadequacy, which results in their focus on superficial and transient issues. Nor is it proof that females are masochistic, weak, passive, unjust, irrational, or envious.

A teen girl's belief that marrying a rich man will insure a satisfying life is based on a childhood of observation. It is the understanding that all American presidents have been males, that if women have money, it is usually because their husbands were or are rich, and that even with all of the changes in society the power difference between males and females endures. It is the understanding that a girl's opinions usually don't count to anybody and that she is not expected to do very much with her life. It is the awareness that avenues to power are not welcoming to ordinary females. It is a teenage girl's observation that she cannot walk home alone from the library alone at night, in contrast to her male friends, and that if she stays in the library studying all evening, this will not been seen as standard teen girl behavior. If she passes up dates for more ambitious pursuits, someone will question the wisdom of her choice. It is the awareness that nobody ever speaks of a woman as a "good catch" or a "good provider" and that there are few powerful females that she can copy or learn from, women who have made their own lives and are self-reliant and happy. It is the observation that it often seems impossible to be her own person. It is the sudden awareness of the status that she holds on the lowest rung of the social ladder, where she has little value for anyone beyond those who love her. These are the experiences that change her responses and may frighten, confuse, or antagonize her.

Ignorance: Why are adult skills so hard to learn?

The number of things we need to learn to be a competent adult, not brilliant, but just able to get around in the culture, is astounding, and most of them must be learned in the years between ten and twenty. For a girl, these include the ability to:

make purchases in stores	pay income taxes	use the washing machine
select items wisely	meet strangers	handle job interviews
wear clothes properly	refuse a date	report a crime
use a checkbook	plan a party	register and vote
travel safely	clean a room	visit a sick person
drive a car	use table manners	handle menstrual cycles
cook meals	wear evening dress	get a prescription filled

There are myriad things that a teen girl must learn, and rarely does she learn effectively from random trial and error. Teaching from skilled and patient adults is far more economical for everyone. Adults generally lose sight of the vast storehouse of knowledge needed to be a functioning adult and are always a bit surprised when adolescents have trouble learning something or do not automatically know it. Reading a map or using a gas credit card are unfamiliar experiences and are best learned through instruction and practice.

For many years it has been the belief that adolescents think differently in the area of risk-taking from the way adults do and that they believe that they are invincible. This is the explanation generally given for their higher mortality and injury rates. Recent research, however, suggests a different conclusion. Looking at adults and teens with regard to tasks of critical thinking, Quadrell and Davis found in their continuing research program that teenagers do not see themselves as invulnerable or at a higher level than adults. This is explainable on two bases.*

First, adults often behave as though *they* were invincible, for example, in their driving habits, sexual practices, and health protection. It is difficult to make the case that American adults behave in ways that assume vulnerability to accident or disease,

---

*M. J. Quadrel, B. Fischoff, and W. Davis, "Adolescent (In)vulnerability," *American Psychologist*, 1993, 102.

and adolescent behavior mirrors adult patterns. The types of risks, however, are very different for the two groups. Teenagers are more ignorant than adults and have less information and experience, and so it is difficult for them to estimate accurately their level of competence and the probability of negative consequences. An icy road to a new driver is not so much a test of logical thinking as it is a test of experience and self-awareness.

In addition, the decisions that teens make are often more critical in terms of risk, with more enduring consequences. Choices about finishing high school or involvement in a sexual relationship are powerful and may structure the rest of a youngster's life, and so they are high-risk issues. Adult patterns are often more routinized, with needs and rewards built into patterns of everyday living, and only infrequent reconsideration of basic life decisions.

Teens are substantially closer to adult competence than they were as children, but what is lacking is experience and the ability to evaluate it in context. Both adolescents and adults see themselves as relatively safe, but adults don't need to take so many risks because what they have is more readily accessible. Adults also have more ways to take healthy risks and to have adventures, whereas for a teen girl there are few ways available.

Are adult levels of competence far above those of teenagers? The daily paper in any city illustrates the problems of adult behavior, and it would be difficult to argue that teenagers have a monopoly on foolishness or that adults always behave wisely.

So when a teenage girl reacts to adults, it is with these perceptions in mind. She has a strong sense of her own abilities in contrast to those of the adults around her. She has begun to notice the power structure of society and her relative place in it, and that her ignorance, more than her faulty logic, makes her inferior to the adults around her. But she is still heartened to notice that there are many things that she can do better than her parents.

What will the other kids think?

Imagine if all of the people around you suddenly shrunk to half their size and began to speak in different voices, so that every time you saw each friend, it was like meeting a whole new person. For a young teenager, relations with the world seem topsy-turvy, and other kids act weird and look and sound different. It is a different self and a different group, and much of a girl's thinking revolves around the meeting of these two. This is part of the reason for the popularity of movies about teens, the voyeuristic wish to see how other kids act, think, and solve problems. Girls learn from watching others, and they may ape or imitate the figures that they see on television or in the movies, which serve as a substitute for skill. There's little point in telling a girl to "be herself" until she has a sense of somebody there to be.

So a great deal of a girl's thinking involves her intersection with other kids. Her newfound thinking skills make it possible for her to imagine all sorts of encounters and possibilities, and she is likely to try out many behaviors in her thoughts before she does so in her behavior. Her obsession is likely to be with anticipating social encounters, and girls often share these experiences in long phone conversations of the form, "And then he said, 'Hi,' and I'm like, well, okay, 'Hi,' and then like he looks at me and then I say 'Hi' and then he looks and I'm like, and I say like, 'So,' and he's like, well...."

Interestingly enough, in cultures where the forms of social contact are tightly prescribed, there is less anxiety about how one should act or the possibility of a misdeed. Sometimes youngsters in our culture attempt to limit their vulnerability to embarrassment by adopting the prevalent group practices, for example, smoking, drinking, or using drugs.

The new forms of thinking available to a girl in early adolescence make thought processes very different. She can think about other kids and think about them thinking about her, and about her thoughts about what they think about her, as opposed to her best friend's thoughts about what they think about her, and what the boyfriend thinks her best friend thinks about what he thinks about her, and so forth. She can compare a number of these observations at once, and the whole exercise is quite captivating.

Other characteristics of teen thought interfere with a speedy resolution to problems. There is great difficulty in separating her thinking from the reality of the situation, so that her feelings and fears become the compelling reality, for example, when she asks a friend, "You don't want to come to my party, do you?"

Her thoughts and opinions may be so firm that they take on the character of eternal verities rather than whimsical reactions. She may be very enthused about some form of clothing or feel that acting rowdy makes her look tough and attractive, so much so that she may be unable to see the way her friends react to her, even though other teens may see it.

To be able to understand what other kids think requires her to put her own thoughts aside, which is a tall order for a girl who has only recently begun to have such unique and interesting thoughts.

The egocentrism that characterizes this period makes her the center of her thinking, relegating all others to the position of audience. Because she notices her imperfections, particularly her physical ones, of which she is likely to believe there are quite a lot, she assumes that they are also paramount in everyone else's mind. It is hard for her to notice that others may not be as interested in her as she is. This leads to the feeling that she is living in a goldfish bowl, under constant close surveillance by others and particularly by other kids. Although this has always been seen as an adolescent delusion, it is in fact an accurate assessment, for teens do closely monitor other teens, noticing their body shape, clothing, hairstyle, and dozens of other details. Adults may not be concerned about a youngster's appearance, but other adolescents will be — and will probably gossip about it.

There are likely to be at least a few scenes of hysterics over clothing and appearance, for a teen girl fears the often cruel judgments of other youngsters. Ridicule and condemnation come far more easily than adults realize to their daughters, and they hurt badly. The anticipation of these is likely to stir up so much anxiety and apprehension that a girl worries about far worse occurrences than usually happen, although there are the occasional true disasters.

Along with great sensitivity to other kids in the later adolescent years comes a developing capacity for relationships at a level that was not previously possible. The ability to put oneself in another's shoes, to understand experiences one has not personally had, and to consider another's unique reactions mean that a teen girl can have new types of relationships.

There is a real capacity for intimate relationships as she approaches the midpoint of adolescence; she can share at a deep level with some reliance on the commitment and sensitivity of the other. She can be very compassionate as well as very cruel. She has a new sense of communication, understands sarcasm, and can use it well.

In the later teen years, reciprocal relationships become possible; she is able to give up more of her internal focus as long as she has exposure to relations with others her age.

If I feel this strongly, it must be right

With the physical changes in a girl's body comes a more reactive sensory apparatus. A girl now feels things strongly, and she is inclined to react with emotion when the situation seems bland, which often surprises adults. These are the days of sudden tears, slamming doors, giddy excitement, and the feeling that she is always "wired." It is a time of excess, when reactions are very powerful, and we may wonder how she can contain all that feeling. A sad movie or even a sad commercial can put a young teen girl deep into the blues, and meeting eyes with a favorite boy can make her euphoric. It is a time of sensation and secret places, when a girl holds many things inside herself, which will later mellow to the finely honed sensitivity of a woman.

It is also a time of superficial reactions; it may be annoying to see a girl terribly upset about a television commercial and have little feeling for a grandparent who is ill. Traumas of minimal proportions dominate the household, and it's all small stuff. Clearly, the strong reactions of the young are time-limited, and can operate only for a few years before the organism begins to mellow in fear of being consumed.

But in the first flush of adolescence, moderation is not a welcome concept, and teens find it hard to balance their responses to stimulation. "That teacher hates me," "He's so unfair," and "You are so mean, Mom," are all part of this period.

When feelings are strong, they have a compelling logic all

their own, and a girl may feel compelled to act. A teen girl's feelings are so intrusive, that having objective thoughts becomes very difficult, for it requires the screening out of emotion.

"If it feels wrong, it must be wrong" is the criterion for many decisions. And with this standard come many consequences. For example, since studying a great deal rarely feels good, a girl may begin to think, "If I have to do something so unpleasant for so long to attain some desired end, there must be something wrong here. Other kids don't seem to be suffering so much, and they get good grades, so there must be something wrong with what I'm doing. It's useless to study this much." Or she may feel that if touching her boyfriend feels this good, it must be right, because her feelings are stronger than her judgment.

The standard of how something feels becomes the measure for the decision rather than the effect of a choice on a girl's well-being. Sensation is substituted for wisdom and implies a superior, intuitive logic, an increasingly frequent practice in the adult culture as well.

It would probably be easier if a girl's feelings always led her astray and she learned not to heed them. But such is not the case. Often her feelings are accurate guides, and she finds that she has tremendous wisdom and enormous insight without working at it. She may overhear the teachers talking and find that a particular teacher does indeed not like her, just as she had suspected. If her intuition receives some incidental confirmation, she may begin to trust her own feelings more than her own judgment, a perilous course.

When her feelings take the form of fears, it may be difficult to prevent them from intruding into healthy activity. The emotional response is so strong that a girl may not be able to master her behavior enough to overpower her fearful reactions. Sometimes a girl may be afraid of her own thinking, since thoughts seem to have a life of their own. She may be afraid that if she thinks "bad" thoughts, for example, thoughts of her parents dying, that this indicates that she is a latent murderer, or that these things will magically happen, and the more she tries not to think a thought, the more it comes unbidden to mind.

The case is similar with good thoughts. The thinking of good thoughts, such as helping others or studying hard, stirs such strong feelings that it appears the same as doing the act itself. Thinking about something becomes the same as carrying it out, so that making a list of chores may make her feel free for the afternoon, because she has given the chores thought time. Intention or fancy substitutes for action and produces the same satisfaction.

When adults ponder teen thinking, there is a strong inclination to say to a girl, in a spirit of condescension, "I know exactly how you feel," or "I felt the same way at your age," two reactions that offend and alienate a girl. They are intrusive and presumptuous, glossing over the very real individuality of different females. A teenage girl will assume that you have little interest in exactly how *she* feels since you are more comfortable with your own observations than with her unique responses. Such reactions also give the impression that her feelings are transient and typical and can be chalked up to a life stage. Trivializing anybody's feelings rarely helps in developing communication or trust.

Many of a teen girl's comments are geared to getting across this special sense of being a person. She says, "You can't understand my feelings, nobody can," and we are doubtful; but in a very real sense she is right. Even if we live with a partner for decades, it is extremely difficult to grasp fully all of the complexities of anyone's thought and feeling.

As adults we are not likely to feel the level of passionate intensity of a teenage girl, and our conversation reflects this. A girl will tell you that something was awesome, outrageous, unbelievable, terrible, amazing, and use all superlatives to describe her experience, while a woman is likely to save her strong terms for unusually powerful experiences.

In her need to get across her special perspective, a teen girl may use music or poetry, either creating her own or referring to those of others. "That's my song!" a girl says and tells you that it sings out exactly what she is feeling and thinking — at the moment, anyway. (So much for uniqueness if the song sells a million copies.) It feels like someone is telling her story, and in an attractive way, no less.

There is an awareness in a girl that her friends also have powerful feelings, and this can be confusing as well as interesting. She may feel put off or frightened or parental at the excessive reactions of her friends, and she may even sound like you when she talks to them. "Take it easy, it's not that important," she says. One of the ways that teens learn to cool down their strong feelings is by talking to other teens and seeing themselves reflected in the others' excess. "Do I sound like that?" she wonders.

Long conversations about feelings are generally rare between male teens and seem to require a female to blossom into full form. So a teen girl may spend a great deal of time listening to girlfriends and boys who are friends, and she may sometimes take the role of counselor. Often this provides a vicarious experience that helps her to learn from others, so that she gets more information about consequences, although this does not necessarily protect her from the same consequences. It may in fact serve to desensitize her to real dangers, for example, when another teen reports, "It was no big deal."

Perhaps the most powerful understanding of female adolescence is the realization that we are essentially alone in the universe and that we are each completely different from others and have to search for the few commonalties. Full contact and understanding are no longer possible as they were in childhood when there was far less of one to understand and share. Now that the mind and the emotions have developed a full range of complexity, it becomes clear that it is no longer possible for another human being to encompass this fully with his or her own thinking. There is also an awareness that few people are interested in trying to do so and that most people care little for our inner workings and ponderings, which to an adolescent girl can seem like a real waste. She is absorbed by the power of her feelings, and it can seem that adults lead a very bland emotional life by comparison. Feelings count as much as actual behavior, and if others say that they don't care how she feels, it seems like a violation. She cares very much how she feels and she considers her feelings as highly relevant to any issue, even though others may not share her perception. She concludes that these others are mean and insensitive.

I wonder why I spend so much time wondering?

Particularly in early adolescence, girls spend a great deal of time in inner reflection. Some of this focus tends to fade as a girl becomes more fully involved in relationships in the later teen years, but at the onset she is likely to become withdrawn and inwardly focused. Thinking itself is a whole new and fascinating realm, and the most superficial youngster develops an inner life that would dwarf that of the great philosophers. It is, of course, the thinking of an essentially untrained mind, so much of what she ponders does not have cosmic significance. It is rather the form of her thought that is intriguing to her, feeling much like a change from pedaling a bicycle to steering a rocket.

Suddenly, everything seems to produce a lengthy and extensive cognitive response, even though this may interfere with her attention to more pressing matters. She thinks a lot, and when she shares her thoughts, only some of them seem worth thinking about to an adult.

A teenage girl can play endlessly with her inner mental workings, and often she uses telephone chatter or talk late into the night at a sleepover to reflect, usually on trivia. But as she is honing her teeth on these small issues, she is mentally preparing herself to grasp larger ones, for example, is there a God and if there is, is God friendly? She is fascinated by the new possibilities her brain can absorb and generate. Sometimes she is interested in the thoughts of others, although this is a characteristically egocentric period.

After the major changes of puberty, a new form of thinking emerges that involves a great deal of flexibility and complexity, so that she goes from being an intellectual dancer to a thought choreographer by about age sixteen. This has little to do with intellectual level and reflects only the glorious miracle of a healthy brain maturing, be it a fast brain or a slow brain. It does mean, however, that certain forms of thinking and reasoning are not possible in the early years of adolescence. "Be reasonable" is a forlorn request to young teen girls.

Childhood might have begun to seem reassuring and simple to a girl at its closing years, but adolescence brings with it a cognitive sense of uncertainty, ambiguity, and the understanding that the world is not fixed and can be reinterpreted. "Oh, look," a high school freshman said as she peered through a microscope for the first time, "there are no labels on things."

This understanding brings with it the perception that there are no absolutes, that everything has exceptions, and that great truths are only generalizations. The stage is set for endless debate with adults and authority figures, which expresses the pleasure of a teen mind now able to take on the universe and feeling up to the challenge. To exercise our intellectual muscles feels good, even though it may be tiresome for adults.

Childhood feelings of security also begin to fade; life is seen as more tentative and uncertain. Things don't necessarily turn out all right, and sometimes they turn out very badly indeed, with no recourse. "It's not fair!" she may scream to an empty sky or a failed exam paper. New thought capabilities in the adolescent allow her to think about a great many eventualities and to admit many unpleasant possibilities: What if you drink at a party and have sex with your boyfriend, and he has a disease, and you get it, and you can't tell your parents, and you get real sick, and you get a skin rash, and they throw you out of school, and the boyfriend won't talk to you....

A teen girl can consider all of the possibilities of a situation and compare them, sometimes in groups, and put some aside to open new possibilities. But the dexterity with which this is done takes a great deal of time to develop. The early teen years are a rapidly changing and confusing state, and a girl may often spend solitary evenings in her room lost in her thoughts. The center of her thinking is usually herself. Her new thinking abilities may make her feel as though she is seeing herself for the first time; she may spend endless hours in the bathroom or near a mirror and be very concerned with how she looks in photographs. She tries to puzzle out the contingencies of her relations with others, seeing what feelings this or that expression stirs up in the onlooker.

Wishful thinking continues to intrude on her reasoning exercises, even though she is beginning to develop skills for testing hypotheses. As she gets on in adolescence, she develops a larger data base, and can learn from her observations of the contingencies around her.

A primary focus of thought in the early teen years is on

the inherent rightness or wrongness of one's actions, and sometimes of one's thoughts (a chancier business). Girls may begin to express new opinions and judgments or may adopt very different daily patterns, becoming vegetarians, for example. Often a girl's judgments are rather self-righteous in tone and take a dim view of parental behavior that does not conform to her current standards. Political opinions begin to be formed, often with great conviction and little information, making a youngster vulnerable to embarrassment. "Jimmy Carter is a Buddhist, and that's why I like him," said one girl.

Her values and standards may change suddenly, making her seem whimsical in portentous matters, but the process generally represents the first excursion into constructing a moral steering mechanism for one's life, and learners need support in these efforts. Psychopaths, for example, have only their own pleasure as a guiding principle, so we should be heartened by a daughter's attempt to develop moral standards, no matter how illogical. A girl must create her own womanhood, piecing it together from many sources; if an adult does it for her, it will lack sturdiness and resilience.

With her new mental structure, a girl's approach to figuring out what is right and what is not tends to be rambling and unending. She often confuses being good with what her parents expect, until she becomes connected with peers; then she begins to see being good as the same as getting peer approval. She is likely to be intrigued by the idea of different moral standards among people, for example, doing right means doing God's will vs. doing the greatest good for the greatest number vs. having all people do the same in the same situation. It helps to encourage her to gather a great deal of information and to think about things in small pieces.

Through all of this, her values are not yet related to her behavior, and she may not see any immediate connection between the two. Intention becomes important, so that the thought component of behavior may take on more significance than the outcome. (If I didn't mean it, it doesn't matter that I did it.) This is a complex question for the law as well; for many crimes the motivation of the individual is a consideration.

Nobody knows the inside of me

The splendid isolation that is characteristic of adolescence usually develops from an awareness of one's unique feelings and reactions and the loneliness that goes with it. Girls in early adolescence are easily humiliated as they feel exposed, sensitive, and unprotected. What to an adult seems like a small nick may feel to a teen girl like a shattering assault. Her sensitivity makes her all the more reluctant to expose herself, and so others often have no opportunity to understand her better.

Much of the thinking of adolescent girls is focused on trying to figure out what is on the "inside of me." To puzzle out her feelings, values, affections, and needs often preoccupies a girl for lengthy periods. Nobody, including our heroine, knows the inside of her. But she feels, perhaps, more of a sense of urgency in remedying this situation.

Sorting out the "who am I" question usually involves more specific questions, such as:

- Did I mean what I said to my best friend?
- How come I said something different to my boyfriend?
- Does that mean I'm two-faced? schizophrenic? dishonest?
- What will I say to her when she asks me?
- What will I say to him when he asks me?
- Why am I such a phony?

Often teenage girls have great difficulty with the concept of roles, and so they expect everything they do to accurately represent their feelings, which keep shifting. They expect a "foolish consistency" in their feelings and reactions and are unnerved when they contradict themselves, feeling as though there is no stable ground under their feet. In addition to their actual behavior, they are able to imagine many situations and their reactions to them, and so their feelings become even more complex. They have not yet located the unifying threads of their personalities that will make structural sense of the hodgepodge.

Most of all, teenage girls want to feel genuine, as though what they do and say fits with how they feel. The worst is to be *phony*. Childhood thought, being more limited, was much easier to sort out, for it didn't involve all of the shades of feeling and imagined responses. Some of a teen girl's anguish comes from the change at about eleven, when girls begin to realize that their spontaneous reactions are not necessarily and always the best choice. To say what one thinks instead of what one is supposed to say is a decision fraught with consequences; and it is difficult enough to figure out what one thinks.

Similarly, to say what one thinks with friends is a risky business, indeed, since they rarely appreciate an unbiased commentator at this vulnerable life stage. To notice, for example, that a friend is overweight or rude seems to require expression, but if she speaks honestly, a girl risks being seen as uncaring or cruel. Not to speak makes her feel like a manipulator or ingratiator or generally not herself. The choice, as Carol Gilligan points out, is whether to speak one's own truth or to stay connected to others.* Often nobody knows the inside of her because she doesn't have enough courage to expose it to another person.

Teenage girls often feel that their internal reactions are bizarre, that no one has ever felt so strange before. If the sight of father shaving disgusts her, she will see this as uniquely her reaction, one that others would find unnatural. But the sense of strangeness also helps her to define herself, because she sees herself as distinguished from others.

For teenage girls, privacy, secrecy, and deception all are part of the same developments, ones that begin at about age twelve or thirteen, when girls begin to withdraw from those around them and to keep their inner reactions secret. They become less communicative, spending more time alone. They tend to close the bedroom door and when walking with adults, to walk a few paces ahead or behind. Not surprisingly, adults may experience this transition as a form of rejection and assume it is a sign of hostility or depression. It may seem that the only time a young teen wants to converse is to argue or debate some parental requirement, and a girl's emotions become excessive. Often she seems to be brooding and morose, causing parents to wonder what is making her so unhappy.

Part of being independent and self-reliant is not telling all

---

*C. Gilligan, A. Rogers, and D. Tolman, *Reframing Resistance* (New York: Haworth Press, 1991).

of your feelings, which children do. If a girl is to have her own thoughts, truly her own, she probably needs to protect them from wiser heads, who would challenge her and point out her faulty thinking or be alarmed or disappointed at her thoughts. To keep them secret protects her sense of having genuine feelings and ideas, unadulterated by reason or logic.

There is also a need to have thoughts that are outside those of the family. How disappointing to hear, "You're exactly like your mother" when you want to be your own new and special person. This may be part of the reason that girls in the early teen years like to change their names, as if to say, "I am different from the person my parents created." A girl also likes to think about things that are detached from the family, thoughts that are not discussed by the family, so that she can't hear their reactions in her own head. Then she truly has her very own internal life.

But as one mentally explores all of the permutations and iterations of reality, it becomes progressively harder to establish what is truth. In childhood, it was relatively simple: truth was the way that your parents saw things. But for a girl dealing with the entire cognitive complexity, it is harder to define and often requires a long conversation instead of a single-sentence answer inside her head.

A girl becomes aware of the possibility of concealing her thoughts and reactions and realizes that society expects girls to behave in certain ways: to be helpful to adults, to smile, to be friendly, to be passive rather than aggressive, to be kind and gentle, and when her feelings do not correspond to these behaviors, she is expected to conceal her feelings.

She also learns that adults and her peers cannot tell when she is lying, or that a lie serendipitously sometimes turns into a truth later, or that lying is often a better solution that telling the truth:

Why don't you want to go see your grandmother?

[*Because she has bad breath and body odor and wants to hug me.*]

Because there's nothing to do at her house.

Girls are aware that they are being treated as inferior or unimportant beings when people ignore their reactions or speak of them as though they were absent. They can tell when they are being belittled or criticized by the tone of the speaker, and often they conclude it is better not to respond to the communication. On the other hand, the refusal to respond further supports the concept of a hidden self.

I better do this, no I should do that; well, actually, I better do this

With the change in the child's thinking to the more complex forms of adolescence come more alternatives in making choices. This is not necessarily an easier situation, since decision-making becomes more complicated. There are more "on the one hands" and "on the other hands," and the ability to keep many thoughts in mind at once often prevents a youngster from surrendering to the compelling logic of one dominant thought.

The upshot of this change is that a young adolescent girl may feel flooded with alternatives, finding it hard to weigh all of them and select the most logical one. She may lose sight of the most obvious and practical solution to a problem and come up with some tangential or irrelevant alternative. It is now possible to consider many possibilities at once, but that does not insure that one's logic has become better developed, and in fact it may become more confused.

Thought does not change all at once, and there are still a number of continuing childish patterns, particularly in early adolescence. It is difficult to separate assumptions or possibilities from fact, and a premise may be treated as data rather than surmise. Thus a girl may say, "Tomorrow will be a snow day," meaning that she believes the statement to be true and classifies it as such in her thought process. But it does not have the same implications as "Yesterday was a snow day."

This is probably a partial explanation of adolescent "wisdom" ("If you want to know anything, ask my daughter, she's got all the answers," one parent said). A teen girl seems to "know" things about which adults have doubts. Adults would see it as possible that she will not get invited to a certain party, while she sees it as certain and plans her behavior accordingly.

If she is shown to be wrong, she does not doubt her thought process, but only assumes that sometimes things go awry.

Systematic thinking, while allowing her to see the consequences of logical choices, does not make her thinking automatically more reasonable.

The whole process of thinking becomes burdensome at points, particularly where it involves making decisions that stir anxiety. Some girls deal with ambiguity and ambivalence by making sudden, impulsive decisions that are announced to parents as faits accomplis.

- "I'm not going to camp this summer."

This helps girls to wrestle with all of the options by placing the listener in the position of having to argue for the discarded choice:

- "What do you mean you're not going to camp? Camp does you a world of good."

Then the girl can take the negative side and play out all the possibilities,

- "I hate camp. The counselors are mean, the place is dirty, and the kids are boring."

The parent represents the other side of her thinking:

- "You loved it last summer. Remember all of the kids who wrote to you?"

In this way she doesn't have to do the processing alone:

- "All right, all right, but don't blame me if I hate it."

She can feel vindicated for the failure (or success) of the decision because she seemingly chose to protect herself but was overridden. When a choice provokes a great deal of indecisiveness, it is more satisfying to arrange the outcome so that the inner angst is lessened and so that the responsibility or blame is muddied a bit.

Sometimes indecision shows up as procrastination, the putting off of things that need to be done. We can remind a girl endlessly that things are easier if you do them quickly, but this usually involves some sort of risk-taking in a venture of uncertain outcome. When, for example, she puts off making plans for the weekend, she is probably weighing the relative risk of being rejected with the relative risk of being lonesome all weekend and trying to decide which is worse.

As adults, we are usually able to prioritize decisions so that we avoid wasting our time or energy on those issues that are either insignificant or unsolvable, and often we have developed routines that save us from too much decision-making. We know, for example, that we will always go bowling with the church on Friday night, which takes care of our social outing plans and saves us from having to generate new plans each week. We are often immobilized, however, by tasks that require many decisions, for example, cleaning the garage.

Teenage girls are seldom so economical about their mental energy, often wasting it on issues over which they have no control or using it up on hypothetical cases like, "What if she tells him that I like him and he doesn't like me?" Since human beings generally cannot handle more than three important decisions in a day before cognitive fatigue sets in, it is wise to save our energy and to use it on only those issues where it is well spent.

One of the ways that girls avoid the quagmire of ambivalence is to follow whatever is the standard for other kids. This can work well in some areas, like, for example, where to go on a Friday night, and poorly in others, for example, how many boys to have sex with. It may seem to a girl that the judgments of others are more valid than hers and that she would be wiser to apply their solutions to problems, but it is wise to keep in mind the nature of the age.

Adolescence is a time for learning, and the only way to learn to make decisions is to practice: to make many decisions and to make many mistakes. Success is a poor teacher, and so are good decisions. It is the bad decisions that will teach her the most about the process and the workings of her own mind. Her worst decisions are better than someone else's good ones. But experimenting with decisions is best done where the risks are limited and the costs small.

Vacillation and change are also part of the decision-making process and may be a sign of wisdom rather than anxiety. It is wise to expect these as part of the process of learning how to make choices and to encourage a girl to change her mind, to back up or reverse herself. There are many poor judgments that we can hope she will reverse, but if reversal is seen as a sign of immaturity, she will stubbornly cling to them, no matter how difficult the consequences. It is wise to avoid making a particular decision into a test of her intelligence or integrity.

Why are parents so mean?

Sometimes parents, like all humans, are thoughtless or insensitive, and a teenage girl may be hurt or embarrassed as a result. More often, a girl is hurt or embarrassed from what others would consider the normal behavior of adults. It is difficult for a girl to understand why parents would disapprove of trendy clothes, when her friends are very positive about how good they look, or why they would insist on rules that keep her away from teenage fun. When they require that she concentrate on school work, it can seem as though their intention is to make her miserable.

It is difficult in adolescence to separate the pleasures of the moment from the preparations needed for a satisfying future. It is often the case that good times as a teen do not lead to fun as an adult, and hard times as a teen lead to a more satisfying adulthood. For a girl who has difficulty understanding long-term consequences, what leads to what, it may be incomprehensible that we must be deprived in the present to be satisfied in the future. Far from seeing her parents as looking out for her, she may see them as out to get her, particularly in the younger teen years. In the older years as adulthood nears, she may accept the truths they speak, but resist hearing them because of denial or a perception of condescension.

Girls have little understanding of the life of an adult, the subjects that preoccupy, the issues that confront, and the pressures that serve as the motivators for daily routines. Even if a woman shares her thoughts or brings her daughter along with her for a day at work, her daughter is unlikely to grasp the subtleties of the situation until she is in the same position herself.

But something significant has happened in adolescence to the parent-child arrangement that prevailed for over a decade.

From the beginning of her life, the deal had been that they would be good parents and she would be a good child, and everything would turn out all right. And this is roughly what happened, that she behaved more or less, and they did more or less what was needed, and things were usually okay.

Parents were available in some form, and they usually had answers or solutions to problems, or maybe told her to find them herself, but at least they replied. It was clear that they knew better than she did, and that they had an interest in what was going on. And occasionally they were truly marvelous.

In adolescence, this all changes. Parents come to school for the high school open house and stand in the hall looking at their map and trying to find the rooms, looking stupid and lost, and they don't understand what the teacher explains in math, and the guidance counselor has to keep reminding them that things have changed from when they were in high school, and a girl may wish they hadn't come at all. How can she possibly turn to them for help when they are so obviously inept?

But do they acknowledge this and back up? Not for a minute! They bulldoze ahead and try to tell her exactly how to run her life and generally give useless or harmful advice. What's wrong with them anyway? Why, she thinks, do they have to be so dumb?

And parents' failure goes far deeper than just their stupid behavior. They have few easy or realistic solutions to problems, they tend to be bossy and intrusive, and they express a low opinion of teens. Their advice rarely protects or saves, and sometimes they let a daughter get in trouble to "learn for herself." And then, some of the time, when she is really unhappy, it seems to matter little to them. As adolescence begins, a girl is able to conceive of what life would be like with a nicer set of parents, and it is easy to demand self-righteously that parents be that way, or be outraged that they are not.

The fundamental problem lies in the shift in relationships between a girl, her parent, and the outside world. Dependency begins to fail in adolescence, as parents increasingly fail to intervene between a girl and the outside world and she begins to act directly on the world, with more or less success. By the time she is in her mid-twenties, if she succeeds in becoming self-reliant and creating a satisfying life for herself, then her parents will have virtually nothing to offer her, beyond their memories and affection and lots of good times in the present. In making the transition, a teenage girl may often feel as though the rug is being pulled out from under her, which is indeed the case, because the foundation of her security, her parents, is crumbling and will be unable to take care of her as she becomes a woman.

As a child she was cared for more or less automatically. She was the focus of her parents' attention, and perhaps her siblings', and she did not have to adjust to outside realities because provisions were made for her. If she was away from the house for the afternoon, Mom always packed a snack so she wouldn't get hungry, but now she has to wait and deal with a growling stomach. There was an easy understanding that she would be taken care of, but now she increasingly experiences situations where there is no one else to turn to, where she must deal with frustration or come up with a solution. If she was not cared for as a young child, then the feelings of inadequacy, shame, panic, and anger will be easily stirred by the common problems of the teenage years.

It may seem an overload, this increasingly heavy responsibility for herself, and often she has great condemnation of more powerful others, including parents, who could have made her burden lighter, but didn't care enough to do so. The moralistic *should* that underlies these complaints — e.g., "The teacher *should* only give me tests on things I understand"; "The neighbor *shouldn't* expect me to baby-sit on New Year's Eve" — are disguised attempts to reestablish the old relationship called, YOU SHOULD TAKE CARE OF ME. And of course, it would be nice to have parents endlessly take care of one, without the responsibilities and risks of adulthood. Parents will spend a great deal of time with a daughter in adolescence helping her to explore the intricacies of relationships between caretaker and dependent as well as between equals.

But to have a relationship among equals requires that a girl understands her parents, which is unlikely in the early adolescent years. It is helpful for parents to explain briefly their perspective and feelings about a situation, but to depend upon a girl's experience to teach her. Some of the greatest success in counseling comes from an objective outsider interpreting a parent's behavior to a teen girl so that she begins to see it more objectively. To see parents as independent people with their own motivations and reactions and a life that only partly and briefly coincides with hers is the beginning of more peaceful dealings.

The second major shock to a teenage girl comes from the realization that although she may have read many Cinderella stories and has the implicit expectation that she will be supported throughout her life, either by parents or a "good provider husband" (and this may be a belief that her parents have shared) it generally is unrealistic.

The idea that a girl must be able to support herself and her children is not a radical feminist idea, but rather a reflection of current U.S. census statistics. The fastest-growing poverty group in the nation is single mothers, and it is not difficult to understand the problems inherent in raising a child and holding a job at the same time. For women who marry, the great majority will hold jobs at the same time that they raise children, because of the increasing cost of childrearing in this society.

But the income level of a young person generally depends upon one of two factors, either the ability to work long hours or the amount of preparation one has. For young women, having children precludes both, so that a young mother who must work is generally limited to low-paying jobs. The preparation one has for the job market is crucial in determining one's standard of living for life.

As girls enter adolescence, their interest in adult women increases, and they begin to notice the connection between the ability to command well-paying jobs and the lifestyle one leads. Often they see marrying a high-income spouse as a substitute for providing for oneself and may attempt to pursue this approach with vigor, finding it more satisfying than the alternative. Or they may fail to establish independence from their parents, feeling that it is unsafe to give up this security.

But the shock of understanding that a girl will one day be responsible for her own support, in a society where women are seen as weaker and less capable, is difficult to absorb. Rarely is there any urging by the adults around her to prepare herself in this way, for the newer market realities for women are not commonly understood. A girl's reaction may take the form:

- "I should have to support myself in the next few years? Are you kidding?"

- "I should have to support a family? That's not a woman's job."

By age eleven, a girl has begun to think about a specific life interest, but this is expressed as a hobby or otherwise optional interest. Nobody asks, in insistent tones, "What are you going to *do* with your life?" as though it were important. These interests are not seen as the basis for a self-reliant and autonomous life, but rather part of a personality. The view that a woman should be prepared to support her family is seen as heretical, a violation of femininity, which it may be, but it is nonetheless a requirement of many American families.

The idea that a woman will be solely responsible for herself as an adult is not part of what girls are taught, even though the typical American woman will spend an average of sixteen years living alone. To suggest this actuarial future to a girl implies that no one will want her or that she cannot establish relationships rather than simply acknowledging the probabilities.

Without a solid foundation of self-support, a woman has no choice but to depend on others to care for her. If a teen girl learns to become self-reliant, then she can choose from many types of relationships as an adult and create the ones that best express her unique needs and talents.

Instead, it is common a girl and her parents to believe that "someone" will support her and to waste the teen years when preparation would be most effective. Girls are often frightened by the understanding that their parents' care will end and they will be forced to shoulder the burden of their own support.

There are few opportunities or requirements that girls focus on the long haul of their lives, and when asked, most girls have no images of what their lives should look like when they are fifty. Even less common is the laying of plans to help girls move toward the lives they would like to have in adulthood. Instead, there seems to be a "wait and see" attitude, which generally means, "wait and see who you'll marry."

Security for girls requires economic empowerment for girls, and this translates to job training. But teen girls, with their limited perspective, cannot be left the responsibility of arranging their lives in a way that will give them the skills they need. It may feel mean to require them to prepare for a secure future, but it is the truest expression of love.

I'm not a baby anymore and I never was

When you begin to notice that a girl looks more like a woman than a girl, it is easy to forget what the child used to look like. But the mind plays curious tricks, and easily leads us to expect that the creature that looks like a young woman will begin to act like a woman. But change takes time, and growth takes longer, and it will be years before a girl emotionally grows into her body.

She will also feel the great expectation her appearance stirs and will expect to be treated like an adult, even though she acts quite childishly. She may demand privileges for which she is not ready, speak in ways that are provocative, or insist on acquisitions that are inappropriate. It will be hard to convince her that growth takes time and that patience is a wiser course than demanding. Teenage girls are used to an electronic age where fax machines transmit messages in seconds and a line of three people at McDonald's seems like an endless wait. Human development has changed very little over the past millennium, and it still seems to take about twenty-one years for a girl to become a woman in a process that cannot be speeded up, no matter how impatient we may be.

For a girl, the sense of urgency is likely to be very great, fueled in part by a society that treats girls over thirteen very much as though they were equivalent to women. Most of the clothes, activities, music, and hairstyles of this age are the same as those of women, even though girls of this age do not have the intelligence or experience to handle a woman's life.

A girl may bridle at the idea that she is not yet who she hopes to be or imagines herself to be. Without actually stating our perceptions, it is wise to keep in mind that girls need a great deal of time to become women, and what they think of themselves in the process, the image of themselves that they carry, is not terribly important or worth quibbling about, as long as the image is a fairly positive one.

A girl will strongly resist being thought of as a child or spoken of that way, and it is a courtesy to respect her wishes, just as we might not wish to be referred to as senior citizens, even though we might technically fit that category. She will also avoid situations where her prior childhood status is highlighted because it will remind her of the disquieting proximity of her former immaturity.

When we see a girl looking very mature, it is easy to assume that all of her childish habits have been abandoned along with her smaller body. But in fact, all of those habits that were problems in childhood, for example, whining, blaming, shouting, pouting, and crying, are likely to continue and be more upsetting in a larger person. But change takes time, and her habits will change if we help her to acquire more adult patterns. It is fruitful to avoid reminding her of her closeness to childhood.

How do I look?

"Don't you ever think of anybody but yourself?" we are inclined to wonder when we notice how often a teen girl thinks about her appearance. And actually, it is not uncommon for girls to focus rather heavily on themselves in this period of life, in part because they have a totally new self to think of and in part because they need to make many decisions about how to present themselves to the outside world.

It is a surprising realization to feel at some point that one is a girl, most clearly and most definitely, and to feel obligated to define exactly what kind of girl one ought to be. That takes a great deal of trying on different types of girlhood, usually before a mirror. There is a whole lot of new equipment to deal with in the form of a body that has recently changed and is taller, chestier, curvier, and sticks out in places that were formerly straight. There are new mine fields to be negotiated; she used to be able to slip through many places that will no longer allow her passage. A woman's body is a new ship to steer and doesn't fit in the old places, and a girl may feel awkward or fat as a result.

Girls generally notice gender differences for the first time at about age four, although they may not see them as enduring. "When I grow up I'm going to be a boy," said one three-year-old girl. Girls learn at that age that they use a different bathroom than boys, and they begin to notice the distinct feminine characteristics of women, such as jewelry or they way they swing their hair.

Now, as a new woman, a girl must decide which feminine characteristics belong with her and whether to look demure, tough, studious, or otherwise is a daily choice and leads her to wonder what she is inside.

The changes in her body and her experimenting with styles do not go unnoticed among those around her. People call attention to them in one way or another; relatives often notice that she's grown and comment in rather insinuating tones. Hairy men turn to look at her, and she has power over them. Her mother notices if her clothes are too revealing, whereas before there was nothing to be revealed.

Do I look good enough to attract the right males? she wonders, and this leads her to develop an idea of who the right male for her might be. She projects to the future, imagining who would be a satisfying mate, and her projection tells much about how she sees herself. In choosing partners, the most common choice is one very much like herself or the imagined self. By age twelve, most girls begin to notice whether boys find them attractive and to dwell on ways that would make them more attractive. It is from these thoughts that the images of herself as a future wife, mother, and homemaker will develop as she pictures how a household should go together.

Her body frame is always there as an issue, sometimes a burden and sometimes an opportunity, but inescapable and irreversible. It's one more thing for her to think about.

Suggestions for dealing with a teen girl's thinking patterns

1. Move over. Ask for her opinions and listen to them. Don't have all the answers. Get used to saying, "I'm not sure..." or "It's only my opinion...." Don't set yourself up as the final au-

thority on everything or the voice of divine truth. Don't pull rank when you get into a disagreement with her or you will lose the opportunity to get her to listen to her own reasoning and correct it. Save your marbles for the truly important fights.

2. Strengthen her reasoning ability. Challenge her to think and hold her own; get her out of being the good little girl, the agreeable accommodating female. Think of all the drug pushers, predatory males, harassing employers, and exploiters in her future, and teach her to stand up for herself with dignity.

3. Don't transform disagreements into tests of your authority. Your real authority rests in how reasonable and caring you are. Give her room to make mistakes, back up, change her mind, and find out she is wrong, and expand this space as she gets older. Don't *ever* say "I told you so!" when she stumbles, or she won't show you that part of her again. Let some of your mistakes show, and show her how to handle them gracefully.

4. Don't judge her character yet. Accept that youth is a time of blemishes of the complexion and the soul. What's more, get into the habit of accepting other people's shortcomings, since even adults are not perfect. Humility is easier on everybody.

5. Teach skills and competence. Offer information at every opportunity. Adulthood lasts for a long time, and there is so much to know. Get curious yourself, and learn some new things, unless you know everything. Make family outings to places where people learn things. Ask you daughter to teach you something that she knows, and learn to be lesser than she is. Go to the library and take your daughter with you. Watch television with her and talk with her about what she sees.

Two

CHANGING
A DAUGHTER

IT MAY SEEM SOMEHOW SUSPECT to set out to deliberately change a daughter, her personality or her behavior, as though to do so implied a sort of rejection. But for a child to become an adult, there must be a great deal of change. Childish ways must change into adult ways, although not entirely without residues and colorings of the child that was.

It is appealing to think that children naturally evolve into adults, that nature provides for this transformation, and that we can remain observers. In physical change, this is accurate, for a girl develops a woman's body and rhythms without much outside intervention. But intellect and affect require something different, something uniquely human, and that is learning.

Parents often complain, "But I don't want to change my daughter, just those few objectionable things!" ignoring that she is a whole, and no one part can change without the others changing too. The best cure for the trials of a teenage daughter, after all, is womanhood.

Is it disrespectful to change her, a violation of her individuality and unique nature? Is it manipulative and exploitative? It certainly can be, and if we determine that she needs to be a political activist or a debutante, then we are discarding her essential humanity for our own gain.

If instead we help her to grow stronger and more skilled, create the structure of adult character, and allow her to fill in the content, then we enhance rather than destroy her individuality.

Life is filled with influences that shape us, randomly it would seem, so that we become adults of one sort or another largely by chance. And she is far too important to be left to chance. But if the purpose is to help her become a full adult, complete with talents, dreams, and skills, and to move her along from the incompetent and limited child she is, then helping her change from child to adult is a profoundly loving thing to do.

Are we the best teachers? Probably not, since there are bound to be other adults who are more skilled and more experienced. But life has given her to us, and perhaps our love for her makes up the difference. It is possible that we will do psychological damage by shaping her and that we will hear about it in our later years. But the danger of not shaping her at all is equally perilous, and it handicaps her. At least when she sets her own course, she has something to discard instead of an abyss.

Changing dependency to self-reliance requires skills of all sorts. There are so many things one needs to know to have a chance at a happy life. A woman must be able to drive a car, walk safely at night, apply for a job, run a meeting, manage her finances, learn social etiquette rules, buy clothing. To be able to maneuver through the world involves developing one's own set of skills that can be applied and built upon to instill flexibility and competence into the system. Universal free public education is a powerful resource in this, but parents are far more powerful.

But often, even in this decade, we encourage girls to transfer their dependence to others rather than developing skill themselves. We assume that they needn't learn about health insurance, paying taxes, or fixing cars, since when they're married, these will be taken care of. Girls too have the same belief that a man, be it father, brother, boyfriend, or husband, will take care of things, except in those settings where they have observed women handling such matters, and then their attitudes are different.

With boys, we have expectations of self-reliance, and when we ask a high school boy his plans for his occupational future, we listen as though we expected him to have plans and to follow through with them. With a girl, both the question and the response are likely to be somewhat different. Girls often go from being a daughter in their parents' home to a parent in their own home, with little time or expectation in between for becoming an adult person apart from a family setting. Girls learn the game from both sides and operate in this setting throughout their lives.

Women who have made notable contributions to the human race are usually raised with different expectations. Eleanor Roosevelt, Leontyne Price, Florence Griffith Joyner, Margaret Thatcher, and Benazir Bhutto were prepared for important roles in society, not ones that replaced being a wife and mother, but ones that expressed their unique talents and abilities in many realms.

If we do not prepare our daughters to be something in this culture, how can they have a choice when they are adults? How can they feel value in themselves or see themselves as necessary to the direction of the society?

In this society, there is no formal recognition of a girl's transition into womanhood, with all the promise that those sixty years hold. The only clear symbol is a girl's becoming a bride, which many girls see as an achievement, an opportunity to fulfill lifelong dreams. Interestingly, boys have no such view in becoming a groom.

Some troublesome teen girl behavior may be rooted in a culture that does not hold girls in very high esteem and expects little of them. But when we set out to change a daughter's behavior from that of a child to an adult, we are expressing high regard for her, high enough to compel action.

If girls are more concerned with relationships than boys, it may be because they are a source of advancement and security. Girls notice that a woman with children is limited and needs help, that women are weaker than men, usually control less money, and are not as tough as males.

Most girls find it hard to conceive of survival without males, since boys or men seem to have what is needed to be safe and successful. But if a girl becomes a self-reliant woman, then relationships with males become far less prescribed and need not always support her dependency.

What makes behavior change? We conceive of behavior as static and fixed, particularly when we don't like the behavior at issue. In fact behavior is a state of dynamic equilibrium that the organism reaches with its environment. Like an ice skater or a bicycle rider, a person's behavior is a reflection of a large group of forces that must all be held in balance, and it must be a balance that changes from moment to moment. Static, unchanging behavior is characteristic of mentally ill people, who respond to their environment in the same way, regardless of how it changes. There is little relation to the present in this form of behavior, since the person has given up trying to balance all of the existing forces and instead spews out behavior according to internal drives.

We may see the same lack of balance in another type of human: the learner. When we are trying to find ways to coordinate opposing forces and competing pulls, we may see a great deal of lurching and a high level of arousal as the person seeks to find a balanced state.

Changing a girl's behavior so that it is a woman's behavior is a difficult task; it touches on a central conflict in the culture, that of the proper behavior for a woman. For a mother, in particular, this is a difficult area, for it brings out all of a woman's feelings about her own life and what she is preparing her daughter for.

All parents will say, "I want my daughter to do whatever she wants, as long as she is happy," which seems to negate the role of defining a future. With boys, necessity speaks, so that a parent will say that a son must be able to earn a living, support himself, and support a family, should he choose to have one. And in delineating these goals, many others things lay themselves out clearly: he needs preparation for a job, he needs to stay free while he prepares, etc. To focus on a daughter's happiness as a future goal leaves one drifting in how to help her organize her time: taking flute lessons becomes equally as valuable as getting a part-time job, while for a boy the choice is much more prescribed.

In another aspect, parents worry a great deal about their daughter's safety, for girls are much more vulnerable to rape, assault, and kidnapping, as well as to poverty, than boys are. And so parents naturally look for ways to secure their daughters' lives, generally focusing on helping them to find protection.

Is this wrong or prejudiced? Certainly not, for the realities are what they are. But there may be better ways to secure our daughters' futures. If we can teach girls behavior that will enable them to take care of themselves and their families, then we are likely to provide them physical security as well, since safety is primarily in the mind of the victim rather than in the hands of those who would threaten.

Look at what affects her behavior

THE CULTURE TEENS GROW UP IN

Teen girls growing up in different cultures or ages experience unique demands and influences. In the United States at the turn of the second millennium, girls are heavily influenced by their families, friends, television, neighborhood, and teachers. In recent decades, girls have had a great deal more unsupervised time, time in which they are free to make choices about their behavior and in which they may be alone or with friends.

An American teenage girl spends an average of 21 hours a week watching television, or about 3 hours a day, and far, far less time talking with parents and being influenced by them. She spends about 5.6 hours per week on homework, and about 1.8 hours in pleasure reading. Girls have about five hours per day of discretionary time, time that is unscheduled and that a girl may fill as she chooses. According to Nielsen Media Research, by the time the American woman reaches age fifty-five she will watch an average of six hours and nineteen minutes of television each day.[*]

That girls spend far more time without parents than with them is apparent in many figures. Thirty percent of eighth graders are home alone after school for two or more hours, and low-income students are home alone for more than three hours, according to a Carnegie Corporation study. Not surprisingly, unsupervised time after school is the most common setting for sexual intercourse among teens.[†]

It would seem that parents are a relatively minor influence on a girl's behavior since they spend little time in direct contact, although they may be physically present in the same space.

---

[*]*Parade Magazine,* May 23, 1993, 17.
[†]Barbara Vobejda, "Study Sees Potential for Trouble in Teens' Lives," *Albany Times Union,* December 17, 1992, C1.

THE FAMILY SETTING AND ITS TONE

If you grow up in a religious family or a football family, then you react differently to Sundays, and so it is with a teen girl's family. What kind of childhood has she had? One filled with sunny approval and encouragement or one marked by criticism and failure? Does she see the world as a trusting place or one full of mean surprises and tragedies? What ways did she develop to cope with whatever she encountered? Did she cling or throw tantrums when things went badly? Whatever behavior she practiced in childhood will come most naturally.

Of additional interest is the physical structure of the family, the number of adults and the number and ages of children. If she is the oldest of five girls, she will have a very different family experience than if she is the youngest of five girls. It is very different to have an older brother than to have a younger brother. In this regard, those families where a girl is the youngest of three children and the two older ones are boys seems to be a particularly difficult constellation for a girl.

IS SHE CRAZY OR STUPID?

Much of a teen girl's behavior becomes easier to understand if a parent remembers her astounding lack of information. Her knowledge is often based on misinformation, poor logic, inexperience, hearsay, and immaturity, and it may look insane at times — when it is merely stupid. And it is worth noting that when a human being acts stupidly, her first response is to hide it.

A girl is in the process of revising her early theories about life and the universe in adolescence. Children develop attitudes and hypotheses about how the world works, and they must then reexamine them as they mature. Often their earlier experiences no longer apply, as in the assumption, "I shouldn't have to study for a test for four hours; I never did before." The rightness of events is measured against these archaic beliefs, and she behaves accordingly, eventually formulating new beliefs based on much sounder foundations. If beliefs have worked well enough, it is very difficult to abandon them. It helps to be somewhat uninformed about her motivation for doing things, for presuming to understand a teen is generally perceived as condescending.

Teaching, not discipline, is required to get good at things

We have choices to make in raising a teenage girl: whether to make her comfortable or strong, whether to keep her safe or encourage experimentation. Ironically, when we teach kids, we help them to leave us behind, for they no longer need what we provide. A teenage girl who can do little for herself is half of an equation looking for the other half, which may take the form of parents, a parental partner, or the law.

By teaching our kids we lose them, because they are no longer dependent. In losing kids, however, we then are closer to having adult companions and family members through the remaining decades of our lives. Our adult children need to be improved forms of our young children, and we create them by teaching them.

During adolescence, however, when there seem to be so many more perils for a youngster, our natural impulse is to pull our kids closer, to say, "Watch out!" and "Be careful!" There seems to be danger and challenge everywhere, and our new teen seems very much of a vulnerable child. A teen girl rejects this protection at the same time that she wants it and may even invoke it. Such are the mixed messages of this stage.

No matter what we do, in the end our children always leave us. Life is a process of individuation, so that the young always seek a new course and leave the old behind. It helps if we teach our youngsters many things, for then they are capable enough to be with us without feeling threatened. A skilled woman who happens to be your former little girl is a true delight.

YOU DON'T WANT TO TEACH?

Many of us are intimidated by the idea of having to impart wisdom and skill to a young person when we don't feel totally competent ourselves. But is it any easier to have an eternal child to care for? A little one's mistakes can be charming or amusing, but the same mistakes in a woman are rarely so, and they are sometimes darned inconvenient, if not tragic. And there are only two ways to learn, by instruction from somebody else or by trial and error. Either way becomes a habit, and learning from others' experience is more economical to the human organism since there is less wear and tear on the system.

It is wise to be realistic in our assessment of our teaching ability. Good teachers set limited goals, and they accept their own shortcomings without self-denigration. Some days are better than others, but most important is advancing the learner and gaining skill as a teacher. It makes sense to assume that your daughter can benefit from your being her parent and to impart whatever you know to strengthen her. She may later discard what you've given her, but it will have served its purpose.

Good teaching might take as its model the way that coaches help girls in the Olympics, which is by remaining in the background, being careful not to intrude. They enable a girl to reach her goals by helping her to overcome obstacles and develop strength where she needs it.

If you feel you have little to offer, you may ignore a girl's neediness. But teaching does not require one to have all the answers; rather it is a form of facilitating learning. Sometimes expressing concern and interest and raising questions are the most powerful forms of instruction.

The ways of managing children are likely to undergo profound change in adolescence. Before it was possible to direct a child without her cooperation. This is no longer feasible with a teen girl, for direct and complete control are harder to achieve when a girl has more power accessible to her. Old forms of punishment will have different consequences now. For example, perhaps you used to send her to her room, but now that is where she wants to be.

SETTING OBJECTIVES

All good teaching is teaching toward some achievement or end state. If we teach a child to read, we want her to be able to read, and if we offer a health course, it is so young people will take better care of their health. So in this job of teaching a girl to be a woman, it is important to identify what we want her to be.

If we can define small, short-term objectives, then we have a far better chance of achieving them. To decide that we want to make her table manners more adult, we might focus on conversation practices at dinner and stay with this before moving on to using the right silverware.

To set more global objectives, for example, "to change her attitude," is usually more frustrating, since this is too intangible and gives us little help in planning a course or knowing when we get there. Better by far to set limited objectives, for example, to get her to ask a parent in the evening, "How was your day?"

While we are deciding which of these goals to work on, it is worth remembering that our teaching days with an adolescent are limited, and after about age eighteen, it will be very difficult to help her develop new skills.

It is also important to figure that good learning always involves *doing* and not merely listening or understanding what is being said. When you teach her to drive a car, it will require a great deal of practice with her behind the wheel, and so it is with virtually all life skills. If you only demonstrate or do things for her, she will be no more skilled, no matter how well she understands what has been imparted to her. Like roller skating, most of the skills that require balance involve a great deal of practice. Getting her into positions where she is doing, instead of watching or listening, is one of the great challenges for a parent of a teen girl.

It is for this reason that belonging to organizations or processes that require a great deal of doing benefit a girl enormously. A girl who has a bas mitzvah, for example, learns public speaking, composing thoughts, greeting guests, and arranging entertainment. This kind of event is a great economy for a parent, since it enlists the resources of adults in the wider society to teach a girl skills that will benefit her. It also pulls her along with the current so that she unavoidably is exposed to skill-developing situations.

LEARNING FROM MISTAKES

Surely the most powerful form of learning occurs in those painful moments when we learn from our errors. When a teen girl makes a mistake that causes problems, it is most helpful to use the opportunity to ask her:

- What have you learned?

- What can you do to set things right? (to restore self-esteem)

- How could you avoid this problem in the future?

When we take away the horror and the shame that she feels at mistakes, then the mistakes can teach. Most adults can recall those powerful experiences that led them to new understandings and new behavior.

When, for example, a girl goes too far sexually, it is wise to help her come up with a good solution to the problem. The solutions she can generate may be less promising, for example,

- Tell all my girlfriends and see what they think.

- Make a joke about it with boys and pretend I don't care.

- Vow to stay away from all boys forever.

- Take the boy on as a boyfriend since at least then somebody approves of me.

The more we help a girl to deal with her errors productively, the fewer and less serious they will be. A teen girl who uses any of the above solutions to her problem is likely to be overwhelmed by the difficulty of both the original problem and its solution.

Often teens hide their errors because of shame and fear that control will be imposed on them if they are not competent at all times. They may feel that they are unable to control their own lives, and so they fear someone else may take over. By keeping mistakes secret, they end up raising themselves, learning in hard and sad ways, rather than benefiting from the experience of someone who has been there.

Change yourself

One of the most reliable indicators that we need to begin changing ourselves is when we begin wishing that someone else would change. This usually serves to point out that we are dissatisfied with conditions and the best way we can figure to change them is to shift the work load to somebody else.

And it may be a wonderful outcome if somebody else changes, whether it be an unresponsive husband or boyfriend, a disapproving parent, or a difficult teenage daughter. Since adolescence is a time of transition, change is built into the period. Those girls who fail to change at all from childhood will later be diagnosed as mentally ill, trapped eternally in the confusion and excess of this period. So a girl's changing is a fine idea.

The problem comes in trying to effect change *in another person* to suit our preferences. To use up our energy and creativity on what we don't control is a sad waste. To control what we *do* have access to, namely, our own behavior, is a powerful investment.

But why change ourselves? Is that not an acknowledgment that we have been doing everything wrong? Isn't what we do good enough? Aren't we catering to a whining child?

Adolescence presents a marvelous opportunity to examine ourselves and decide, from the maturity of middle age, whether adulthood is what we want it to be, what we had in mind the last time we looked at ourselves carefully, back around age twenty-one or twenty-two. We become aware in middle age of those personal attributes that hold us back, perhaps laziness or lack of courage or problems in relating to others.

Just as our young people must change to fruitfully use this period of their lives, so we must change for the next decades of our lives. This is the time to clean out our character closets. When you notice your daughter eating badly, it's a fine reminder to look at your eating patterns. If she seems passive and withdrawn, evaluate your own activity. After all, we become like the people we spend time with, and she has spent the past decade or more with you.

Does this mean that you are to blame for every one of her shortcomings? Certainly not. Does it mean that by changing your shortcomings, you serve as a model, teacher, and inspiration to her? Of course!

If you are locked in a power struggle with a daughter, with both of you refusing to give up your ways of behaving or your opinions, you might try to understand yourself better and more compassionately. It is an opportunity to find an easier way to live your life so that you are not always responding to her, but instead to your own needs.

You need to be the kind of parent you respect, even if she makes it difficult or does not go along. You don't need her agreement to adopt new attitudes or behaviors, and you can be the parent you admire even if she responds badly.

By changing ourselves in the ways that we know are best for us, we unbalance the tensions and standoffs in a household. When we try out new ways of relating and spending our time, we provide incentive for those around us to be different. It also points out to a teenager that there is rarely one right way to do things and that life is an experiment rather than a test.

It is wise to reevaluate the stance you have taken on controlling behavior. Parents of small children must exert a great deal of control, but parents of adolescents need to teach youngsters to manage themselves. The problem is not in having rules, but in having inflexible or unreasonable rules. We can take the opportunity to do a thorough and unflinching survey of our beliefs and to modify those that fit in the following categories:

1. *I must have control of what is happening to my child. If I don't, it means that I'm neglectful and irresponsible, or that I let my kid walk all over me, and I don't deserve any respect.*

Most of our shaping of children is done in the first five, or perhaps ten years, of their lives. After that, our control lessens, and the world begins to intrude dramatically. The ways that we affect a teen's behavior depend in large part on the rapport and mutual concern that has grown up over time between parent and child. Parents may feel neglectful of teens because suddenly parental services and care are unnecessary or are rejected. To have a person in the house who suddenly exerts influence is an unnerving experience for an adult, who is accustomed to being in a position of power. When children are small, adults must control them, and if they do not, the children suffer greatly. But in adolescence, the shift must be made to teaching them. In dealing with female adolescents, we may feel a stronger need to control since society seems to stress that teenage girls need more limits, while boys need more freedom.

Along with the idea of control goes the belief that children must respect their parents and not challenge them. But teens are in the business of displacing our generation with their generation, and a little jostling is called for. To have long discussions exploring religious beliefs, to listen while a youngster tells us how she would raise her daughter, and to expect a daughter to have feelings and express them clearly and civilly is not to give up our position in the household; rather it is to establish mutual respect rather than power as the basis for family relations. If our daughters are to grow into strong women, we must give up the idea of winning struggles with them and teach them how to win for themselves. For if they don't win, we surely lose.

2. *I'm not good at this job of parenting. I could work harder at it, and if I don't, it proves that I'm a bad parent. If my daughter turns out badly, that's the final proof.*

It's not hard to feel inadequate as a parent in this culture. The newspapers are filled with stories of parents who have mistreated their children, and the assumption that notorious criminals are created by parental mistakes is pervasive. On the other side, the media are filled with often conflicting suggestions of how to raise better children. Although parenting is an important job, it is wise to keep in mind that parents have less than complete control over how their kids turn out and that there are no warrantees on any childrearing methods. Most child abuse and neglect laws describe good parenting as staying with one's children and showing concern for them. Furthermore, parenthood is not a test, but a way to live. It gets easier with practice, and it is highly influenced by the hand one is dealt.

3. *If my daughter is unhappy, it means I'm a lousy parent. Happy kids come from good homes with loving parents.*

Children seem to differ from birth in the valence and intensity of their moods, with some children typically more exuberant and optimistic than others. Constitutional factors have a great impact on mood, with thirteen-year-old girls generally quite negative and fourteen-year-olds more positive. Parents don't have the capacity to make a daughter happy or unhappy in these years, not as they did when she was a child, for they have no control over those factors that are most influential: her body, her talents, her social sphere.

Is unhappiness bad for teen girls? A continuous, unrelenting depression certainly is and must be addressed. But when a girl is blue and disheartened, it may serve as the beginning of self-wisdom and can energize her to make changes in herself or to take action on her own behalf. It is wise to be sympathetic and companionable but to avoid being responsible for a daughter's happiness. To keep our own mood as happy as possible by arranging life in satisfying ways helps to lift a youngster's mood.

> 4. *If I ask for help as a parent, everyone will know I'm a failure. Everyone else knows how to raise their kids.*

Most people are more concerned about being embarrassed by their own kids than they are in evaluating others' kids. There is a general confusion about what to do with teenage girls, and the most skilled parents seem to be those in professions that offer training with young people and those who have raised several teen girls. People who need to rate others usually find a way to criticize and condemn, and even raising the perfect child doesn't protect one from others determined to ridicule or disapprove.

> 5. *If my daughter is mean to me, I probably deserve it. If my own child doesn't love me, it's because of the way I've treated her. If I don't shape up, my daughter will abandon me to a miserable, lonely old age.*

No matter how you behave, your daughter will abandon you. That is, if she's healthy. For the job of a parent is to raise children who are strong, self-sufficient, and different from their parents. The better parent you are, the more likely that your daughter will go off on her own. But the good news is that happiness in middle or old age never depended on the ministrations of grown children in the first place. And, indeed, the happiest of elders are those who have created a life that is self-sufficient and that maximizes their enjoyment. Ironically, those folks seem to have offspring who love to be around them.

6. *Criticizing my child is criticizing me. I will protect my own from the world. My child is never bad, and if she is, I'll handle it.*

In families where adults feel a great deal of powerlessness and insecurity, defending children becomes a reflexive act. Sometimes adults live out their own adolescence and take pleasure in watching a girl flaunt authorities or break rules and get away with it, particularly if they have been harshly controlled as teens. Parents may be unable to see their offspring's shortcomings, because acknowledging them seems to cause a loss of self-esteem for the adult. Sometimes parents are afraid that their offspring are too delicate to withstand negatives of any kind, and so they temper every consequence and provide endless reassurance, making it impossible for a girl to develop a conscience or initiative. In any of these approaches, a girl is kept a child within the family rather than growing and developing in the ways that she needs to.

7. *She'll have to learn from experience. She'll grow out of it. She's an individual and she'll change when she's ready.*

Passive parenting, where we wait for a girl to attain a certain level of development before we teach her more, is sometimes a useful approach, for example, in learning to drive at fourteen. As a general strategy, however, it leaves a girl to find her own way, a lonesome, painful, and confusing process, even when a girl insists on it. To most girls it feels like nobody cares very much about them or cares enough to put energy into teaching them and saving them from the errors in a trial-and-error approach. Girls certainly do learn from experience, but only if someone helps them to learn, arranges experiences that they can utilize, and shows them way to express their own uniqueness within the context of getting where they want to be.

Avoid power struggles

It is not hard to tell the family that a girl comes from. When she hates to lose and fights, even cheats, to win, it means that she has grown up in a win/lose setting, where coming out ahead counted. When a girl blames others when things go wrong, it generally means that there is a blaming atmosphere at home, in which everybody is on the defensive.

The great problem with power struggles in a family is that everybody loses, because a girl needs to be powerful for her parents to feel safe and secure. And parents are always more powerful, because they have the power of wisdom and experience. Girls look for ways to feel powerful, and if nobody helps them to find good and effective ways, they develop their own: they ignore consequences, becoming reckless and self-defeating; they attend only to the present and disregard the future; they accept any consequences that result from their behavior rather than submit to authority.

In a power struggle between parents and a teenage girl, adults challenge with the tone of their voice and their reactions. Their words convey that there is something wrong with her, that she had better do what she is told, and that she doesn't measure up. And adults often refuse to try new ways of relating, because to do so feels like giving in to her, like a defeat.

There are a few places in adolescence where adults must predominate, and there is no room for teenage errors. When these occur, and they occur rarely, it is important for adults to be in control. Parents should not use themselves up on trivial issues, on shouting matches about "the way you spoke to me," or "how lazy you are," because when the great issues emerge, there will be little influence left to use. Many adults have broken themselves trying to prove that they could make a teenage girl do something, and something trivial to boot.

It helps to be tolerant and accepting but very clear about your limits. Great teachers are doorways, not doormats. To see a girl's frame of reference is not to abandon your own, and you must keep your vision of how things should be, for it will guide you both.

Perhaps most importantly, acceptance works to change the power struggle into a struggle to make her strong, as in the old verse:

> He drew a circle that shut me out, heretic, rebel, a thing to
> flout;
> But love and I had the wit to win — we drew a circle that
> took him in.

Be optimistic

If you understand that the teen years are a time of learning through experimentation, then the value of healthy risk-taking becomes clear. Without risk-taking, a girl stays with what she knows, what is familiar from childhood, and does not learn her own limits and capacities. And in fact, a close look at teen behavior indicates that most of it is rigid and repetitive. Adult beliefs about sexual freedom in adolescence, for example, seem to be more a reflection of adult fantasy than teen reality, for most teens are extremely conservative and inhibited in their sexual practices.

For a youngster to dare to do what her intuition and good judgment tell her requires optimism about how things will turn out, and with so few years behind her, it is difficult for her to feel confident. It is also hard to believe that things will get better or easier over the years, since the change from childhood to adolescence sometimes seems to a girl like a turn for the worse, with everything much harder.

When girls experience the natural tension and uncertainty of adolescence, it is difficult for them to listen to advice or to try new approaches. It helps if adults have a bright outlook and communicate their acceptance of a youngster, thus giving her hope. It is wise to start many conversations with:

- You know what I like about you...

- You're different from other teenagers; you seem to...

- You're really good at...

- I don't know what I would have done without you...

- It will be interesting to see you a few years from now, when you can...

It is possible to find reason for optimism even among teenage girls who are parent abusers, juvenile delinquents, convicted felons, or just plain nasty. It may take effort to overlook the one hundred bad things to find the one ("You certainly have remarkable persistence..."), but it is effort well invested. It has to do with developing a prejudice in her favor, so that her behavior is always interpreted in a kindly light, while teaching her better, more effective behavior.

Since this is a time of mistake-making, a response must be made, and we cannot congratulate her on her errors, although we may commend her for her boldness in trying something new. It is wise to ignore the foolish things that she does; most of her errors will disappear in the same way that her baby talk disappeared as she listened to adults talking. Where there are mistakes to be discussed, it is wise to minimize them and to avoid making a fuss over the minor ones. About three serious fusses a year are all that a teen psyche can absorb, so it is wise to save up for the big ones, when you can be shocked, frightened, appalled, and terribly upset, thereby leaving her with a memorable and very rare consequence that will mark her behavior as unacceptable for all time. To be upset frequently desensitizes a teen to a parent's reaction.

It is effective to react with this sort of shock if you usually see her in a highly optimistic light, as a person with good judgment who is respectable and admirable. To lay the groundwork, it is necessary to cling adamantly to a positive image of her, which allows you to say, when she does something truly awful, "You just weren't yourself. You must have been out of sorts. That's not like you at all."

It is also useful to predict the future for her as a way of working against her forlorn outlook and her unrealistic enthusiasm for her judgments. When you look ahead, you can probably see ways that her weaknesses can become strengths and her shortcomings can change to assets, even though at this time it may be a reach to do so. If you look ahead and foresee a powerful, effective woman emerging, it helps her to reach ahead in her efforts. Too often we predict negatively for girls, letting them know that we think they are headed for dire outcomes, and we can't see any way that they can succeed. Impressionable former children may secretly respect our experience and lend credence to our words, believing that we must be right to worry about them But worry is a poor teacher.

When you have a decisive vision for a girl, believing that she is headed for a great future, it helps to put the awkward present into perspective. After all, the greatest of women all went through a gawky, foolish adolescence, and so hers is not unique or indicative of a disastrous outcome.

If you find that you are always disappointed in her, it means that you are not seeing her clearly. When all else fails with a teenage girl, lower your standards. Even if she doesn't turn out in ways that you like, this is still only a part of your life, and it is bearable. To be disappointed in her is the same as blaming her for not being what you want. What she needs is hope and help to get there.

If you can't find *anything* to be optimistic about and you are repulsed at the idea of trying to see her good side, it is useful to try to understand your feelings better. You may notice that you spend a lot of time justifying your parental decisions to others and looking for their agreement, or complaining about how unfair and unreasonable your daughter is.

Underneath these reactions is likely to be an adult who feels very much to blame for problems with a teenage daughter and inadequate at solving them. When we were kids and something went wrong, often somebody was to blame, and we may believe that it is us.

It is helpful to accept that having a child means tolerating childish behavior for about eighteen years, and that there are no shortcuts. Nobody has yet found a way to turn girls into women rapidly. But we can be optimistic about the women who will eventually emerge.

Be friendly

If we are to change behavior, then it is critical to cultivate a pleasant atmosphere for the relationship. Otherwise, all of our teaching turns into a power struggle. Trying to change behavior out of anger or fear rarely produces positive results, and arguing and bullying generally stir up resistance rather than co-operation. The concept of the payback, in which every action produces a reaction, is appropriate here. If you are unfriendly to a daughter, there will be a payback of some sort. She may forget to help you with a heavy package, she may laugh at some sensitive issue of yours, or she may not get around to her chores.

The form of the payback may vary, but there will always be a negative given for a negative received.

You can get away with saying many things with a teen girl, for example, "You look like a hooker," and you may be clever as well as accurate with sarcasm or ridicule, but the message she gets is that she is belittled and stupid. If we want her to learn, then we have to show the best manners in teaching her, or otherwise she will pay too much attention to our tone and not enough to our message. When we are arrogant or pompous, she spends too much energy in trying to protect her self-image and to avoid feeling inferior. And when we are condescending or patronizing, making her feel like a child, her anger is likely to distract her.

It is worth avoiding criticism and instead voicing our concern or questions, or stating our disagreement forthrightly. When she behaves in a way that is problematical, it is wiser to ask about her reasons, review her judgment and what she hopes to gain, and predict outcomes with her. This puts us on the same team with her and is much more likely to move things along.

Teenage girls have little to offer emotionally, because they are so preoccupied with the changes occurring in their lives and the new demands on them. The adults need to fill the affection gap by supplying what is missing.

If we show that we care, it helps to cushion her feelings of inadequacy, and she is more likely to see us as a helper and not the enemy. We will endure a great deal for those who truly love us, and if you can get across the level of your caring, you may move her closer to trying the things you suggest or listening to your point of view. Changing behavior is far more than manipulating someone else to please us; it occurs out of genuine concern for another human being and a willingness to become invested in that person's welfare.

Some teens are continuously combative and hostile and show resentment at all turns. The most powerful way to stop hostility is to be friendly and impervious, which is an unassailable position. If there is a clash between your friendliness and her hostility, it is worth considering whose feelings are powerful enough to dominate the household. For the adolescent years, though brief, do last and last. We might as well make them pleasant.

Be determined and reasonable

Raising an adolescent child can give us a much clearer view of ourselves and tends to remove illusions, partly because teenagers react spontaneously and genuinely to their parents and partly because this is a trial-and-error process in which the results of one's beliefs are clear to see. The reward at the end of the process for the adult is a much more realistic view of oneself, as long, that is, as one remains involved.

It is important to avoid being drawn into the powerful emotional currents of adolescence by remaining outside the range of strong feelings, and certainly out of target range. When a parent reports having screaming battles with a girl it is worth noting that battles always require two combatants. If a parent can remain calm in these situations, it is possible to be a port in a storm for an upset teen girl, and to offer her a different track that she can follow.

Determined and reasonable behavior on the part of an adult removes the excuse for teen irrationality. When an adult speaks courteously and directly, it is difficult for a teen to lapse into screaming, childish hysterics, or angry verbal assaults, for the tone has been set. Parents are enormously helpful when they hold the line in this way, since they make it possible for a girl to regroup and respond in a more mature way. The opposite is also true, that when an adult becomes sarcastic, attacking, belittling, and unreasonable, the adult feels a drop in self-esteem, the teen's behavior degenerates, so both suffer.

By holding the line on what is determined and reasonable, an adult outlines a course of action that is in a girl's best interest. It makes sense, for example, to set clear limits on how long an issue can take up space in the household, lest the entire family pivot on a girl's minor crises. Without demeaning her or disapproving of her excessive emotional reactions, it is nonetheless wise to shift the focus after due consideration and help have been given.

Giving too much attention to teen problems, a tendency of grandparents and stepparents, can intensify or prolong a girl's reaction to problems, when it may be more helpful to offer distraction or productive activity. In this sense, school is a powerful remedy for teenage girls' emotional excesses since it sets limits on their reactions. Wise parents follow the general expectations of schools, which do not accept emotional turmoil as a valid excuse for nonparticipation.

Sometimes adults feel that a girl is provoking them with outbursts and emotional reactions, and it may seem that she is deliberately forcing them to respond. This is sometimes true; a youngster afflicted with powerful and distressing feelings may so upset an adult that the adult is forced to take action for both of them. Because bad behavior makes a girl feel stupid and ashamed, she may act so badly that an adult has to react and rein her in, thereby helping her. It seems much wiser to do the reining in before she embarrasses herself and upsets everybody; this can be done in pleasant ways, by giving her a chore, sending her to her room, asking her to take a shower, or other control diversions.

When a girl acts up and makes demands, it may be that she doesn't really want her own way, but that this is just the best that she can do and she doesn't want to relinquish power to a parent. It helps in these situations to get her moving, to get her doing whatever will be helpful in solving the original problem.

A parent does not need a teen's agreement to adopt a certain course. It makes sense to be assertive for yourself, to be the final judge of your parenting decisions. It may be that a teen does not agree, and while it is wise to listen to her opinions sensitively, it is not wise to seek her agreement and good will. Doing a good job as a parent requires a great deal of wisdom, and much of it will violate a youngster's fondest fantasies. A parent can decide whether it is necessary to make her comfortable at all times or whether learning begins with discomfort and dissatisfaction.

Parents are entitled to change their minds, to make mistakes, to be uncertain, and to reverse themselves. A sign of high intelligence is the ability to change course when the circumstances require it, so it helps to get into the habit of saying: "I was wrong, and now I know differently," or "I changed my mind."

In doing so without shame, we teach a girl to do the same. So that she is able to say, "I was going to get high tonight, but I changed my mind," or "I used to think that sex with my boyfriend was cool, but now I don't think so."

Although parents would prefer that a daughter have adult wisdom in her decisions, human growth is always erratic. If we support a girl's self-respect when she changes her mind, we help her to grow.

Recognize a new person emerging

Often we speak of teens as having an identity crisis and wondering who they are, but this is not exactly accurate. The description may seem apt, however, since a girl seems to change randomly. All of the childish parts of her do not disappear; she still retains a lot of the preferences and anxieties of that earlier time, and most of the same attachments as well.

It is useful to consider that all of the most interesting women started out as children indistinguishable from others, but that somewhere along the way they began to take on a shape of their own. An eccentric self begins to emerge in adolescence, a person who is unlike the former person and different from the family. She may seem to be at war with the culture or her family, but the process is more akin to that of a flower growing toward the light, even though it may get bent from trying to go around or through obstacles. For the human being, growth is an inexorable process; it proceeds without stopping, although not necessarily with a steady rhythm. But change, inexorable as it may be, takes time, which cannot be shortened.

It is not solely a matter of developing an identity, which we all need, but more a matter of becoming a complete person. A teenage girl cannot live out her life under her parents' care and supervision. To live in the world, she needs a strong sense of herself, who she is, what she is good at, and where she needs others.

Much of this finding out happens privately, without being exposed to others, like the time she spends in the bathroom examining her face and trying to get an idea of what she looks like. She needs to have a good deal of privacy in these years, which may represent an uncomfortable change for parents used to her tagging along everywhere. She needs to have secrets, keeping to herself some things that are rather trivial, but that give her a sense that there is a self that one can keep things to.

Privacy to a teen girl means control and the power to make her own decisions. For adults, a girl's privacy represents a loss of power, for how can parents give their opinion or direct a child when they don't know what's happening? But a teen girl still needs a great deal of help, and therein lies a primary conflict of these years, for adults know that she needs help, and she doesn't.

Save her good view of herself

Often the image of ourselves that we develop in adolescence becomes part of an internal language and orientation that is underneath conscious thought, but that shapes a great deal of our response to the world. Unfortunately, inadequacy is the hallmark of this period of life, and the feeling of being insufficient can persist into adulthood, undermining all attempts at achievement, or worse, preventing a person from taking any risks at all.

To help a girl develop a good view of herself requires that she have a realistic view, one that casts her as a person who does good and bad things, similar to the adults in her surroundings.

After age nine, girls generally experience a drop in confidence. They sometimes act as though they have no value to the family or school and may seem to deliberately provoke rejection and disapproval. It is also a time when they may seem ungrateful, unfriendly, and suspicious, perhaps out of defensiveness and self-criticism. There is an awareness at this age that things don't necessarily turn out well and that the world may not be understanding or forgiving.

Ironically, a teen girl may behave much better in the family if she can see her mother behaving badly, perhaps because it allows her to forgive herself for her own transgressions. What appears to keep a girl fighting is the wish to save her good view of herself, so that even if she does bad things, it is for understandable reasons.

The world rarely notices what a teenage girl does well, or what an adult does well either, for that matter. We get reactions for our errors rather than our good behavior; we get traffic tickets rather than driving awards. Looking for approval is the beginning of anxiety; it takes us away from ourselves and makes us put our own standards aside, substituting someone else's as better. Feelings of inadequacy come from looking for approval, not the failure to find it.

So in helping a teenage girl to learn all that she will need in the years ahead, it is wise to gauge how much she can tackle as a novice, making sure that she takes some risks, but not enough to flatten her. When we begin to teach driving, we need to get out of the driveway, but the superhighway must wait for an appropriate skill level.

It is wise to emphasize what is learned rather than success. Even though American education is based on the idea of grades as the criteria for learning, it is helpful to emphasize a more useful standard. To help her to be daring and to avoid perfectionism, we might adopt a different response to her descriptions of school, showing approval for increasing sophistication of thought and applauding her efforts to develop good work skills, rather than responding only to her grades.

She is likely to hold grades as the standard for approval and be upset if we do not revere them in the same way that she does. And if we ask her if she knows how to fail a test and suggest that knowing how to fail is knowing how to pass, she will be truly appalled.

If we help her to deal more comfortably with failure and point out how often successful people fail, she may begin to see life as a trial-and-error process, in which nobody has all the answers. If we avoid judging her learning and instead react with interest, we are likely to hear a great deal about the reasons that underlie her judgments. The girl who eats paper in class may seem bizarre until we learn that this is the only way she can invent to save embarrassing exposure of her note to a friend and to preserve social relations with her friends. Failure is the great teacher if we have enough confidence to learn from it; for a teen girl to do so, we need to help her keep her good view of herself.

Along with feelings of inadequacy go feelings of shame, the child's reaction to being revealed in public and being found wanting. A teen girl fears losing the love of others, but she needs to try to be a person at the same time, a difficult juggling act. We need to help her make decisions about what is right rather than directing her behavior. When she fails, we need to help her avoid harsh judgments of herself. We need to help her avoid the things that lower her self-esteem and to teach her the difference between shame and self-correcting guilt. One way to help her stay on track is to predict her feelings with her for the future and conduct some experiments to check the predictions, for example, to test what happens to her self-esteem when she doesn't do her homework for an evening.

Another job in this realm is to help a girl to separate ignorance from protective self-deception. Girls sometimes comfort themselves with fantasies of the form, "My boyfriend is a bad guy, but he's good to me." If we can help her sort out her wishes from her observations, we give her a better basis for her decisions: "What does he do that's good to you? I notice that he hasn't shown up when he says he will."

Another way that a parent can help to support a girl's good view of herself is to help her to accept responsibility and follow through. Girls who handle household responsibilities generally have higher self-esteem than girls who do not. By teaching a girl how to follow through, we are showing her the respect implicit in high expectations.

With strong emotions, listen

Strong emotions are the norm for teenage girls, and they may be expressed in many forms, including verbally, with body language, and with facial expressions. Often we can tell how she feels by what a girl does or does not do, for example, not quite getting ready in time for a party. When we notice inertia or lack of direction, we can't help but wonder if underneath there are strong feelings of inadequacy, fear of failure, or refusal. At times a teenage girl may be hypersensitive or overexcitable, laughing too loudly and speaking too stridently.

When we ask about her feelings, it may be quite difficult to listen with open ears. Culturally, listening is not a prized behavior. Most people don't enjoy listening and instead wait for the time to pass while you speak, or wait for their turn to talk, or finish your sentences for you to hurry you along, or nod at your comments as though they already knew what you were going to say, or change the subject, or interrupt you. Parents mirror the culture in their conversational habits.

It can be even more difficult to listen to a teenage girl, since much of what she says is likely to sound trivial, boring, over-blown, exaggerated, or ridiculous. It is particularly difficult to listen to a girl who is trying to understand her feelings and whose feelings are provoked by seemingly unimportant events. No wonder that a parent becomes exasperated and says, "Is that all you're worried about? I wish I had your problems!"

But in the same vein, when she was a toddler and shrieked with disappointment at being deprived of a cookie before din-ner, we probably recognized the difficulty a small person had in absorbing a large feeling, and so it is with girls of this age. The feelings are often too large for their small psyches, and so they emote.

Listening with attention is helpful, because when a teenage girl is talking, she is also listening to herself and revising her conclusions and perceptions by seeing what she says through the eyes of another. But she can do this only if she doesn't get tied up with justifying her feelings to you or trying to convince you that she has a right to feel as she does.

Feelings come and go and they change continuously, unless they are frozen by defensiveness. When we say, "Your feelings are way out of proportion," "Brighten up!" "Don't let it up-set you," "You don't mean that," we put a girl into a position of having to insist that her feelings are real and that she has a right to feel them. The nature of feelings is such that she has no control over emotions, but they will change if they re-ceive a sympathetic hearing. What's more, since her feelings are not under her control, if you insist that she change them — "You hate your brother? Your don't mean that. Go tell him you love him" — you make her feel guilty over something uncontrollable.

It is best not to argue, criticize, condemn, mock, make light of, brush off, or analyze her feelings, but instead to show inter-est and concern and to listen with courtesy. Listening doesn't mean that you agree with her reaction or that you support her feelings or behavioral choices, and it doesn't commit you to a course of action. You may be quite empathic when she describes her anger and embarrassment at a teacher who scolded her for not doing her homework, while not offering the opinion that homework should be done. Listening to her feelings does noth-ing more than clear the deck for the next stage of the process of changing her behavior. Without this listening, her feelings are apt to lie underneath and stir up resistance and turmoil whenever you try to effect change in her behavior.

When you can describe her feelings well enough so that she agrees that you know how she feels, it is time to move into problem-solving with her: "What then can we do about this?" It may mean that you consider several possibilities and sleep on the question, deciding the next day. And of course with some problems you can decide to do nothing. Or it may be a time to ask her if she wants some help from you, in whatever ways you feel ready to offer. It is best not to pressure her to solve a problem, but to show concern and offer help and creative options.

When she is anxious or afraid, you may agree together that it would help her to have more contact with the things that she fears or avoids, for example, social events or dealing with strangers. Exposure is a teacher, and a girl's mind keeps integrating new data and updating her conclusions.

Sometimes if you do the feared thing or an adult version of it, such as meeting new people, you can ask her for advice on how to proceed. A parent can go on a job interview, and have a girl involved in the preparations; if your youngster is shy you can invite new friends to the house and ask them to bring their children.

When there are strong feelings at play, you might ask her to predict what will happen from trying a new behavior as compared to sticking with the old behavior. You can then observe what actually does happen and help her to become more knowledgeable about herself. When you ask her to make a judgment about what is best for her, she must confront her own childish reasoning and wishful thinking.

Show her how to care for others

It seems to come naturally to some girls, almost as though it were in the genes: they are kind to animals and small children, remember Mom's birthday, are considerate of Grandma — and then when they become teenagers, it all disappears. We are at a loss to explain how this great personality change or character decline occurred. Sometimes it seems like she's just mean all the time.

But adolescence is a time of learning many new ways of doing things and finding new ways to be oneself. Old ways seem childish, and it takes time and practice to develop new ways. Most girls have difficulty with caring because they have not been taught caring habits. And since behavior always comes before feelings in adolescence, if we wait for her to feel motivated to be kind to others, we may have a long wait. When she was little, we didn't wait for her motivation to teach her how to brush her teeth, and similarly altruism is a matter of habit. Later on it will seem natural and right, when she has been doing it so long that it seems a part of her.

Although there are many good reasons for teaching girls to care for others, the major reason for discussing it here is that it makes behavior change easier. Engaging in behavior that benefits others achieves much for a teenage girl who needs to change her ways to more adult behavior.

Altruistic behavior raises her self-esteem and her faith in herself as she notices herself doing things unselfishly for others. Taking care of others gives her a chance to use her talents, to impress others, and to hear people talk about how helpful she is: "My dear," said the little old lady in the nursing home, "you brighten my whole day when you read to me."

She hears quite enough that is negative about her and about teens in general, and here she is in a situation where everyone, herself included, agrees on the goodness of her acts. Altruistic behavior is always therapeutic, regardless of the motivation.

Taking care of others helps her think more maturely about taking care of herself rather than merely trying to make herself feel good. When she takes others seriously and tries to do her best, she is more likely to take herself seriously. When she sees people who are more needy than she is, she is likely to see herself in a different light and to estimate her strengths more realistically.

It also teaches her that loving is active rather than passive. The child loves passively, by pleasing others and letting them take care of her; the woman loves actively, reaching out, thinking of others, and acting on their behalf. When we require the behavior, there is more of a chance that the feelings will follow.

Getting her interested in things and people outside herself exposes her to new experiences and learnings. It helps to distract her during this time in her life when there is so much turmoil, and it allows her to come back fresh. It also gives her more data about life, a better understanding of what leads to what.

The self-centered aspect of adolescence has to do with the press of internal feelings of great intensity and is not limited to this one time of life. At other periods of great change, for example, when a woman becomes a mother or is widowed or loses a job, she is likely to be quite self-involved and to have little room for the needs of others. Crises tend to increase our focus on ourselves.

All humans want love and approval, but a great deal depends on how much of ourselves we have to spend. Teen girls, with their sketchy view of themselves, often have little self to expend, and so they seem very miserly with their caring. Helping others helps a girl to expand her view of herself by giving and stretching and learning. She comes to understand that she is far more than she thought.

At the beginning of middle school, and certainly in high school, it is useful to require community service and for parents to find ways for a teenage girl to be useful to the community. As one parent told his daughter, "Either you pick it or I'll pick." The activity needs to fit the maturity level and the talents of the girl and should be in clear contrast to earlier childish activities.

For reasons not altogether clear, when we look at the histories of kids who get into serious trouble, we rarely find altruistic activities among their past behaviors. Perhaps this is because, like tooth brushing, this habit can develop only if an adult values it highly enough to require it of a girl and to help her with it.

Three

PROBLEMS

NY LIFE TRANSITION INVOLVES PROBLEMS, as it combines
challenges and changes. For a teenage girl, the growth
experiences of these years are a mixture of good and
bad; the period itself is a microcosm of life experiences. Rock
music is a good indicator of the emotional tone of adolescence,
describing in its lyrics the loneliness, despair, excitement, and
existential confusion of the age.

In modern Western culture, there is a sense of urgency
to all human needs, so that Americans have come to expect
immediate satisfaction in major and minor areas of life. Advertisements for fast pain relief, fast food, and computers that
process in nanoseconds, all give the impression that, no matter
the problem, relief is just a moment away.

But adolescence takes ten years, a full decade of life, to do
its work in transforming a girl into a woman; there is as yet no
known way to speed up the process and no reason why there
should be. Nature launches its creatures at its own pace, and it
is only the human wish for immediate gratification that would
interfere. And there is wonder in the process of a girl becoming
a woman, a singularity in each iteration of the eternal process.

Sometimes we slow the pace of this process when we lose
sight of the goal and react to the frustrations of the moment. If
we demand more than a teenage girl can offer, we disrupt her
learning.

Relationships with teenage girls can be turbulent because a
girl is not a full person, no matter how she may look. An adult
must fill the gaps to relate to a partially formed personality and
make up the difference in wisdom and patience if there is to be
a full exchange. At times, this may feel like psychotherapy, and
it can come close to being so. For although a girl of fourteen

may have the appearance of a woman, her mind and emotions are far closer to those of a child.

The foundations of adult life are being formed in the gangly undergrowth of her personality, and they will serve as her lifelong roots. Here, at the beginning of adolescence, at twelve or thirteen, the dreams and imaginings that occur randomly, her picture of the good life, will form the basis of her motivation and the objective of her ambitions. All of the setbacks she encounters and the achievements she attains will be measured against this implicit, unverbalized standard.

Some sense of her vision can be gleaned from watching her reactions and listening to her opinions. Who are the people that she admires? An older sister? A teacher? A father? What seem to her to be the elements of a life well-lived? of a satisfying life course? To find the dreams of a grown woman, it is necessary to go back to these days of early yearnings and imaginings, for it is here that a female begins to lay down her vision of the complete life. Rarely can a young girl articulate this, for it is preverbal and unformed in her thinking, but it operates nonetheless.

The job of a parent is not to make this vision, or to create it, although a girl's dreams will necessarily reflect the family in which she grows up, but instead to help a girl to find the ways to reach *her* vision, or some approximation of it. In particular, a parent needs to help a girl use the problems and challenges of adolescence to become more skilled at reaching what she wants and better able to define it.

How can an adult help a girl get to a place that she can't articulate, or even help her define what she wants? ("I don't know. I don't know! Why do you keep asking me what I want out of life?" one girl shouted at her parents.) Patience is the beginning and listening the constant requirement.

Most of all, parents can offer reassurance and guidance. Reassurance that the future is brighter than it might sometimes seem, and guidance on how to make it come out her way. Reassurance gives a girl hope, for whatever we tell her, she is likely to believe us, and if we are optimistic about her and her future, she is likely to believe. Conversely, if we tell her she is hopeless and useless, she will trust what we say and behave accordingly. Reassurance helps a girl to find her strength, to develop her skills, and to set goals for herself.

Guidance helps a girl to see herself clearly, to devise solutions for overcoming obstacles, and to help her to get back on track when needed. It is a major leap of faith to trust a girl to undertake such a major project as fashioning a life, but our alternative is to try to stop growth and keep her a child. No matter how unready she seems, life proceeds inexorably.

But the responsibility for reassurance and guidance need not fall solely on parental shoulders. There are structures we can add to a young life that support our efforts and offer reassurance of their own. One is the use of family rituals and the other is the help of spiritual observance and exploration.

Family rituals, like family dinners and outings, or ceremonial observations of changes, like graduations, baptisms, weddings, and bat mitzvahs, offer continuity and rebalancing in a time of turbulence. They reinforce a girl's sense of belonging in the family and in the culture, and they legitimize changes that require psychological adjustments.

When girls participate in these types of activities, they are reminded of the bonds of affection and mutual reliance that connect families, and they can grow up without losing their foundation. A family need not be a traditional nuclear family for rituals to be effectively observed, and they may add a double measure of security where there has been disruption or loss in a family. Celebrations and family patterns need not involve great expense either; often the frugal efforts of family hands are more meaningful.

These patterns stress the continuity and reliability of family bonds and offer a sense of stability during times of change. In stressful times, they can seem like an anchor and a way to structure one's decisions.

Mainstream religious institutions generally take the same perspective of the family, even though they might see humankind in the universe quite differently. Their suggestions for fruitful and serene living typically involve the same ideas of caring for one another, compassionate sensitivity, and fair treatment. As such, they offer support for the guidance and wisdom of parents and make parental suggestions seem less idiosyncratic and personal.

Spiritual involvement often stimulates a girl to think about herself, her relation to others, and her place in the universe. A fruitful period of personal inquiry, adolescence is also a time when a girl sorts out values and ideals and shapes her own view of the way the world should be and what she has to offer.

Sometimes parents feel that a girl should figure out her own religious values for herself, without participation in organized religious activity. Just as we teach a girl to read so that she can figure out what sort of literature she likes to read (or write), so it seems wise to do the same with spiritual issues, rather than letting her fend for herself. Religious teaching usually supports parental teaching and reiterates the important questions of those who love young people:

- What is best for you?

- What is right and preserves your self-respect?

- What is fair and protects your relationships with others?

In this framework of support and structure, a girl can more productively encounter the challenges of adolescence. The continuing difficulties and frustration of teenage girls are the exercises through which we help a girl to know herself and set her life course. They are the setting in which we give her guidance and reassurance through the practical problem-solving they necessitate.

Care of self and surroundings

PERSONAL HYGIENE

Young adolescent girls are just emerging from childhood, and much of their ability to care for themselves will depend upon skills learned in childhood. Learning about body care usually begins in the third year when it is taught in small and large ways, such as brushing teeth, bathing, and so forth. By age nine, girls have usually achieved some autonomy in body care and can shower alone and care for teeth, hair, and dressing.

With adolescence comes a new set of requirements beginning after the tenth birthday. Breast development generally begins to show before age eleven, followed during the next two years by the beginning of menstruation, although there is great variability in the pace of development. Girls who mature unusually early or late will have a more difficult time because they feel alienated from the mainline of peer development.

Physical changes lead a girl to sense that her body is not the same as the body to which she grew accustomed over so many years. She is likely to spend a good deal of time in the bathroom with the door locked, particularly if there is a mirror, as she tries to familiarize herself with her new person. Comments about her growth and development will not be welcomed, and a girl may fear that there is something wrong with her body, that her changes are actually diseases, like cancer. After her breasts begin to grow, she is likely to experience an overall growth spurt, in which she adds inches and pounds.

The onset of menstruation raises a new set of worries, among them that she will be publicly embarrassed by staining or leaking. The use of pads, belts, and tampons will feel foreign and uncomfortable, as though she were suddenly wearing the apparatus of an old woman, and she is likely to feel very much estranged from a body that requires such. Even though her first periods will typically be irregular and painless, she may feel sick, dizzy, weak, or otherwise unable to cope. She will need teaching to learn to care for herself, and it will go most smoothly if she develops daily and monthly routines.

The following will be helpful:

1. Set up routines on a calendar, one at a time, to care for: teeth, hair, toenails, fingernails, body hair, and body odor. Begin with the easiest routine and add others gradually.

2. Help to develop her personal taste by discussing her preferences with her as she uses various products and tries new routines. Let her choose a shampoo, soap, and toothpaste. Leave some room in routines for personal variation. Set aside specific times when you can be alone with her to help her.

3. Take her to purchase the products necessary to care for her body and discuss her choices with her. Avoid little girl imitations of what is needed, for example, play nail polish, and instead, buy the real thing as a woman would use it if this is in accord with parental values. If using nail polish is part of the family routine, purchase clear polish, polish remover, and pads.

4. Ask a friendly relative or older sibling to teach her some of their habits for self-care, so that she can begin to fashion her own routines from a variety of options.

5. Don't discuss her bodily changes or new patterns as a matter of conversational interest with others in or outside the family. Keep the experiences private and avoid boasting about how grown up she's becoming.

APPEARANCE

Since most American women are dissatisfied with their body contours, girls coming of age come into this legacy as well. Displeasure seems to focus on the lower trunk and upper legs, with females in general complaining of feeling fat. But true deformities are relatively rare, and instead it is imperfection that is under attack.

Young teenage girls, emerging on the serious feminine scene, measure their appearance against media images, which can leave them feeling profoundly imperfect and hopeless as well. In American culture, there is an enormous emotional investment in appearance and a belief that this determines relations with others. Contrary to the themes inherent in American advertising, there is relatively little that can be done to alter appearance since one's height and general body shape are genetically determined. Although weight can be lost, this rarely changes overall appearance unless there is a serious weight problem.

When the body seems out of control during the rapid and dramatic growth spurts of adolescence, a girl may turn to makeup and clothes as aspects of herself that are changeable and, hence, under her power. Often clothing choices are used to hide defects in weight or height. Sometimes, unintentionally, clothes highlight body problems.

Unusual choices in hairstyles and clothes can sometimes indicate group membership for teenage girls. These may identify her as belonging to a particular cluster of kids or may highlight her age. With clothing, a girl can clearly differentiate herself from younger and smaller children, as well as from adults, and she can also publicly reject her parents' preferences. Sometimes, the right to make these choices is more important than the alternatives selected, so that clothing ensembles are a celebration of freedom rather than an expression of artistry.

In each grade in school, there are fashion choices that describe one's relation to other youngsters. Clothing items, such as a particular type of shoe, jacket, or purse, are a symbol of belonging to a group or of affiliation with peers. In urban areas, for example, the way that a baseball cap is worn can indicate gang membership.

By the time a girl is sixteen, she has usually developed her own style and preferences in dress, and although it difficult to predict her choices, they are likely to be distinct from those of her parents. At this age there is also more interest in adult forms of dressing, for example, evening wear or business dressing.

For parents, appearance is a difficult subject, and one of the first arenas where we begin to differentiate ourselves from our young people; we don't want others to believe that we deliberately turned out a youngster who looks like *that*, particularly when we look normal. Our only hope is that onlookers have dealt with teenage girls and understand that our tolerance and patience take precedence over our sense of good taste. Of greater concern is the use of makeup, jewelry, perfume, and other embellishments that can make a girl look hard and coarse. These may do more than stir others' interest and can provoke reactions that are difficult for her to handle.

The following will be helpful:

1. Talk with a teen daughter about her preferences and help her to make decisions about appearance, rather than making them for her. It is wise in any conflict with a teenage girl to avoid issuing edicts that cannot be effectively enforced and that invite her to test her creativity in avoiding your rules. If she becomes focused on getting her own way and avoiding a parent's control, then the opportunity is lost for her to explore her own thoughts and values and to observe the consequences of her behavior.

2. Avoid constant conflicts over appearance since it can seem that you don't like the way she looks. Do not inspect her as she goes out the door and learn to overlook minor details of her appearance.

3. Instead of talking about what a girl is wearing, discuss how she wants to appear and the impression of herself she wants to leave with others. Ask about the people whose appearance she respects, and ask if she is different from them.

4. Don't tease her about her appearance or make sarcastic or

intrusive comments about breast development, weight gain, or acne. As a matter of etiquette, make no references to her physical characteristics at all, for these are in poor taste in dealing with women, and she needs to be treated with the same courtesy due any female. Conversations about body functions and parts are always held in private, and with dignity preserved.

5. If a daughter always dresses in a way that pleases parents, consider whether she is bold enough to develop her own individuality.

6. Help her to make a yearly clothes budget, anticipating needs as much as possible. Avoid wishful items, like a smaller size bathing suit, and structure the plan according to how she actually lives rather than how you or she wish she would live. Don't, for example, invest in expensive exercise clothes or sports equipment if she has not already begun these activities. Help her to anticipate seasonal wardrobe renewals and planning for special occasions.

7. Find ways to help her develop her artistry in clothing by encouraging her creativity, helping her develop a style, and using sewing or crafts as a way to experiment with additions to her wardrobe.

SLOPPINESS

Young teenage girls often seem most comfortable in messy rooms and rumpled clothes. In later adolescence, there is a more studied, stylish, composed messiness, which may require several hours to create. The disarray in a young teen girl's appearance is representative of her internal chaos, a mixture of thoughts and feelings in seemingly random composite.

During adolescence, a child's personality structure loosens and reforms in a somewhat different pattern, with new ideas, feelings, values, and behavior. There is continuity from earlier times, with some characteristic aspects carried over, but much is new, and experimental as well. Aspects of a youngster that were quite familiar may seem to disappear entirely, to resurface years later.

The way that a girl keeps her personal space reflects much of this internal disorganization. The adolescent's feelings of disintegration and coming apart are often vividly illustrated in the condition of her room. When an adult imposes order on this outer expression of a girl's insides, rarely is it appreciated, and instead a parent may hear: "Now I can't find anything!" The mess has become a cherished and familiar representation of her uniqueness and the basis for an emerging order.

Some of a girl's sloppiness may be simply a carryover from sloppy habits in childhood, which seem legitimate because they have been practiced for so long. But when teen guests begin to come to her room, a parent may feel a sense of urgency to insist that things be cleaned up. Sometimes a girl's messes are meant to communicate how loose, casual, and relaxed she would like to appear.

On the other hand, some girls may become obsessively neat, with picture-perfect rooms that seem to belong in show windows, in which there is upset if items are rearranged. This can be symptomatic of a personality that is too tightly organized, with insufficient risk-taking and opportunities for growth.

The following are helpful:

1. Adult concerns about sanitation, infestation, and property values should not be ignored, but attempts to clean up a teen's things are best done with good cheer and without scolding and criticism. Better yet, set a household cleaning time in which all family members tidy up their share or their things, with peppy music to keep things rolling and a snack available. It can be interesting to use a timer to determine how long it takes to complete a task like changing a bed.

2. Where criticism is called for, make it constructive by sandwiching it between praise:

- "It's interesting to see how your taste has changed in the way you like your room." (praise)

- "But it needs to be cleaned each week." (criticism)

- "And I think you can take care of that." (praise)

3. Avoid descriptions of your own teen years and your family's rules. Instead, talk about how a daughter will probably choose to keep her home when she has her own apartment, and how she will decorate it, for this will be in just a few years.

4. Prepare a redecorating effort at age thirteen or fourteen, and let a teen girl choose from among your nominations. Sup-

port her taste, and help her find ways to express it, using old sheets, paint, and rummage sale finds. Point out how different she is from you. If she shares space with other children, find ways to set off or screen apart her areas.

5. Remember that healthy, responsible adults vary considerably in their degree of personal organization, and that messiness is not the province solely of adolescence. It is also not a particularly feminine or masculine habit, even though the standards for each are different.

6. Teach a girl to be responsible for her own clothes, and once a week, on the same day, go through the closet with her and figure out what needs cleaning, mending, straightening, laundering, or ironing. Do the same with your closet.

7. Tolerate black lights and posters, souvenirs and old flowers, but not candles or incense in her room.

PRIVACY

A girl's need for time alone appears suddenly, with a closing and sometimes locking of her door and a wish to bathe and dress in solitude. A girl's patterns force the family to change theirs, so that others must knock before entering and avoid intruding, which may be a problem where youngsters share bedroom space. It is these responses that help a girl to relate to herself in private, and so make it possible for the adult woman to have intimate relationships without losing a sense of herself.

At thirteen there is a noticeable retreat inward for a girl, which can be alarming for parents who may feel hurt and deserted because of a girl's withdrawal and negative attitude. A young teen may seem to vanish within the house, spending a great deal of time in her room, moving quietly into and out of the bathroom, and raiding the kitchen in secret so that nobody sees her eating.

During this stage there is an internal renovation of thoughts and behavior as a girl ponders and often is obsessed by her changing body, social life, and personality. For if parents are mystified by her feelings and reactions, a teenage girl is completely baffled. When asked why she needs to be alone so much, she will have no explanation. In the early teen years a girl is growing what she needs for the rest of adolescence, and this period of great introspection begins to diminish as she gets closer to sixteen.

The wish to be alone may also be seen in her changed response to being touched by others. Physical expressions of affection from adults may cause her to shrink back or pull away, and she is likely to feel childish and uncomfortable in these exchanges. Touching and hugging seem to obligate her to return the affection and its expression, which she may resist.

It is unwise to ask girls to accept the touching that goes with social niceties when they do not want it, for it leaves them feeling powerless and discounted. Far better to teach a girl to react to touching in ways that make her comfortable, even if relatives are disappointed.

Sometimes the wish for privacy is expressed in the ready acceptance of time alone at home after school, when parents are working. This may be a way of enjoying newfound independence and the solitude of an empty house or apartment.

There is less sharing of secrets and confidences about social experiences in early adolescence, whereas the child might have been in the habit of describing them in detail. At thirteen, girls begin to become guarded in talking about their friends, and by fifteen they are much more so.

The following are useful:

1. Although a girl may seem moody, sullen, and sour, it is wise to remember that the business of rebuilding oneself from the inside out is a somber task, and it is often intimidating and disheartening.

2. Allow a girl to be a stranger and to have her mysteries. Do not insist that she reveal all or share with you on your terms. Above all don't say, "You never talk to me anymore."

3. Knock before entering. Don't disturb her things. Don't read her letters. Don't ask intrusive questions. Don't assume she's sneaky. Give up ownership of her insides.

4. To encourage her conversation, show minimal interest in her secrets, and avoid intense concentration on what she says, acknowledging only rather absentmindedly that she's talking. It will help if you are absorbed and somewhat distracted by projects when she is conversing, and if you avoid a great deal of eye contact. Communicate in more casual ways that you love and esteem her.

5. Find other, more detached ways of communicating. Share a movie, and offer an opinion that invites comment, for example, "I bet teenagers aren't really like those kids in the movie

EATING HABITS

In adolescence, a youngster suddenly has far more freedom and choice than in childhood, with many options available that were not there in earlier years. To go with friends to fast-food places, to have money of her own to spend, to be able to prepare her own meals means that now she is more in charge of her eating habits. Initially, all of a girl's childhood wishes can be realized, since she can, in her teen years, purchase or prepare her favorite foods. The result may be frequent, erratic, or nonnutritional eating, which establishes itself as a habit.

Also appearing with adolescence is a concern with appearance and weight. To control weight is one way to control a changing body or to produce a pleasing shape. Dieting in young teen girls may be related to the drop of confidence that appears in girls at about age eleven, when there is a sudden sense of inadequacy and helplessness. By controlling her weight a girl can force her body to appear proper.

The sense of self-doubt about her appearance and general worth is often heightened in early adolescence by the withdrawal from family and consequent isolation, which further reinforce feelings of alienation and rejection by others. "I must be a loser," she concludes, "or else I wouldn't be alone so much," overlooking the fact that her isolation is self-initiated.

About two-thirds of teen girls between thirteen and eighteen actively strive to lose weight, even though obesity afflicts only a small proportion of teens. Often it is not weight itself that is a problem; instead, it is the emotional discomfort with one's body or relations with others that provokes the need to renovate oneself.

These patterns are different from those of anorexia or bulimia, although eating disorders generally develop from unstable eating patterns involving an excess of emotion and difficulty in decision-making. Many girls, for example, at the beginning of swim season, feel uncomfortable in a bathing suit, and so they begin a diet. However, it is usually a diet that supplies insufficient nourishment and bulk so that it cannot be adhered to, and after a few days normal eating patterns override it. Feeling uncomfortable now because of her deprivation and her lowered self-esteem at failing to lose weight, a girl returns to her former patterns to cheer herself up, thereby guaranteeing a return to unhealthy eating. In time, the dieting/reckless eating pattern establishes itself, with alternating cycles and gradual weight gain.

Often the problem is very much influenced by the nutritional structure of their surroundings and the availability of food. When teenage girls are away at camp, for example, either as campers or counselors, their eating habits usually improve because of the limited choices and downplaying of eating as recreation. Meals are available three times each day, with no choice of foods and few fatty or sweet items available. The stomach and appetite adjust, and girls develop the habit of regular, limited eating, with little other thought of food.

In contrast, when girls attend a high school where there is a cafeteria and a fast-food store, the supply of food is constant and unhealthy. School lunches, according to the U.S. Department of Agriculture, have too much fat, too much saturated fat, not enough carbohydrates, and hence encourage poor eating habits. The U.S. school lunch program is the dumping ground for surplus agricultural commodities; as an example, the law until recently required schools to serve whole milk.

Outside the school as well, a girl's surroundings may encourage unhealthy eating. Fast foods, with their heavy fat, salt, and sugar content, increase appetite rather than satisfy it, and they support an eating pattern that includes frequent, high calorie, low nutrition meals eaten sporadically during the day. Missing are the fruits, vegetables, and grains that make up the nutritional backbone of daily eating and that provide energy and reduce appetite.

The following will be helpful:

1. Visit the library and find educational materials, including books, pamphlets, videotapes, and magazines, that outline healthy nutrition and the relation between eating well, feeling good, and looking right. Leave written materials on the table where breakfast is eaten and on counters or tables where snacks

are eaten. Watch videotaped material with a teenager, and ask her for her comments about what is presented.

2. Restructure the family's eating patterns. Eliminate sweets and high-fat foods and saturated fats. Avoid foods that can be eaten without preparation, such as snack foods, which are usually high in calories, fats, and sugar. Keep on hand and within sight fruit and vegetables for snacking. Cut up fruit for snacks and arrange it in tempting ways, asking a daughter for artistic help. Avoid eating in restaurants, and if you do, go to slow food places where nutritional food choices are available. Better yet, eat out by picnicking and have a good array of healthy, attractive food choices.

3. Get into healthy eating habits yourself and enjoy them. Eat three meals a day and no more. Avoid prepared foods or mixtures. Choose foods that require minimal preparation, such as fish, vegetables, potatoes, salad, and fruit juices.

4. Change your language patterns. When you describe a pleasant evening, don't refer to the menu. Discuss your experiences in terms that do not include oral or abdominal experiences.

5. Plan family menus together to include food choices that are appealing to everyone. Point out the need for including each of the food groups, including grains, protein, dairy products, fruits, and vegetables. When all nutritional requirements are met, rarely is there much appetite for the nonnutritional items. Most careful research points to undernourishment as the basis of obesity.

6. Discuss eating outside the house with teenagers and help them to deal with school cafeterias and outings with friends in a nutritional way.

7. Notice aspects of a daughter that are nonphysical and comment on them. Help her to feel attractive because of her personal qualities and her intelligence.

NERVOUS HABITS

The early adolescent years often include nervous habits that remain from childhood: biting nails, sucking fingers, blinking, sniffing, touching or playing with the hair, tossing the head backward to clear the hair from the face, facial tics, and speech habits, including, "You know..." or "Like...." When twisting or pulling of hair leaves bald patches, this is termed trichotillomania and requires professional help.

Nervous mannerisms most often occur in girls who are overly dependent on others and likely to be restless, sensitive, stubborn, excitable, and easily embarrassed. For a small proportion of girls, these habits will continue into adulthood. Where muscular tics are combined with uncontrolled verbal noises that sound like barking, a girl may have Tourette's syndrome. Nail biting is more a source of embarrassment than a physical problem; nails may become sore or break and communicate a girl's tension to others. About a third of college girls bite their nails, a much more common habit for females than males. For most girls, nervous habits that developed in childhood will disappear at about age twelve, although they may return when a girl is tired or upset.

Nervous habits sometimes develop in a setting where a girl is under more pressure than she can productively handle, be it internally or externally generated. Where a girl feels inadequate, either because she has set unrealistic standards for herself or because the requirements are beyond her abilities, she may feel humiliated and tense. If parents are anxious, rigid and demanding, or intolerant of her childishness, her physical mannerisms may communicate a system in stress.

Other factors that influence the development of tension habits include exposure to trauma, in which a girl is confronted with circumstances that dramatically overwhelm her resources. A car accident, household fire, or constant teasing by an older sibling or friends at school may disturb her sense of personal adequacy.

Under these conditions, a girl's self-doubt may turn into constant, gnawing apprehension about the embarrassments, whether private or public, with tension release possible only through nervous mannerisms. These habits are mildly self-destructive. Nail biting and hair pulling, for example, are damaging to body parts and represent a refusal to respect oneself.

The following will be helpful:

1. Talk with your daughter about what you observe and, with her, keep a record of her habits, for example, how often

she bites her nails. Discuss with her how she feels about her behavior and how other kids see it. If possible, record her nervous mannerism on videotape. If it is a speech mannerism, audiotape can be used.

2. Ask her to imagine how she would like to appear, for example, in terms of her nails, her blinking, or her hair play. Notice whether women or girls that she admires exhibit these behaviors. Observe whether anyone else in the family exhibits these behaviors. Keep track of what she is doing while these behaviors are occurring. Ask her to set goals for herself in the form of how she would like to appear in her behavior. Set realistic objectives that involve a gradual decline in the behavior, not an abrupt end.

3. Avoid all scolding, admonishments, or warnings. Instead, substitute encouragement and praise for the tiniest improvement or express optimism about the future when the habits will be mastered. Find ways to be warm and supportive.

4. When she insists that she can't stop the behavior but it is clear that she would like to get control of it, ask her to do it deliberately for ten minutes at a stretch, for example, chewing her nails for this period of time. This paradoxical instruction restores her sense of control over her own behavior, for knowing how to start something implies knowing how to stop and takes away the compulsive nature of the act.

5. Encourage the expression of feelings on a variety of issues, regardless of how difficult it may be to hear them. She may hate her brother, feel that you are unfair, or feel sad with no one to blame. Feelings do not need to be resolved when they are expressed. So it is wise to refrain from offering her solutions to her problematical feelings. Expression alone helps.

6. Reduce stressful demands on her and help her to recognize when she is feeling overwhelmed, overtired, spent, or overexcited.

7. Help her to develop ways to calm herself when she begins to feel tight and tense. Teach relaxation skills and ways to develop serenity. In particular, be calm yourself, and avoid getting tense or overly concerned about her nervous habits. Practice smiling at her when you talk and putting some warmth into your voice or perhaps a hand on her shoulder.

8. Encourage regular physical exercise that is aerobic and

oxygenating, for example, running, brisk walking, swimming, or bicycling.

9. Help her to develop good habits for her fingers, such as knitting or crocheting, so that when she is restless, she can do something that raises her self-esteem.

10. Identify those situations in which she feels helpless or lost and where circumstances make her particularly tense. In an anxious setting, where there is little structure, she may be particularly vulnerable to nervous habits.

Emotional issues

IMPULSIVENESS

All teenage girls are impulsive in some aspects of their lives, most often where there are decisions to be made and an absence of structure. Impulsive responses are usually fast, often ill-considered, and seem to reflect a much younger form of reaction, where little judgment operated. A girl may burst into sudden giggles or loud raucous laughter, suddenly collapse into tears, jump up from her chair, knock something over, physically grab something, or answer much too quickly, hurting feelings with a clever or rude answer or starting an argument. Impulsiveness may also be seen in the quality of decisions made, with impulsive spending that leads to buying things suddenly and without planning, buying things she can't afford, and being ashamed of her decisions in this area.

The opposite of impulsive behavior is reflective behavior, which can be difficult in a body overflowing with newfound hormonal energy. To some extent, reflective/impulsive inclinations are a personality dimension, so that some youngsters are constitutionally more impulsive than others. And the childhood years have had an effect in shaping her, either to practice fast responses or to think before she acts.

Family patterns have a great effect on behavior, since when both parents are highly impulsive, it is difficult for a youngster to be different. Considered judgment and reflection take training, which require patient teaching. It is wise to take a close look at how the family solves problems and whether there is adequate room for each person to think and consider before acting.

Television watching too has an impact on a girl, since it usually presents fast solutions to problems and encourages fast behavior in making choices in its advertisements. The inherent passivity in watching is offset by the impulsivity that it promotes after the watching is over.

The following will be helpful:

1. When a girl acts impulsively, ask her to repeat the sequence, but to substitute reflective or controlled behavior. For example, when she jumps up from her chair, ask her to get up again, but slowly and gracefully. When she stuffs food at the table, ask her to go through the eating again, but slowly and gracefully.

2. Respond in a low-key manner when you are correcting her, adding encouragement of course. When she impulsively interrupts your conversation, politely ask her to wait, and then have her repeat her question slowly.

3. Teach techniques of learning to wait, and share with her how you deal with those frustrating situations where you must wait, for example, when you are placed on hold on the telephone.

4. Develop a routine for situations that evoke impulsive behavior, for example, having teen guests in the house, which can be overstimulating to an impulsive girl. A routine might involve spending time in her room with the friend, followed by a walk outdoors, followed by a snack, and then cleaning up. The structure of the schedule saves her from too much decision-making and helps her to make reasonable choices beforehand.

5. Ask for her considered opinion on a variety of subjects, and listen without judgment to her ideas. As a practice, ask her to take the responsibility for working out some household needs, and ask for two different solutions to a problem, for example, how to arrange the silverware drawer so that it stays neat. Ask her to discuss her two plans with you so that you can evaluate them together before she actually does the task. Use this format for small chores, and begin to develop it as a way to solve bigger problems, for example, what sort of birthday party shall she have?

6. Help her develop a problem-solving set, where she iden-

tifies her feelings, generates possible solutions and evaluates them, constructs a plan, and finally evaluates how well it worked. Start with small problems, for example, how much allowance raise should she ask for or when should she clean her room each week. The same format can become an internal guide for other situations requiring solutions.

7. Find places where impulsivity can be put to good use, for example, in sports, artwork, or dance, and encourage her to develop her skills in these areas as well as to learn the control needed to satisfy herself.

FEARS AND PHOBIAS

Teenage girls sometimes appear so bold that it can be surprising that they have a variety of fears. But childhood ends slowly, and it takes many years to get over fears of the dark.

There are many other worries that preoccupy youngsters, some of which are left over from childhood and some of which are new in adolescence. Some girls will still have a child's fears of animals, like dogs, or may be unduly concerned about injuring themselves, or about the dentist or doctor. For most girls, however, these fears will have gradually been resolved as they grow stronger and more adequate in these situations. A girl learns for example, that she can frighten a dog with her shouting and that the dentist will usually stop to listen to her.

Some fears may linger on, especially fear of snakes, the dark, or heights, or worries about being kidnapped, and often these persist into adulthood. By fourteen, there is a general lack of fearfulness and an overall optimism for teenage girls, although new worries begin to replace old fears. Fearing rejection or a bad reputation becomes more common. With the increasing distance from her family, a girl is likely to feel very dependent on other youngsters.

Fears about being unpopular, rejected, or criticized by other kids are strong for young teens and may become consuming. By sixteen, fears are more reality-based and include worries about safe driving and post-school plans, and there may be childhood holdovers as well, such as fear of bugs or heights. In addition, there are fears that develop in response to new situations, such as fear of competition or very large crowds.

When adults are asked their greatest fears, they often list public speaking, death, and divorce, in that order. Not surprisingly, teens are also afraid of the same types of problems — social embarrassment and loss or rejection by a loved one.

Phobias are intense fears that have little basis in reality and set off seemingly uncontrollable behavior, such as running away, disrupting daily routines, and interfering with normal living. Most phobias are related to natural occurrences, such as storms, insects, animals, and the dark, and generally decrease as a youngster matures, but some remain, as seen in the 10 percent of the adult population who have phobias. Women seem to be especially vulnerable to phobias; they make up 75 percent of agoraphobiacs, 95 percent of animal phobics, and 60 percent of those with social phobias.*

Phobias generally originate in traumatic experiences that are connected to and symbolized by the stimulus. The events need not actually have happened to produce a strong response in a youngster, and it is this strong response that the phobia endlessly repeats in an anticipatory fashion. To some extent, phobias are conditioned; the body responds with a set of automatic changes in blood pressure, pulse, and respiration, so that the feelings can occur separate from conscious awareness.

The initial event that precipitates a phobia may not seem to cause much upset in a girl, for example, when she has to have blood drawn. The resulting reaction, a needle phobia, may not become apparent until the next encounter with the same event. Sometimes phobic reactions underlie other types of behavior such as shyness. When a girl seems frozen in a social setting and cannot unlock herself, she may have intense fears of dealing with strangers.

One of the ways that a young mind may cope with excessive and unwieldy anxiety about a particular situation is to project it onto an object, and then develop a routine surrounding that object. A youngster who is afraid of the dark, for example, may have an elaborate bedtime ritual that includes touching the door so many times or getting under the covers before the light goes out, and she may be extremely upset if her rituals are disrupted.

---

*Robert DuPont, *Phobia: A Comprehensive Summary of Modern Treatments* (New York: Brunner-Mazel, 1982).

These reactions are not problematic in young teens, but if they persist, they can interfere with normal activities.

Panic disorder is an adult malady that often begins in sixth or seventh grade, when a youngster may start to have heart palpitations, difficulties in breathing, and a feeling of great apprehension. For most girls, the incident passes with no further repercussions. But in about 5 percent of girls, anxiety develops about having the experience again, and a fear of fear develops.

Girls who are most vulnerable to panic attacks are those who are sensitive and timid, anxious in new situations, and react to stress with fear or great apprehension. For those who develop phobias or panic attacks, professional help may be needed to build more constructive patterns for dealing with anxiety.

For other youngsters who show excessive fear in everyday situations where others are comfortable, the following will be helpful:

1. Don't scold, criticize, or humiliate a girl who is frightened, even if she has no reason to be. Feelings have their own logic and must be respected. Instead, listen compassionately even if you don't understand, and reassure her that she's still a good person, no matter what she's feeling.

2. In a calmer setting, discuss the incident and ask her to describe the worst that could happen. Distinguish between what is possible and what is probable. It is possible that the dog will break his chain and attack you, but not probable.

3. Help a girl to be powerful and act in her own interest. If she is afraid of bugs, give her something to swat with; if she is afraid of the dark, help her to maneuver without illumination. Explore with her the responses she would make to threatening situations and what she would do if the feared thing occurred. Suggest alternative approaches with her and act them out.

4. Teach her the relaxation response to help her to get comfortable, and then use it in those situations where her apprehension builds.*

5. Help her become better informed about the feared object or situation. If she is badly frightened of needles, help her to learn to give shots. If flying is frightening, find ways to learn

---

*This highly useful self-relaxation technique is described in detail in the short book *The Relaxation Response*, by Herbert Benson, M.D. (New York: William Morrow, 1975).

about the sounds and sensations of being in an airplane and what they mean.

6. Where a youngster appears to be using rituals to control fears, discuss with her the level of tension in her life and her ways of dealing with it. Reassure her that compulsive behaviors do not mean that she is crazy, and that if they are troublesome, there are ways to help reduce them over time.

7. Encourage risk-taking in areas away from her fears or phobias. If she is nervous about calling a friend, help her to find ways to help herself do it. Help her develop ways to estimate the likelihood of success in her endeavors, and to plan accordingly.

8. Communicate to her that life involves many fearful experiences, that taking risks, and occasionally being hurt, is part of living, but that the greatest risk is to take no risks at all. Help her to understand courage as the triumph of will over fear, not the absence of fright.

DEPRESSION

There are many indicators of depression in girls. Sadness, loneliness, apathy, listlessness, feelings of worthlessness, guilt, pessimism, hopelessness, and changes in appetite, sleep, or emotional responsiveness may all indicate depression. Girls may complain of being tired and unable to sleep, having a headache or backache, or feeling irritable.

Teenage girls experience much higher rates of depression than teenage boys, and usually in the later teen years. Some of this is related to the change in self-concept as girls go through puberty. For boys, self-concept goes from low to high through puberty, while for girls it is more likely to go from high to low in eighth grade,* so that as a girl makes the transition to adolescence, she feels less and less happy with herself.

One way to conceptualize depression is that it is based on a cognitive perception of personal helplessness, and indeed, a depressed teenage girl will reply to all your well-meaning efforts by telling you that it's no use, that nothing will change or improve things. She is expressing the seeming futility of her ef-

---

*From the National Center for Education Statistics, *A Profile of the American Eighth Grader* (Washington, D.C.: U.S. Government Printing Office, 1990), 17.

forts against her perceived problem. Depression is more than the "blues," in that it endures and appears to structure a girl's life, and she may arrange her day so that she can sleep as much as possible.

The following will be helpful:

1. Have a complete physical exam to rule out any problems that may appear to be depression, for example, mononucleosis or thyroid disease.

2. Deal with your own frustration, fear, or guilt at her depression. Remind yourself that teenage girls are affected by many factors besides their parents. Be optimistic about what you have to offer; you may not have caused the problem but you may be able to help.

3. Reassure her that she's a good kid, and that you notice all is not well. Ask her to talk it over with you because you're concerned. How long has she felt this way? Are some situations harder than others? Do her friends know that she feels bad?

4. Listen to her when she speaks and avoid making suggestions. Instead, as far as you can, commiserate and be optimistic about her finding solutions.

5. Focus on the present. Ask her, "What can you *do today* that will help you feel better?"

6. Help her to make a list of all of the things that are wrong in her life and give them a priority label starting with the worst as number one. Deal with the first, and think about things that might be done to ameliorate the situation. Put off the rest for another day.

7. Where are the places that she feels powerful and competent in her life? Where are the places that she feels unable to make things happen? These can sometimes more easily be explored from a distance, for example, by thinking about an earlier time such as eighth or ninth grade, in which she can identify what helped her feel strong or helpless.

8. What is the communication tone around a girl? Does she hear optimistic and encouraging things about herself, or does she hear fatalistic, hopeless reflections on her or the world? Is her home a helpful place, a refuge, or a place in which to be cautious? Are parents allies or the enemy? If she falters, do they close in for the kill or help her stand up again?

9. Where depression continues for more than a week, seek

professional help for her, and ask for recommendations on how you can be helpful.

EXCESSIVE ANXIETY

Excessive anxiety to one teenage girl is creative tension to another. Tension in the system can help a girl to overcome inertia, laziness, and fear of risk. When anxiety begins to interfere, rather than facilitating productive activity, it becomes counter productive and requires intervention. Anxiety usually takes the form of low-level chronic tension that deprives a girl of relaxing and joyous experiences.

Anxiety can appear in many forms. A girl may be dependent on family or friends, unable to take reasonable risks on her own behalf, or she may be highly suggestible or cautious and indecisive. When she chooses a course, she may be rigid and inflexible, unable to alter her plan when new options present themselves. Sometimes she does little and broods, or is apprehensive. Her body language may express anxiety, and she may seem agitated, sweaty, or tearful much of the time, ready to explode, or she may have poor patterns of eating and sleeping. Sometimes when anxiety runs high, she may have an upset stomach, diarrhea, nervous tics, or breathing difficulties.

Anxiety develops when a goal is blocked, and a girl must choose between equally unhappy alternatives. When she is anxious about homework, for example, it is because her goal is to get good grades, which require attention to homework. To deal with her inadequacy about homework, she must either ask for help, which makes her feel more inadequate, or puzzle it out on her own, which also makes her feel inadequate. So the blocked goal and equally unappealing alternatives stir up indecision and anxiety. A favorite teen solution for this problem involves long telephone conversations with friends until the evening has been used up and the necessity of decision avoided.

The same scenario is repeated in many settings and applies to anxiety about controlling eating, doing chores, making friends, and so forth. What is lacking is the perspective on one's behavior that allows a girl to structure her responses differently and the creativity to come up with alternatives that will be less costly to her.

Sometimes anxiety is part of a more enduring problem that determines a girl's response to virtually all life situations. She may have great apprehension about any new or novel circumstances, and anxiety and worry may be the predominant form of emotional response. This may show in physical tension, restlessness, fatigue, or frequent deep breaths. She may be keyed up, startle easily, or always be irritable. In such cases, it is wise to seek counseling for her.

The following will be helpful for a girl with excessive anxiety:

1. Listen sensitively to her thoughts and concerns and avoid trying to persuade her to be more reasonable or optimistic. If she could, she would, and her feelings are not accessible to her conscious control. To try to persuade her to change her feelings only leads her to feel more inadequate.

2. Stay calm yourself and keep her anxiety in perspective. Work on your own serenity and try to be optimistic about how she will cope.

3. Be clear about what you expect from her, so that she knows what pleases you and what angers or frightens you, which she can then put aside in order to focus on herself. Be open and direct, and avoid hiding your feelings about her behavior, for this will only stir more anxiety. On the other hand, be tactful and supportive when you communicate your viewpoint. When she appears to be focusing on pleasing others rather than pleasing herself, ask her what pleases her and listen with interest to her answer.

4. Help her to choose sane and predictable circumstances, for example, in applying for a job or choosing a course in school. If the environment is predictable, then she can be comfortable in knowing what she needs to handle and planning accordingly. Help her to avoid those situations where she feels off balance.

5. Encourage her when she fails, and help her to learn that she will survive. Think of failure as a learning experience, and one that we can tolerate. Repeat endlessly that she is more than the sum total of her successes and failures and that you like her because she is herself.

6. Limit her worry load, and let her know that some things are not her affair. If Grandma is mad at Mom, it's not for her to

solve. She has her own business to do, primarily school, friends, and self-care, and the rest is up to others. Teach her to butt out.

7. Help her with decision-making, sometimes by using paper and pencil to outline pros and cons and to figure alternatives and costs. Encourage her to establish a time line for making decisions, since procrastination only feeds anxiety and feelings of inadequacy. Remind her that most decisions are imperfect compromises.

8. Help her to take risks and take them yourself. Ponder first, assess the actual risk, and then act. After she takes a risk, for example, raising her hand in class, talk about what happened and how it felt to her.

Family relations

TEENAGE GIRL IN THE FAMILY

"I really wish my parents would just leave me alone," the fourteen-year-old said tearfully. "They pick on me for everything, and they never stop telling me about all the stuff they hate."

"Like what?" asked the counselor.

"Like my mother's always complaining that my room's a mess and that I don't do anything except watch TV. Or that I fight with my sister, the little brat. And then she tells me that I have a rotten attitude. You can't ever be good enough for her."

Why are teenage girls so difficult to live with? The moodiness, self-absorption, and disregard for others that mark the period can be extremely trying for adults, but they usually represent a youngster's attempts to cope with the problems of their age, both real and imagined. A majority of teenagers are difficult: two-thirds of girls experience moderate or severe turmoil during this period, leading some professionals to claim that adolescence is not a life stage, but rather a psychiatric diagnosis. Sometimes it seems that a girl's adolescence is more difficult than a boy's. She seems more vulnerable, physically and sexually, her feelings appear more volatile, and she experiences puberty at an earlier age than boys.

At times parents feel manipulated and provoked into angry responses by their daughters. "She knows exactly how to push my buttons," said one mother, "and when I come home and see all the dirty dishes in the sink, I can't understand why she goes out of her way to make me mad." A youngster's attitude is often the underlying irritant; if she cheerfully ignored her chores, pleasantly disagreed with others, and misbehaved with a friendly smile, it would be far easier to forgive her transgressions.

> "My daughter acts like she hates everybody. She hasn't smiled in this house since she turned thirteen. When I try to sit down to have a talk with her like I used to when she was little, she says leave her alone. I know that there's something in there that she just can't get out."

It is the appearance of hostility that seems to cause parents the greatest distress: the readiness to snap, the sarcastic arguing, and the rejection of loving overtures. Parents often wonder if something happened to their daughter that they missed that causes so much sourness, and they wonder why it has to be a secret from them. Or a teenage girl may become passive, withdrawn, and quiet, responding with little interest to anything in the household and preferring to spend hours alone in her room, doing nothing.

> "Family? What family?" the distraught woman said. "I don't have a family anymore. I have two girls who spend their lives in their rooms or on the phone or with those damned Walkman earphones on, and pretend that I don't exist, and I have a husband who ducks out every chance he gets so that they can't ask him for money or rides."

It may seem that teenage girls have little use for their families. They complain at having to participate in family activities, and they usually prefer to spend time with their friends. But adolescent females need their families as much now as they did in earlier years, although they are unable to admit it.

> "Would you drop me off down the street, Dad? I don't want anyone to see that I'm with my parents."
> "Who do they think you live with? At fifteen, they think you have your own apartment?"

Parents are critically important in the adolescent years, because in this very short time a girl must prepare for the sixty or more years of adult life ahead of her. It is in this time that she must learn the elements of personal care, the foundation of occupational habits, the skills of relating in families, as well as a vast storehouse of practical information: how to set a table, drive a car, deal with rude people, make an appointment, and handle money.

During these years, a girl will form an internal image of herself that will remain intact, unless challenged, throughout her life. She will come to see herself as attractive or physically unappealing, as intelligent or slow, and most important, as able (or unable) to meet her own needs. If a girl views herself as limited in competence or power, she will look to others to do what she cannot do for herself, which for some marks the beginning of a lifelong habit of childish dependency. On the other hand, if a girl has the opportunity and the obligation to develop her skills and talents, she is more likely to see herself as having something to offer others and as able to find or create for herself what she needs, which is the only real basis for self-esteem.

Girls as learners: While all of these momentous developments are occurring there are other people in the family who are experiencing their own lives and their own challenges. Teenage girls are essentially learners, and the ignorant are hard to live with, as anyone who has ever driven with a student driver knows. When adolescence is most fruitful, the irritations, worries, and crises that a family experiences are all used to further growth. They are grist for the mill, a chance to make a girl a more intelligent, responsible, and creative woman. Parents have the choice of either enduring adolescence, or using it to encourage the emergence of a more viable human being, for this is an incubation period.

So the family becomes a crucible, a place in which great ferment and seeming chaos produce an adult who is capable of what Freud saw as the two essentials of a psychologically healthy life: to love and to work. Families teach both of these when they operate well, because contained in the family's internal processes are experiences that generate the competencies needed to love and to work.

Adult love requires at least two skills, the ability to commit oneself to others and facility in expressing and meeting needs. Relationships between adults flourish when there is a willingness to work to keep things going smoothly and when each person takes the responsibility of getting his or her needs met.

To be able to work requires behavioral habits that must develop early in life and optimism to energize them. All four of these elements — commitment, need expression, work competence, and optimism — need to be operative in families so that teenage girls can develop as healthy adults.

Teaching commitment: In teaching a youngster to love, we are not teaching her to feel love, which can be stirred up by a powerful movie or even sometimes a good television commercial, but rather we are teaching the skills of acting lovingly, out of practice and principle, because we are committed to a relationship. If as adults we acted lovingly only when we felt love, we might not always tolerate our children, respond patiently to our spouses, or forgive our friends. Acting out of commitment holds relationships together because it forces people to keep working toward solutions to problems and conflicts, and it lessens the anger, anxiety, and depression that can develop from conflict.

As adults, however, we may often be unsure of what to teach our daughters about commitment and conflict resolution. With a teenage girl, this is often new ground for us, and we may seriously doubt our own ability to keep the family running smoothly, much less teach a reluctant learner how to do so. Although we may want a daughter to make a useful contribution to her future family, we may be leery of implying that this is her only choice in life or that her gender requires her to shoulder the responsibility without sharing it.

What then do we teach? What makes a family strong and able to work out its problems? We can often tell what makes a family weak or ineffective, but we cannot make girls competent by teaching them a list of don'ts, any more than we can teach a new language by telling a learner what not to say.

Individual families explain their strengths differently. Some stress the feeling of comfort and acceptance or the open communication that they find at home; for others, the family's ability to handle conflicts and crises is basic. From a sociological perspective, the family's function is to care for all its members and to launch the offspring into self-supporting adult lives. Popular mores suggest that families are strong and successful if they can remain intact, avoid divorce, or produce children who attend prestigious colleges or obtain high-paying jobs.

Tolstoy said that unhappy families differ, but that happy families are all the same. There are universal attributes of functional families that can be taught to youngsters so that they carry within themselves the seeds of future strong families. These elements are the same four that allow families to teach their offspring to love and to work: commitment, need expression, competence, and optimism or faith.

In healthy families, there is a strong commitment to and respect for the family as a living organism. The welfare of others is as important as one's own, and although there is room for individuation and growth and separation are encouraged, emotional membership in the family is a constant. Kids do not get lost from these families, and both parents and teens know where each other are at night. If there is an obvious unity in the family, a youngster can safely leave when the time comes. Emotionally unhealthy families never seem to let go.

Teaching commitment requires little discussion, but a great deal of attention to behavior. It is important to demonstrate committed behavior, with an explanation if necessary:

- "I may be angry, but I'll still help you with the dress."

- "We'll all work together on dinner."

- "Call me if you need a ride tonight."

It is important to insist on family-sustaining behavior from our youngsters, no matter how much we enjoy indulging them or how frustrating their resistance may be, for it is through supporting the family that they develop a sense of responsibility and self-worth. To know that our contributions are essential to the operation of the whole gives us a sense of belonging, competence, and importance.

We may, for example, require that a daughter occasionally cancel her own social plans to baby-sit for a parent's night out; we may give her the job of helping a younger child with homework; we may teach that when a sibling is truly in need, rivalries are put aside and help is generously given. We may insist that on a birthday our daughter provide some sort of gift and share in the celebration, allowing another to have the place of honor. We may require that she learn to express appropriate condolences for another's heartaches, even though she may not yet have developed the capacity for compassion or true empathy.

Commitment is a behavior, not a feeling, and it reflects a shared belief in the value of the family. We cannot teach commitment by asking accusatory questions: "You don't give a damn about this family, do you?" or "How can you care so little about us after all we've done for you?" It is useful instead to insist on certain behavior and to have faith that at some point a youngster will develop the appropriate attitudes. When we teach kids to brush their teeth, it is our insistence, not their philosophical agreement, that sustains toothbrushing. After many years of good dental care, healthy attitudes develop. If we do something for long enough, it begins to seem right and natural to us and our values fall in line to support it.

Teaching commitment requires many small lessons and demonstrations, all of which point to the central fact that the family is the sum of its parts and more than that. Many of these lessons involve the commitment of others to a youngster: taking over her chores when she gets a last-minute invitation, attending her school functions and teacher conferences, helping her with homework and projects, and showing interest in and respect for her dreams.

Throughout all of this, we should emphasize that the family, whether it is a traditional nuclear family or a variation, requires all of us to work, that the family is not a parent project, and that for the family to succeed, all must help. We teach ways in which the family benefits us all and requires our self-sacrifice in order to continue. We also teach that the family is there in times of trouble and sorrow or sometimes just to share fun.

Teaching positive language: We can teach kids how to commit themselves to a family, and we can teach them to help to make the family a pleasant place by insisting on a positive tone to communication and exchanges in the household. We can emphasize the value of reassuring, helping, encouraging, finding the good, praising, showing appreciation, and seeing the potential in others instead of their shortcomings.

These ways of talking are habits that we develop or bring with us from our families of origin; they form a family language that comes to seem like the normal way to communicate. Complaining, whining, nagging, criticizing, condemning, shaming, ridiculing, demeaning, and blaming are also habits and can become a damaging, pervasive influence. We can choose to develop either language in our household, although the semantic content of our messages may be the same:

- "I'm sick of your messy room! Why can't you ever clean up that filth? You'll always be a slob!"

or

- "When you get older, you'll learn how to take care of your room. You're changed a lot since you were little, when you used to mess up the whole house. You're a good kid, and I'll help you learn."

Human feelings vary enormously from day to day and include a great deal of negative emotion like sadness, anger, envy, despair, and discouragement, and although all feelings need expression and acceptance, there is always an optimistic bottom line that we can add. We choose what to say and what to see; the glass is either half empty or half full, and our youngsters are either half child or half adult. But we must be careful, because they believe what we tell them, far more than we realize.

Emphasizing the positive must include ample room for accepting the negative, although we choose to limit negatives so that they do not dominate the household. We teach empathy, compassion, and the use of kindly words and acts to help others when in trouble, but we insist that individual troubles not take away, for lengthy periods, the right of each family member to have a positive experience in the family.

We cannot force down unpleasant adolescent feelings, however; this type of pressure only postpones and intensifies emotional eruptions. When we begin to argue that a youngster's feelings are unreasonable, inappropriate, immature, crazy, or ridiculous, we push her toward anger. Far better to accept the expressions we hear with sympathy and to remind ourselves that feelings are transitory and once vented and considered in another person's presence often change in tone and intensity. When feelings have been expressed, it is important to move on to more upbeat activities, and to the needs of others in the family.

Maintaining a positive atmosphere in the household includes pointing out the good in a teenager, so that she can have reason for optimism. An adolescent's situation often seems hopeless, for she is too old to enjoy the protections of childhood, she is unfamiliar with her embarrassingly mature body, her peers are often cruel and unfair, she is beset with powerful feelings, and no one seems to understand how hard life seems to her ("These are the best years of your life, dear," somewhat obtuse relatives may sometimes tell her).

Although we cannot fully understand the variety and source of her fluctuating moods, we can be relentlessly optimistic in finding the good in a teen girl, even when she seems determined to show us that there is none:

> Kirsten's face had the red glow of anger, and her eyes were wet and red.
>
> "You know what I think of you?" she said. "I think you suck!"
>
> Her mother eyed her levelly, and then her eyes softened.
>
> "I can see how mad you are, but I don't like your choice of words. You can do better than that."

When we hear anxiety and self-doubt, we can reassure a girl that she will find easier ways over time and that all of us make mistakes. When we see her floundering, we can let her learn from her errors, but we can also add a kind word. When we criticize, we can do so against a backdrop of good-natured acceptance of her and praise for her other good qualities. And when we see even the smallest changes in the direction of maturity, we can point them out as harbingers of the impressive young adult who is emerging before our eyes. By predicting what we wish to appear, we often hasten its growth.

It is important to ask for appreciation and reassurance for ourselves from others in the family, so that the tone of the household is one in which each person has reason for optimism and a sense that he or she is valued. Although we often complain that we feel unappreciated in our families when we have teenagers, it is important that we teach the skills of appreciating by requiring others to find something good to say about *our* efforts, by requiring thank-yous, and by occasionally asking others to trade places with us, doing our chores and taking our responsibilities. Resentful martyrs only teach kids to tune out and to become more insensitive.

To change the tone of a household, it is not helpful to scold and lecture others for their negativism or lack of gratitude; this usually breeds hostility and resentment. Instead we can use as models the most powerful tool that we have: ourselves. We can show our appreciation, find positive potential in hard times, point out the fine qualities of those around us, and voice our optimism about the future. We can ask that complaining be replaced by honest self-evaluation:

"I hate math! That teacher hates me and she'll never pass me!"
"That sounds tough! What can you do to try to pass?"

We can extend sympathy and support for the hard times that others encounter, or believe they encounter, without blaming them for their troubles. Once we have given such a response, we can require that kids stop complaining.

The most important consequence of requiring positives in a household is that all can see it as an emotionally sunny place, regardless of the current crisis. Although there are problems, there is reason for hope.

Regular religious observance is an important support for a positive atmosphere in the home. All of us need to know that there are wiser forces guiding the universe than our woefully inadequate human wisdom. Most mainstream religions also teach some measure of responsibility for the welfare of others and support the concept that we have the power to improve the world around us, even if only in a small way. When teenagers are surrounded by optimism and faith, they eventually respond to the felt expectations, and rarely do they permanently go against what seems to be the natural order of things, although they may make some frightening detours on the road to maturity.

Teaching family members to speak clearly: A third essential of viable families is the practice of straight talk about needs, even when it appears that the surroundings are not receptive. Family therapists have all had the occasional experience of seeing couples who have been married for many years and have lived with assumptions that have never been contested. ("But all these years, I thought you liked sleeping with the window open.")

Expressing our needs is not a spontaneous, whimsical matter, for if we speak without thinking, then we teach others to disregard us and to ignore our communication. On the other hand, if we proudly hold our feelings inside, self-righteously castigating others for failing to read our minds, then we cheat them of the chance to respond.

"She should know that the music is too loud and turn it down. I work all day and I go out of my way to pick her up at school. She knows I'm tired and that music gets on my nerves."

"Did you tell her that?"

"I shouldn't have to say it."

It is often difficult for parents to deal honestly and assertively with their teenagers, particularly if they harbor guilt at being less than perfect parents. Candor is often easier with young children than with teenage girls, who can disagree, criticize, explode, or cry. But it is parental clarity that helps girls to speak more clearly themselves.

There is always some self-sacrifice in a family, and no one person ever gets a full measure of everything he or she needs or wants. Particularly in families with teenagers, parents are often worried or inconvenienced, and there are periods of crisis or stress when feelings run high. But if a parent is angry and frustrated for long periods, there may be important parental needs that are going unfulfilled. The following are indicators of a parent who is failing to speak clearly about his or her needs:

1. A parent finds that he or she is often angry or anxious at the thoughts of the daughter.

2. A parent withdraws from contact with the youngster to avoid having negative feelings stirred up.

3. A parent avoids eye contact or physically facing the daughter.

4. A parent has fantasies in which the daughter is taught a lesson or in which the parent in vindicated.

5. A parent engages in continual complaining about the daughter to others or in justifying his or her parenting practices.

Where any of these are present, they indicate that a parent needs to make his or her needs known.

Brevity is an important characteristic of clearly communicated meaning. Long pauses, "uhms," lengthy explanations, self-righteous lectures, apologies, and false emotions only confuse the message. Three sentences are usually ample for conveying our needs:

- "I want you to take shorter showers. Long showers are expensive and inconsiderate. I know you enjoy the warm water in there, but I want you to limit yourself to ten minutes."

How something is said either supports, qualifies, or negates the message, so it is worth watching ourselves on videotape or in a mirror when we are trying to speak assertively, asking the following questions:

- Does my posture show that I am sure of what I am saying?

- Do my arms and hands reach out or do they threaten?

- Is my gaze direct?

- Is my voice clear and definite?

Just as our children must learn new ways of behaving in adolescence, parents must also change. We can help girls to express themselves clearly by doing so ourselves.

Teaching teen girls to live in our families and eventually to build healthy families of their own means teaching them to deal directly and effectively with their own needs. But this is a complicated process, which involves first identifying what's wanted and then evaluating its necessity, cost, and obtainability. Teen problem-solving needs to develop if girls are to become responsible women. Girls may ask for one thing, but need another, so that their meanings need decoding:

- "I need more money" (to feel self-reliant)
- "I need a job" (to feel important)
- "I need more friends" (to feel attractive)
- "I need a boyfriend" (to feel valued)
- "I need to be thinner" (to feel brave)
- "I need a car" (to feel independent)
- "I need to be left alone" (to feel safe)
- "I need better grades" (to feel confident).

When we try to talk to adolescent girls about what they need to be happy and how to obtain it, it is important to listen rather than to talk and to discuss them, not ourselves. In particular, we need to avoid sentences which begin with,

- "When I was your age..."
- "If it were me..."
- "My parents always told me..."
- "I think you should...."

These responses fail to recognize that the girl before us is not the same person we were at that point in our adolescence. We would do better to encourage her to explore her own feelings:

- "Tell me how it feels to be in your shoes..."
- "It sounds like things aren't so easy for you right now..."
- "I don't remember much about being a teenager..."

When her views conflict with our values, it is important to state our standards clearly and briefly, *after* we have clearly grasped her feelings:

- "I think self-respect has to be earned."

- "If you want to be important to others, then you have to be sensitive to them."
- "Jobs go to people who go after them."

In helping a girl to look at her feelings, we are developing a process that she can use again and again on her own, that of combining feelings and values and setting a course that is congruent with both.

Developing competence: The last major characteristic of strong families is that they value proficiency in their members. This does not mean that kids do well on aptitude tests or job applications, although they frequently do, but rather that the family constantly searches individually and as a group for better, more satisfying ways to live life. The family experiments, this year trying Christmas on the ski slopes instead of the way it has always been done, or perhaps by taking language lessons, or teaching a daughter some of the skills of her father's work. The people in the family try new ways of handling problems and feelings, knowing that their efforts will be respected and their courage and creativity applauded.

Skills are taught in these families, so that people get good at things and see themselves as competent and essential. In a crisis, when the toilet overflows or the ambulance must be called, everyone helps. Even the smallest child can feel proud that the picture she was given to draw in the emergency room helped to alleviate the crisis by lifting everyone's spirits.

Youngsters are not treated as interferences in these families, but rather are seen as powerful assets, as people who help things to work out, even when they have caused the problem. Accusations, blame, condemnation, guilt, anger, and resentment are minimized when problems happen, because family members see crises objectively and more quickly take effective action to get things rolling successfully.

Everyone's self-esteem is protected, and therefore solving problems is a mental exercise rather than a witch hunt. Blaming is usually a sign of limited creativity. "If it weren't for what you did, I wouldn't have this problem" is another way of saying, "I have no idea what to do, so it will feel better if I get angry."

In powerful families, the emphasis is off the individual and on solutions. In these families girls can develop a wide range of creative responses to life.

NASTINESS, SOURNESS, AND UNPLEASANTNESS

"What's wrong with her? She never smiles, or says anything nice anymore. Why does she complain about everything? Why does she try to find something to get upset about? You can't do anything to please her. Why does she get so mad? She treats me like I'm the enemy, but if I try to be nice to her, she brushes me off or makes fun of me. Why does she have to be so nasty and sour all the time? It's like there's a black cloud in the house."

The negative attitudes of adolescence seem particularly virulent in a teenage girl, but they generally indicate more about a youngster's self-image than her opinion of her family. Parental encouragement, a powerful catalyst for change, is not nearly as effective as a girl's experience of success in those things that she values. No matter how often we tell her that she is wonderful, she knows her own truth.

But parents cannot become casualties of her tension by having the household's harmony, work schedules, and relationships disrupted by arguments and nastiness stemming from a girl's unsteadiness. Like anyone, teen girls like power, and the heady feeling of dominance over others is particularly appealing to those who have an excess of self-doubt. Crises are additionally useful for teenage girls as topics of conversation with friends.

Teen girls cannot manage too much power within the family, because when they believe that they control their parents, they experience insecurity, guilt, and a loss of self-respect. Sometimes behavior that seems senselessly provocative serves the purpose of forcing parents to set limits and controls on a girl who cannot control herself or ask for help.

A girl may often want to argue with parents as a way of finding emotional contact and intimacy, which may no longer be sought by curling up with her parent as she did when small. Intense quarreling allows a youngster to feel adult while becoming emotionally connected to a parent. Where frequent arguing is a problem, it may help to arrange alternative means of sharing, for example, sharing intense drama on screen or stage, participating in athletics together, or working hard at some project.

When conflicts develop, parents need to set general rules and to avoid personal references:

- "In this house, we speak civilly, without sarcasm, when we're angry."

- "I don't want you smoking as long as I'm responsible for you."

Rules and expectations should, for the most part, be stated briefly and privately. A teenage girl's attention span for parental messages rarely exceeds three sentences. Girls need a chance to respond and to give their opinion, which must receive an open hearing:

- "I understand that you disagree with my view on this, and you have a right to your opinion. Even so, I expect you to do as I say."

It is useful to point out the positive consequences of a girl's cooperation, rather than making threats:

- "When you begin to speak civilly, we'll have a chance to talk about the rock concert."

The following are helpful in living with a sour teenage girl:

1. Avoid taking a teenage girl's reactions personally. Loving parents sometimes assume that if they did their job well, their kids would be happier. But for an adolescent girl, most things she wants are beyond a parent's control, for example, popularity, boyfriends, a different shape. Teenagers are often unhappy for reasons that have nothing to do with parents, and in fact they often barely notice their parents. A girl's silence, refusal to chat, remaining in her room, and dour looks at parents are generally not aimed at them, but at an imagined outside world that is not nurturing. Parents need to remain bystanders, rather than assuming the role of target.

2. Sadly enough, parents can offer little to solve a teen girl's problems. Avoid giving unsolicited advice of the form, "It's no

wonder you're unhappy! If you would only...." Far better to ask, "Can I do anything to help?" Sometimes solitude is the best solution for a fretful, irritable girl who needs a chance to rest, relax, and reconsider her behavior.

3. Although a parent may compassionately understand the reasons for a girl's unpleasantness, this understanding does not require acquiescence.

- "I'm sorry that you have a headache, but you can't shout at your brother."

When the focus is on behavior, it makes corrective comments less threatening:

- "I can't have my clothes misused. They're important to me and they have to be taken care of."

not

- "You never take care of anything and I'm sick of it!"

4. It is unwise to voice overpowering anger to a teenage girl, for harsh statements are retained forever in memory, long after our feelings have softened, and cruel words cannot be taken back:

- "I can't stand the sight of you."

- "I'm sorry you were ever born."

Rarely will a teenager learn from such words or be shocked into better behavior. Instead, her anger and self-pity will make her more resistant to a parent's influence. When feelings run high, moderation or time out may be the more prudent choice:

- "I'm too angry to speak with you now."

- "I'll have to think this over and let you know what I'm going to do about it."

5. Sometimes a girl's responses are surly because she blames her parents for anything that makes her unhappy: the party she wasn't invited to ("because all my clothes are ugly"), or the teacher who scolded her ("because you wouldn't let me talk on the phone about the homework"). People in families sometimes cause one another inconvenience, but the core of these messages

is a rejection of personal responsibility for one's own welfare, a childish stance. It is important to reassure a girl that she can succeed even with obstacles and that parents expect her to take responsibility for her problems.

- "It's hard when people don't like you because of your clothes, isn't it? And making friends is always a little complicated, but I think you'll find a way."

- "I hate being scolded too! How do people make sure that their homework gets done in your class?"

6. When a teen girl disagrees with everything we suggest, it can seem like we have taught her nothing or that she is determined to negate all that we have worked for. But it is important to look past her words to her *behavior* to consider whether she generally conforms to family values. Tweaking the lion's tail has always been a way for the mouse to feel powerful.

7. A major milestone is reached when a female adolescent becomes indifferent to disagreements and tolerates her parents, rather than incessantly raging at them. Girls need to practice defending their opinions and standing up for themselves, and this usually begins at home.

MISTREATMENT OF OBJECTS

Personal identity first develops as babies learn about the world and that they are separate from objects, that they have clear boundaries.

Personal boundaries again become an issue in adolescence, as teenage girls work out an internal image of themselves that makes them distinct from others and that may lead them to wish for a different name or a different family. Young teens often have a very fuzzy sense of the differences among people in the family, and so it seems that all members should be treated equally, e.g., "You got a new coat, why can't I?"

Part of growing up is growing out of the family, differentiating oneself from the warm, nurturing human pool in which we flourished early on. But in that setting many objects belonged to everyone: the refrigerator, the bathroom, the comb. When a girl is old enough to use things independently, for example, Mom's hair curler, her clothes, or the car, it may feel right to her to appropriate them without asking.

Some families continue on eternally with no clear distinctions among individuals and their possessions (until young people begin to earn their own income, which they consider to be in special category falling under the general rule, "What's yours is mine and what's mine is mine"). The family is one gross, melded identity in which individuals fail to emerge as separate, powerful figures and never become fully responsible for their own lives, so that parents provide eternal financial support to aging children.

Far better off are those families where parents are able to disconnect sufficiently from their youngsters, recognizing that they may not have done a perfect job of parenting, but they nevertheless allow them to acquire and maintain their own objects. Even if we could easily give girls whatever they wished for, they can only attain competence and self-respect by exerting their own efforts to satisfy themselves. It helps to avoid entrusting girls with responsibilities for which they are not ready, because we endanger their self-esteem when we encourage an unrealistically high view of their judgment and maturity.

- "Is that the suede coat I got you on the floor? I spent all that money on you, and that's how you take care of it? What's wrong with you?"

In some families, when girls reach a certain age, they have access to all the perquisites of adult status, including clothes, cars, and credit cards. Although sometimes unintentional, this type of parental indulgence sabotages a youngster's growth, for her meager income as a young person can never produce the luxuries that her parents may be able to bestow upon her. The result of such treatment is often feelings of profound inadequacy and withdrawal from adulthood. Alison, the twenty-year-old of Jay McInerney's *Story of My Life*, expresses a girl's confusion clearly when her father tries to limit her spending:

"But it's like, these goddamned fathers, they give us everything for a while and then suddenly they change the rules.

Like, we grow up thinking we're princesses and suddenly they're amazed that we aren't happy to live like peasants."*

Part of growing up and becoming independent is the recognition that parents cannot give us all that we want. In families where everything is provided an adolescent, separation and individuation become very difficult. There is a sense of guilt and failure in trying to do things for oneself because to do so appears to be a rejection of a safe and loving family. But when a teen girl is hungry for possessions, she is more likely to try to become financially independent, to care for her things, and to feel confident in her abilities, all of which support her growing competence as a woman.

Helping girls to develop a sense of themselves includes encouraging some degree of personal organization, no matter how idiosyncratic ("It's right here, Mom, I always keep it under my dirty laundry"), and a respect for the possessions of others.

Personal boundaries must sometimes be established for a girl so that she can see herself as distinct:

- "The newspaper is here primarily for me. Either wait to cut out articles until we've read it, or buy your own paper."

Many of the common conflicts with teenagers involve possessions improperly cared for. It is awkward to define what belongs to whom in a family, for it seems to be a refusal of nurturing, but defining one's possessions is a part of establishing identity and limiting misunderstandings.

- "This is your home and it's my house. I don't want your homework papers scattered all over the living room. When you have your own house, you can live however you like."

Monetary issues are often difficult to discuss in families, but kids develop important assumptions about personal labor based on how we discuss money. It is not necessary for a girl to fully understand family finances, but she needs an overall sense of financial expectations and limits. Teaching a youngster to earn money helps her to value her own labor, to see herself as capable of generating her own satisfactions, and to limit her financial dependence on others.

New York: Vintage Books, 1988, 115.

But respect for objects and boundaries must also be accorded a teenage girl. Her room, clothes, treasures, money, and mail should be treated with the respect due any adult in the house.

When you encounter misuse of objects:

1. Assess your own behavior. Teach respect for possessions by demonstrating proper care of your things. Keep track of personal possessions and money, and show your interest in their care. Show respect for your daughter's boundaries by respecting her possessions. Maintain the privacy of her room, her things, her letters. Don't use them without her prior permission, and don't pry.

2. Connect the right of ownership with the responsibility of proper care. Provide a youngster with objects that she can reasonably care for, and postpone other acquisitions until she is ready:

- "When you begin to hang up your clothes, perhaps it will be time to talk about those fancy boots that you want."

3. Have youngsters share in the cost of large individual items with money they earn *before* they make any purchases. The building anticipation fosters responsibility and awareness of their labor and its value. Objects gotten freely with no effort encourage lax treatment and a sense of powerlessness, as though other's whims and not our own work bring rewards. When we agree that she can "pay us back" by advancing money before she earns it, we undermine her awareness of her own limits and ability for self-restraint.

4. As youngsters grow older, allot less money to special-occasion gifts, a practical measure since most parents do not have unlimited funds to satisfy a growing girl's growing wishes. Instead, encourage a girl to work toward what she wants and surprise her with help when she has almost met her goal. Showering a teen girl with gifts may initially be pleasant for parents, but it is bound to end in disappointment, for a girl cannot possibly be sufficiently grateful.

5. Misuse of things, untidiness, and leaving things scattered around the house comes from a belief that objects will be replaced if necessary and that others will look after us endlessly. It helps to have a "charity box," which is a collection vessel for objects separated from their owners, the contents of which

are donated to charity at the beginning of each month. A girl's "donated" possessions are not replaced.

6. To set reasonable limits on clothes shopping, two clothing lists should be made each year, for warm and cool weather, and should include items needed for school and for social and recreational activities. Money can be allotted for the list, with a girl having an increasing say over how the money is divided among the various items as she becomes a more sophisticated shopper. This type of teaching helps a girl to understand her own needs and to provide adequately for them.

7. Give a youngster the chore of tidying the house each week, returning things to their proper place, reuniting objects with their owners, making things orderly and organized. This activity is helpful to busy parents, teaches a lesson in responsibility for one's things, and can also serve as a therapy for a temporarily disordered personality.

8. Trading and borrowing are common among younger teenage girls and allow them to feel closely connected to others their age. Although parents need to limit sharing of very valuable items, it is wise to tolerate the sharing and concentrate instead on reinforcing a girl's emerging personal taste.

9. When a girl is choosing clothes in a store, do not offer opinions until after she has formed her own. Better still, express your views in a question form:

- "Do you think you'd be self-conscious in such a short skirt?"

Where limits must be set, acknowledge her feelings, but hold firm:

- "I know you like this skirt, but I have to overrule you."

10. Do not comment on a girl's body and insist on seclusion when she undresses. Similarly, do not undress in front of her at home or in a store, and do not share bathroom time with her. Showing respect for bodily privacy helps her to develop good habits.

11. Arrange a bank account of her own early in adolescence, and require regular deposits from gift money and earnings. Consider it as savings for the future, regardless of her plans.

12. If college is under consideration, plan financially with your daughter. Even if it is possible, it is unwise for adults to offer complete financial support, for this saps a girl's initiative, ambition, and independence. Instead, expect her to pay part of her expenses, and plan with her how she will do so, beginning in the ninth grade.

CONFLICT WITH BROTHERS AND SISTERS

"My cousins were arguing at the dinner table, and without warning, my older cousin picked up her fork and threw it at her sister. It had sharp tines, and it hit her in the forehead, sticking there for one horrible moment, before it fell down onto her dinner plate."

It seems like the fighting will never stop and that it has no limits when siblings are bickering, particularly when one of them is a teenage girl. In the next century, sibling constellations will probably be identified as more powerful determinants of personality than parenting practices.

Certain characteristics emerge in particular birth order positions and lead to predictable stresses. Middle children in sibling groups of three or more often have greater difficulty in establishing a clear image of themselves. Firstborn children are more aware of parental expectations and voice dislike for the extra responsibility that often makes them junior parents. Last-born children, in contrast, usually receive proportionately more attention and indulgence from adults and siblings, although they also have a surplus of authority figures. So each child in a family has reason to believe that the others are better off.

For teenage girls, anxiety about appearance or achievement leads them to look to a sibling close in age by whom they can measure their progress. Often a good child–bad child pattern develops between two teen girls close in age, with the two striving to be opposites. One must be the opposite of the successful sibling or the shy sibling. Fears of being like a bad sibling can motivate a youngster to be excessively good or to deride the other with name-calling and ridicule.

Sibling conflict is powerful because it involves the intimate and vulnerable parts of youngsters, which are exposed through daily living together. Brothers and sisters are usually aware of each other's sensitivities, what will most easily shame or anger. Kids seem to know how to "get to" a sister or brother, and as each child becomes an adolescent, siblings may react with discomfort or rejection. When a girl begins to dress differently, act differently, and develop new concerns and new friends, younger siblings may feel the loss of a playmate and become angry ("I hate her! She's so stuck up!").

Adolescent girls who need to be radically different, with outlandish clothes and hairstyles, may need to set themselves very much apart from a family upon which they feel too dependent, or they may need to distinguish themselves from their all-too-recent childhoods ("Don't call me one of the kids, Mom!"). Other siblings may resent and resist this obvious, pronounced separation, claiming that their sister is a phony and a fake and a snob, because she still seems like a child to them and is just pretending to be something else.

There are several sibling constellations that seem to pose particular problems for girls:

Two older brothers and one younger sister: The double impact of two male personalities may be overwhelming to a girl who seems outwardly at ease but inwardly fails to develop a clear sense of herself and may be prone to anxiety and compulsive disorders.

Single girl child: With only one child, the household is apt to be more oriented toward adults than children and a girl's perspective may fail to emerge as distinct from her parent's. The shaping of a distinct young woman becomes problematic, and she may seem to be a carbon copy of mother or father.

Many much older siblings: To a daughter this can feel like living with a parental tribe, one that holds all the collective wisdom and expertise possible; it will be particularly difficult where all of the older siblings are male. A girl may establish pseudo-independence in adolescence by spending more time with siblings than with parents instead of learning to deal with her peers. When she does mix with those of her own age, she is inclined to see them as a group substitute for her parents.

Many younger siblings: The risk in this arrangement is that a girl becomes a parental figure with adult responsibility at a very early age. Unable to become truly competent, she is apt to suffer from feelings of inadequacy and anxiety about failure. She may continue to care for her siblings well into adulthood and feel guilty at having her own children and family.

The following will be helpful with sibling conflicts:

1. Establish the wellspring of each child's esteem in her separate and unique identity:

- "You're very different from your sister. I'm interested in your ideas, and I wouldn't expect you two to see things the same way."

Point out often, in a positive way, that she is interesting, puzzling, surprising, and very different from the other children she lives with.

2. Adolescent family relationships often build on the foundation of childhood. Don't expect a change in basic affectional patterns just because a girl becomes a teenager; this is a change on the outside, and her insides are still like earlier times. If she and her brother have never liked each other, they probably won't now or in adulthood. Gracefully accept your failure to control your offspring's affections.

3. Don't transform your wishes into predictions that override her feelings, such as:

- "You and your sister will be best friends some day."

- "Your sister is your best friend."

- "I know you really love your brother deep down."

This is pure parent fantasy and will only create more conflict.

4. For a teenage girl who is in the "black sheep" position in the family, offer alternative interpretations of her behavior that cast it in an esteem-building light:

- "Creative people are often very messy. But I'd like you to try to keep your room a bit neater."

Don't wish out loud that she would be more like her brother or sister. As a matter of habit, don't mention two siblings in the same conversation.

5. When fights between siblings develop, teach conflict-resolution skills, such as expressing one's feeling in a positive

manner, listening to the other person's view, suggesting solutions, and learning to horse trade and take turns. "What," you can ask, "is the quickest way for each of you to get some of what you want?" If kids fail to come up with a resolution in a set time limit, flip a coin.

6. Insist on civil treatment in the house, but reassure youngsters that they are not expected to be friends, like each other, share social activities outside the house, or pretend to have loving feelings. Emotional attachment takes maturity to develop and sometimes never develops at all.

7. Recognize that there are some positive aspects of sibling conflict. It provides practice in dealing productively with aggression, it offers a form of companionship and stimulation, and the continuous exchange often creates a powerful bond. For a girl, it can be a way to integrate power and femininity. When it begins to irritate you, go for a walk, or send the youngsters outside to settle quarrels in the fresh air. It it's nighttime, ask them to sleep on it. Adult life often requires tolerance for conflicts that aren't resolved quickly.

8. Make clear the point at which parents intervene in sibling conflict, for example, if there is a danger of people or things being hurt, if the noise disrupts the rest of the family, or if one person is unfairly overpowered. Once ground rules have been set, stay out of earshot, and don't offer your wiser solutions more than occasionally. Here, as in many areas, kids need to learn from experience.

9. Avoid trying to treat all children equally, which is impossible and unhealthy. Teenage girls, like all children, want to be special, unusual, and unique, and youngsters do better when they receive what they need rather than what is equal. Mercy, not justice, is the byword in raising children. It may occasionally be instructive to schedule an "equal day," on which all kids are treated the same. Youngsters can be required to follow the pattern of the youngest sibling for that day, so that all rise and retire at the same time, with all the same privileges and restrictions of that age. This usually discourages complaints of inequality and highlights each child's special needs.

10. Accept that your love for one child will be stronger than for others, probably the child you see as like yourself. This is

not necessarily to a child's advantage, because you may expect less of her, offer her comfort instead of challenging her, and produce more dependence than for the child who is not the apple of your eye. Children need kindness and predictability, and these are aspects of behavior, not emotional traits. How a parent feels has far less impact than how a parent acts.

11. Recognize that the little girl who was such a pleasure in her early years may have become a burden to her mother in the teen years, and accept that nature helps us launch our young by lessening our delight in them as departure nears.

12. Take time to listen to the content of conflicts between siblings, perhaps by tape recording them unobtrusively for listening at your leisure, before making assumptions about relative responsibility. Sometimes the victim is really the provocateur, and sometimes the subject of the argument is not the real agenda.

13. Avoid being manipulated or monopolized by one youngster's positive or negative behavior. Balance parental attention, perhaps by directing one child to chores while spending time alone with another.

14. Sibling aggression can sometimes make parents feel paralyzed and guilty if they are anxious about conflict in general. If even low levels of hostile exchange seem to tighten or frighten a parent, it may be worth that parent's time to explore the problem independently.

15. When a girl is allowed a clearly favored position as an adorable little girl, she can begin to perceive herself as entitled to center stage in the family. To change this type of self-focus in a child requires a parental reevaluation of the relative importance of the other children. Shirley Temple children often need special encouragement to mature and become more inwardly directed.

16. Children in a family usually have grossly unequal talents and shortcomings, which cannot be balanced by parents. It is possible, however, to react individually to each child's triumphs and failures, setting standards of performance for each child, rather than group standards.

17. Avoid parental fighting in which the child is a proxy. A misbehaving girl deserves consideration in her own right, not as the representative of her mother or father's position. Watch

out especially for those situations where each parent continually takes opposing sides in sibling disputes and the children
become stand-ins for their parents.

18. Consider rivalry as one means, when controlled, of a
girl's exploring the limits of her abilities. In reaching to outdo
a sibling, she learns about herself.

19. Sometimes two sisters get locked into a dance of opposites — "I'm pretty, you're not. I'm dumb, you're smart. You're
good, I'm bad" — and the strong contrast makes each feel secure
in her clear identity. When this type of relationship develops,
separation can be very helpful, in the form of summer camps or
summer jobs or separate schools.

SELFISHNESS

> Dear Mom and Dad:
>
> Sorry doesn't help. I know you finally got a job, Dad,
> but moving a teenager in the middle of high school is the
> worst thing you can do, especially if he or she is editor
> of the school paper, captain of a sports team or just en-
> joying high school. I know how it feels because I am that
> miserable child.
>
> I hated leaving my boyfriend and all the pals I'd had
> since first grade. I'm in my junior year and should be think-
> ing about the prom and SAT scores. Instead, I'm crying my
> eyes out.
>
> I hate you, Mom and Dad, for doing this to me. I will
> never forgive you as long as I live.
>
> Boston Heartache*

Excessively self-centered teenage girls are like hit-and-run
drivers, barely noticing the wreckage they leave behind them
in the family, where they rarely take account of other's needs or
feelings and react to most issues solely on the basis of how they
will be affected. The ability to empathize, or walk in another's
shoes, develops slowly during adolescence, and without help it
may not develop at all.

---

*From Ann Landers, *Albany Times Union,* December 21, 1989.

"I don't care. I really don't care."

"Your mother just came home from the hospital, and it's not fair to insist on having your friends over."

"Why does she always come first? I'm a person too."

Living with a selfish youngster is a trying experience; family members often complain of feeling exploited and misused. A self-centered girl seems to demand so much in the way of clothes, money, makeup, haircuts, and chauffeuring that it is particularly upsetting when she seems unwilling to reciprocate.

It is important to consider whether a girl's selfish behavior represents a change in her attitude or a change in our expectations of her. If she has generally been a thoughtful, considerate child who behaved reciprocally in family relationships, then her behavior probably results from the hormonal stresses of puberty, which can lead a youngster to forget other's needs, a reflection of her enormous anxiety and insecurity.

Some girls are selfish and demanding as middle-aged children (ages seven–eleven), unwilling to tolerate refusals and uninterested in others' needs. Their behavior is tolerated for many reasons: a parent who suffers low self-esteem may feel guilty about disappointing her child in any way and so may accept greedy, exploitative behavior; a parent may be uncomfortable with conflict and so may avoid challenging a young girl for fear she will make a fuss; a parent may be too overburdened or too inept to teach appropriate consideration for others.

When the same youngster, because of physical maturing, begins to look like a young woman, society's expectations and consequently the family's expectations may change. Now she is no longer a cute little girl whose pouting amuses our friends. When a woman-sized girl shows her displeasure in public, we are apt to feel embarrassed and angry.

When our expectations are not based on a view of teen girls as productive, contributing young adults, they may remain prisoners of childhood, forever seeking narcissistically to occupy center stage among peers and family and always to receive immediate gratification for their wishes.

Although an accentuated self-awareness is a normal part of adolescence, excessive selfishness is dysfunctional in several ways. It can interfere with the formation of friendships, it can indicate a lack of mature moral values, and it may give rise to passivity, demands, whining, and depression.

Families operate at a disadvantage when one or more members are excessively self-interested. The sharing, reciprocity, and interchange that makes for fluid exchange of feelings becomes blocked by resentment and deprivation, and family growth begins to atrophy. The family may, however, circumvent the troublesome individual and in so doing pull her back into the mainstream of healthy growth.

What to do with a selfish teenage girl:

1. Ask about and listen with understanding to a youngster's reasons for what appears to be selfish behavior. Sometimes this behavior reflects a fear of rejection or humiliation. "I want" may mean "I'm scared."

2. Allow a youngster to experience a reasonable degree of frustration and disappointment. When a parent saves a girl from discomfort, it suggests that she is fragile and cannot tolerate disappointment. Instead, cheerfully encourage patience in the face of frustration, and point out that the world is full of injustices, great and small.

3. Demonstrate concern for others and instruct a youngster in specific behaviors, for example, "When a friend is in the hospital, you must call before you visit to make sure that she is well enough for guests." Teach courtesy as a routine way of showing concern for others. Good manners and proper etiquette are antithetical to selfishness.

4. Promote a good self-image by accepting empathically a youngster's strengths and weaknesses. Show interest in a teen's views and opinions, tolerate her feelings even if unreasonable, and show some physical affection. Acceptance of oneself fosters caring about others.

5. Avoid constant criticism, even if warranted. Where criticism is necessary, sandwich it between reassurance and encouragement. Particularly avoid contrasting a youngster unfavorably with her siblings:

- "You're a good kid but you need to speak civilly to your brother. I know it's not easy, but you can do it."

6. Examine your own behavior. Do you show real interest in your children and others? Do you take responsibility for the

welfare of others and share your resources to do so? Do you avoid verbally blasting a girl when you are angry, even though it might feel good to get it off your chest? You might tell a teen:

- "You're a selfish brat and you have no concern for anyone but yourself."

- "You don't care what happens to me as long as you have your fun."

- "You think the world revolves around you."

But she will harden her heart and respond angrily, often reacting out of guilt or other temporary motivation. Instead, you might manage the patience to say:

- "When you feel more secure about yourself, you'll begin to think of others."

- "You have to think of my needs as well as your own. We live together in a family and we depend on each other."

- "We all need help in this family. Sometimes you have to put yourself second."

Then she will be stuck with reasonable ideas that she cannot refute and that remain in her thoughts. Heard often enough, they become truths that subconsciously direct her behavior, influencing her over all of her years. As the father of modern hypnosis Milton Erickson put it, "My voice will go with you. . . . "

7. Do you show concern for the plight of others and avoid derogatory comments or sarcastic humor directed at the less fortunate? Are dinner conversations self-centered expositions by parents, or do they include references to the feelings and perspective of others? These are all things that you can change to develop a model for unselfish behavior.

8. Encourage a concept of the family as a team, in which each member contributes and benefits. Require caring behavior for others in the family. For example, when a parent arrives home from work, the children can be taught to ask, "How was your day?" instead of, "Why didn't you pick up my dry cleaning?"

9. Privileges in the household, but not an allowance, should depend upon completion of specific chores that contribute to

the group welfare. As a youngster starts to drive a car, have friends over, and use the kitchen, she needs to assume proportionately more responsibility. She can take over certain of the adult chores, such as running errands with the car.

10. When selfish behavior appears, discuss it and ask the girl to reflect on others' perceptions and reactions to it.

11. Tape record selfish conversations, and after a week has passed, play the recording and ask the girl to comment on her reactions at hearing herself. Ask her to suggest how she might have responded differently. Mention that you sounded the same way at her age.

12. Require that a teenage girl regularly participate in community activities that benefit others and that produce no personal gain. Joining groups of any kind is beneficial; it helps a girl to relinquish her self-focus (unless they are groups that train girls for modeling careers).

13. Under relaxed conditions, trade roles in the family, with parents taking the role of the children and adolescents acting as parents. Act out a girl's selfish behavior and the impression it makes on others; also act out considerate behavior for contrast.

EXCESSIVE DEPENDENCY

> Many women have more power than they recognize, and they're very hesitant to use it for fear they won't be loved.
> —Patricia Schroeder

Overly dependent behavior in teenage girls may be coupled with social shyness or obesity, but within the family, it shows itself as a childish reliance on parents to act and speak for them. Sometimes the dependency reflects delayed pubescence, and a girl may be late in going through the physical changes of the stage. But the whining and pleading for adults to do for her what she can often do for herself, the constant drive for parental attention and contact, and the unwillingness to scale down one's demands are usually a part of stunted self-reliance.

Sometimes a girl may be overly dependent but be pleasant company, a "good little girl" of fourteen or fifteen who prefers to stay with the adults rather than mixing with other teens. She may be quite appealing, but her lack of true independence makes the approval she garners unhealthy, for her future lies in relating to those her own age.

Although teenage girls are limited in their competencies, there is, in some families, an excessive reliance on adults for help in areas where they could take care of themselves, for example, arranging personal appointments by telephone, choosing clothes, or scheduling leisure time.

Overly dependent girls seek a great deal of physical nearness, which is evident in their whining, complaining, and demanding, with little show of initiative. One of the characteristics of this pattern is a girl's physically leaning on a parent. There is a wish for excessive attention as the girl often attempts to monopolize the adults with her achievements, complaints, and misbehavior. To move a girl to more self-reliance stirs up resistance since it feels to her like abandonment. Consequently, she may refuse to ask a friend to visit even though she is lonesome or refuse to participate in recreational activities, even though she is bored.

Overdependent behavior is marked by passivity, and rarely do these youngsters surprise us with aggressive problem-solving. There is often a pleasant closeness about having them with us; they always seem to want to be near to us, and we can delay the inevitable loss that comes when our daughters become women.

Sometimes overdependent girls seem like very good daughters: they are considerate, helpful, attentive, and always participating in parental activities. Or sometimes they appear to harbor hostility that may mask excessive reliance on adults, an ego-deflating condition for a teenage girl, who wants to look, act, and feel like a mature, savvy young woman. Pouting, interrupting, complaining, and whining are all forms of saying, "You're not taking care of me well enough for me to feel good," which may indeed be true. When we become parents of adolescents, we need to lessen our supports, increase our reassurance, and stand back. Growth always involves stress and tension, and a teenage girl is likely to feel the need to take the initiative in her life.

When a girl has difficulty obtaining social acceptance, good grades, or other desirables, she may become accusatory toward her parents, blaming them for her difficulties:

- "You don't care anything about me!"

- "You won't do anything to help me."

- "You're always so mean to me."

These are all accusations that echo a childish wish that Mom or Dad will make it all come out right.

Life for an adolescent girl is complex, and parents no longer have the power to make things right, although some try, instead of requiring a girl to take the initiative in solving her problems. "But she gets all upset, she's just a kid," a parent complains, as though requiring her to take responsibility is an unfair and unnecessary burden. Hearing this attitude, a girl senses that her parents have a low opinion of her competence and courage, and she trusts their judgment, which makes their words a self-fulfilling prophecy. She may then become moody, anxious, and resentful because of her insecurity, and the cycle continues. Insecurity produces parental rescue, which heightens insecurity, which requires further rescue, etc.

If a girl has difficulty developing self-reliance, the following are useful:

1. Encourage, encourage, encourage. Point out what she does well, but speak accurately. Exaggerated praise engenders cynicism and distrust. Nudge her to consider reaching just beyond her grasp. Be less ready with answers and solutions. Refrain from offering solutions to her problems, even when you have good ideas. Instead, encourage her not-as-good initiatives.

2. Take stock of your own behavior. Perhaps dependency is comforting if you are lonely and reassuring if you fear your daughter will not need you as she grows up. Be clear that you truly want a daughter who is absorbed in her own interests and busy developing her talents. Some parents feel valuable only if they are nurturing and guiding youngsters.

3. Closeness that interferes with normal adolescent separation may be reassuring to a parent, but it may stir up intense guilt and anxiety for a teenage girl. A sensitive youngster, narcissistic anyway, who sees herself as very important to the world, can feel unkind about depriving parents of her presence and the joy that she believes it brings. If the parent is unmarried, the situation becomes more intense since separation can seem

like betrayal. Reassure her that you eagerly await her adulthood and the independence you will both feel in a new type of relationship and that you both need your freedom.

4. Bad manners, in the form of constant interruptions, whining, and nagging, mask overdependent behavior. These habits are not usually outgrown and tend to become more irritating with age. Refuse to respond to discourteous or unpleasant requests. Require a teenage girl to speak civilly, allow a few minutes of conversation, and then close the discussion. Give either a clear yes to requests or a firm no, or set a time at which you will render a decision. Waffling responses such as "We'll see" or "We'll talk about it later" invite nagging.

5. Avoid nagging a girl with your repeated requests. Instead, give directions, not suggestions:

- "I want you to clean your room this morning."

        not

- "How about cleaning your room?"

6. Keep a list of all of the directives or requests that you make over a three-day period, and then eliminate half of them. Concentrate your energy on the important ones and plan to get to the others at a later time.

7. Arrange daily time with a girl, perhaps twenty minutes, which can consist of sharing something pleasant. Avoid any serious discussions, and do not point out during this time that you two obviously can get along. Lighten up, relax, and be casual, if only for twenty minutes.

8. Expect a girl to do for herself what most girls her age are able to do. If she appears to have difficulty learning to do something, break the task into parts and teach it in small doses.

9. Arrange household rules to avoid daily negotiation. A teenage girl's bedtime may be left up to her, but you might insist that she be up one hour before morning departures to insure tranquil mornings for all.

10. Avoid criticizing a girl for overly dependent behavior. Instead, stop participating in her dependence, and set clear expectations for her behavior. Learn to become preoccupied, overworked, busy, and otherwise engrossed when a girl asks for help with a problem that is clearly within her reach to solve.

11. Catch her in the act of being self-reliant, and praise her honestly.

12. Parents need to grow out of suffocating relationships and to begin to look for means of personal fulfillment that are separate from their children. For many, a daughter's maturing can signal the return of parental freedom. Begin to imagine your life after she is a grown woman.

FIBBING

None of us is completely honest, and civil relationships seem to require some degree of restraint in expressing oneself candidly. Voicing appreciation for a gift we do not want, feigning interest in boring conversations, giving compliments that exaggerate reality, and making excuses that mask our true feelings are all examples of the polite falsehoods that prevent disruption and conflict in social exchanges.

We want our offspring to be truthful and trustworthy, but there are limits. We do not, for example, want private family information shared, nor do we want others injured by excessive candor. As parents, we often need to soften our comments because our youngsters are not prepared for blunt truths:

- "That's an unusual lipstick color."

- "Large stripes aren't very flattering to your figure."

- "I'm sure your young man has some redeeming qualities that we haven't noticed yet."

It is unwise to insist rigidly on "the truth at all times," because this leaves girls unable to protect the privacy of their thoughts and feelings. To insist on absolute truth also leaves a girl open to the influence and intrusiveness of others and implies that there is something wrong with her if she needs to keep her thoughts to herself: "Why don't you want some beer? Have you got a problem?"

It helps instead to acknowledge that as girls develop, they will have "secret selves" that we will respect and not try to expose. There are many areas that we all keep private, and direct questioning may elicit falsehoods, because a girl cannot adequately shield herself in any other way. Adults are used to fending off inappropriate questions — "How much money do you make?" or "How old were you when you first had sex?" — and can generally find a way to maintain their composure, but this is an acquired skill. Small girls are used to responding to intimate queries, for example, "Did you have a bowel movement today?" and during adolescence, the habit of revealing the inner self must change.

Fibbing is a part of relationships rather than a part of people. When a girl is seen as a "compulsive liar" it is usually because she reflexively avoids exposure of her thoughts, feelings, and behaviors. To let all of these parts of her be seen would be to risk criticism and control if she feels very fragile, and so fibbing becomes an extensive and entrenched habit.

Most girls are able to distinguish fact from fiction and to tell the truth at the appropriate moment, when they feel safe. Girls who lie continually are usually attempting to avoid conflict for which they can see no better resolution. They may be anxious or hostile, but they are refusing to participate in hammering out acceptable solutions to disagreements.

Fibbing, in the form of exaggeration or what has been called "embroidering the truth," is a standard part of adolescent female language:

- "My father screamed at me all night!"

- "That teacher hates my guts!"

- "I could kill my sister!"

Language at this age reflects the powerful emotional currents and the hormonal fluctuations of puberty, and it sometimes seems that all of a girl's sentences end in exclamation points. Although we may encourage moderation, we may as well ask for serenity in a hurricane as hope for emotional balance in adolescence.

When there is more exaggeration and fabrication than seems usual for girls in general, it may be an indication that a youngster is seeking a way to achieve more status in her own eyes. Perhaps teenage girls will always feel deprived until they can reach the full power of adulthood, and so this will be a period of striving and struggling. A shortcut to adult status may take the form of becoming the deliverer of important or shocking news, and so becoming important oneself, a person worth listening to:

- "Judy's mother is dying!"

- "My boyfriend's parents threw him out of the house!"

The problem with these headline announcements is that girls often feel guilty and self-conscious once they listen to themselves and uncomfortable with the appearance that they have presented. Girls sometimes frighten and embarrass themselves with such attempts to be important.

The following are helpful in dealing with fibbing:

1. We should look closely at our own behavior as parents and consider whether it is appropriately respectful to ask for certain kinds of information from a girl:

- "Do you have your period?"

- "Is your best friend having sex with her boyfriend?"

Intrusive questions that cause conflict or humiliation in a girl will usually elicit an evasive or dishonest response.

2. It helps to suggest ways for a girl to deal with prying questions (even yours) politely:

- "I don't want to talk about that."

- "I can't answer that question and still be a good friend."

- "Why do you ask?"

Encourage her to refuse some questions directly, without any explanation or apology. Requests for sexual information or telephone requests from strangers fall into this category.

3. When we become aware of intentional falsehood, it is wise to inform a youngster directly, without questioning, trap-setting, or accusations. We need to indicate that we know the truth or that we have good reason to believe that things are a certain way and to refuse to debate whether adequate proof exists to support our conclusion:

- "My best guess is that the stereo broke while you were using it."

- "I think the plans for tonight are different from what you're saying. I think you hope to meet boys at the mall and take off with them."

It is then best to move quickly to settling the underlying issue, without dwelling on the fibbing. Assume that a youngster's growing self-respect and your high opinion of her will lead her to speak more truthfully as she matures and express this to her directly:

- "As you get older, honey, you'll start to handle these things more directly, and maybe you'll come and tell me when you break something of mine so we can settle it."

Focusing on the core problem instead of the deception, a parent can describe it as a problem that must be resolved together:

- "I need to protect my things and to know that you won't take them without asking me first. And that goes for everybody in this house, including you. So what are you going to do about my broken stereo?"

4. Fibbing is often the result of a girl's personalizing disputes and disagreements, so that attention is drawn away from the conflict and refocused on defending herself. She may want to concentrate on explanatory fabrications: "It couldn't have been me who broke the stereo, 'cause I wasn't even in the house yesterday, I mean not much, or actually, I was only home for an hour and...." Instead, though, we want a girl to evaluate the utility of her behavior, in this case, to look at her wisdom in using others' possessions without asking. In a disagreement, we need to keep reminding her of the issue at hand and ask her to form an opinion on the issue.

5. For a girl who slips easily into fibbing, a good deal of reassurance and support for sagging self-esteem that takes a beating when girls fib, will help to encourage forthrightness. To dig hard to find good attributes that can be optimistically pointed out helps a girl to change old habits.

6. Sometimes fibbing is a form of wishing out loud:

- "I'm on a diet."

- "My homework's all done."

- "I'm gonna get a great report card."

It helps to point out how difficult it is to be objective about our own behavior. Small children find it impossible to distinguish their feelings, thoughts, and behaviors, and consequently they often fear that because they think about something, it will slide over into behavior, or that if they intend to do something, it is as good as done. Similarly, sometimes adults feel that to form the resolution to do something gives the same gratification as actually completing the act.

7. To help a girl express unpleasant feelings or experiences, it helps to be a supportive listener, without condoning misbehavior:

- "It sounds like it was upsetting when the policeman got angry at you."

After a great deal of listening, bits of truth emerge and a parent can begin to offer guidance, but judgments and directions offered too quickly often close down a girl's sharing.

8. Where discrepancies in a girl's comments suggest misstatement and involve important distinctions, it is important to express one's view:

- "It doesn't make sense to me that you'd be given detention only because a teacher doesn't like you."

It may be appropriate to offer help in clarifying the issue:

- "How about if I call the teacher and help you understand this better?"

9. Encourage a teenage girl to describe her feelings about her experiences and remind her that kids often get into hot water because of mistakes and misjudgments. Avoid undue solemnity in your replies and get to the core issue:

- "What are the rules for behavior in school?"

- "How can you avoid detentions in the future?"

Strongly support her responsibility for her behavior and discourage helpless victim talk, for example, "I had to do it or I would have gotten in worse trouble," or "It wasn't my fault,

I fell asleep." State and repeat your faith in a girl's ability to handle her responsibilities creatively.

10. Never play police detective and cross-examine a girl, trying to trick her into self-incrimination. Although such approaches may be satisfying to an outraged, injured parent, they damage the relationship with a daughter, further weaken a girl's self-respect, and usually strengthen the lying pattern. They also diminish a parent's own good view of himself or herself. Instead of cross-examining, encourage a girl to discuss her feelings and behavior with you when she's ready, and voice faith in her developing maturity. Be sure to set appropriate limits and consequences for the core issue:

- "Perhaps when you feel more relaxed, you'll discuss the baby-sitting incident with me, and I think you'll be able to come up with some interesting opinions about it. My best guess is that you had company while you were supposed to be watching your brother, and so I have to do something about that. But I'd like to hear your thinking before I make any decisions."

11. Remember that assaultive questions are more likely to produce lies:

- "Who the hell do you think you are using my stereo!"

- "You little liar! You had kids over here while you were supposed to be baby-sitting!"

Allowing a girl to maintain her self-respect produces more learning; one of you has to keep a cool head, and it's not likely to be her.

12. When teen girls lie, it can seem like an exciting game to them, in which they play Robin Hood to your Sheriff of Nottingham. It makes for exciting conversations with friends, in which their daring exploits can be recounted, part of teenage folklore. Unfortunately, the posturing can become more important than a girl's integrity, and so it can be helpful in these situations to discuss with her what she finds most admirable in women and what she respects most in herself.

13. As a general rule, when girls seem intent on adversarial relationships with adults, constant reminders that a parent

is her strongest supporter and her best fan will help discourage deception.

CHORE AVOIDANCE

- "I'd like a job someday where you have a nice office, and wear great clothes, and not have to do much. And also where you can go out to lunch a lot with your friends. And I don't want to have to work late, either, like my dad does."

A girl's first experience with work is likely to be the household chores that are her responsibility. Adolescent girls, bigger and stronger than several years before, become a potential asset to the family, because they are able to share in family and household responsibilities. The heavy work required in a residence, for example, vacuuming, dusting, bathroom cleaning, dishwashing, laundry, and cooking, all come within the capacity of an adolescent girl.

Most teenage girls will react to chores according to the understandings laid down in childhood about how the family operates. A family is a complex organization that requires a great deal of input to sustain life and to launch children. All of the chores can be performed by adults, or by hired servants, or they can be shared, with gradual shifts in tasks as children mature.

In families where parents provide all supports throughout childhood, hostility develops during adolescence because parents often resent the parasitism of their offspring, and teenagers are apt to feel a lack of competence and value to the family, sentiments based on a realistic assessment of their limited contributions. There is also a guilty defensiveness regarding one's poor habits. Parents who have been uncomfortable requiring their children to contribute to the family because of guilt, fear of abandonment, or hostility will find it more intimidating to require an uncooperative teenager to do so. Parents often underestimate the capabilities of their offspring, and so are inclined to see most household chores as beyond the capacity of a teen, concluding that it is easier to do the job themselves. A girl who is considered incapable of using the washing machine or the vacuum will see herself in this limited way, and her self-esteem will drop accordingly. Protecting a teenage girl from life's demands is likely to make her less secure rather than more so. All chores take teaching and supervision, but a job well done is a good remedy for anxiety, depression, or boredom.

There are families in which all members participate in chores appropriate to the level of their abilities. Small children may do very simple tasks such as carrying objects to various rooms, or announcing meal times, but the concept develops of the family as a living organism sustained by all. Although no one relishes hard work and there may be bickering about relative contributions, all see the necessity of contributing in order to keep the family running smoothly. Over time, youngsters see themselves as necessary, significant, and important to the family. A sense of integration and belonging emerges from long-term sharing of household responsibilities.

To prepare a girl for adult employment, we need to develop habits that will help her to be productive and successful, habits like punctuality, attentiveness, thoroughness, and enthusiasm. Exposure to work in the family is the first experience most youngsters have, and we can begin to cultivate appropriate habits while we have a strong influence. Girls are most likely to imitate what they see, so it is important that they observe our approach to work.

As a girl reaches fifteen or sixteen, part-time jobs become an important source of learning about the real world. Ten hours of work weekly is maximum for girls with academic obligations and social needs to meet as well. Summer work is also a powerful learning experience. Two effective ways to encourage reluctant workers to find and keep a job are to provide little or no spending money and to use youngsters for household chores at no pay.

To teach a girl the value of money, we need to connect it to work, for money is the representation of labor. For a girl to associate the cost of a new sweater with a full day of baby-sitting or housecleaning helps her to think realistically about her own needs and to take care of her possessions.

When dealing with a reluctance to work at chores:

1. Keep a sense of perspective. Most of us are unenthusiastic about physical labor. Teach strategies for reducing the unpleasantness of work, for example, playing music while working,

doing chores quickly, using a timer to shoot for a record, arranging a reward at the conclusion of a chore, breaking a task into smaller parts.

2. Work alongside a girl, particularly in the learning phase, so that you can monitor and shape her activity with a lot of encouragement, which all learners need.

3. Concentrate on teaching the task and its requirements. Before starting, make and post a list of what constitutes a completed job. This helps to depersonalize the activity and limit the tension:

Washing dishes is finished when:

- All dishes are washed clean of food and grease, drained, dried, and put in cabinets.

- Pots are scrubbed and draining in the basket.

- Food is covered and put away.

4. Do not link allowances to chores because girls need spending money for routine minor expenses. Chores are part of family needs and cannot be optional for any family members.

5. Set times for chores so that procrastination and arguing can be avoided. Choose times when other activities are not likely to interfere, for example, Saturday mornings rather than afternoons. Insist that chores be done even when more attractive opportunities present themselves. A girl who wants to go to a pajama party on Friday night can do her Saturday chores on Friday afternoon before she goes.

6. Occasionally, once every few months, do a youngster's chores when she is pinched for time. Heartfelt appreciation stems from help that is seen as purely voluntary rather than expected.

7. Adolescent girls spend a great deal of time in the bathroom, and chores should include cleaning and straightening out this area on a daily basis.

DISCOURTESY

Dear Miss Manners:

My favorite cousin's daughter and her best friend's visit to me last week is the cause of my present unhappiness.

Mary and Jill arrived from a tiny country town on the bus, and my husband and I planned a wonderful week for the two girls. After four days, in which I learned that these two were capable of anything just short of delinquency, I called my cousin and asked if they could return home — not giving any of the real reasons we had for wanting them to go. But here are a few: When I asked for a napkin at a local restaurant, Jill said — loud enough for everyone to hear — "I didn't come down here to be her maid," and "These two oldies are weird." They ransacked the refrigerator as we slept and left half-filled Cokes under the bed, dripping all over the new wall-to-wall carpeting. They left the guest bathroom in worse shape than did Elvis Presley and his entourage at a Holiday Inn....*

Inside a family we are used to tolerating and even being amused by childish behavior, and we may fail to notice that the behaver is no longer a child. Teenage girls increasingly deal with the larger world, which judges them without the softening effect of parental love, and sometimes their behavior closes doors.

A fair proportion of this society's psychological disorders could be eliminated by the early and systematic teaching of good manners based on consideration of others, which would certainly make relationships more satisfying all around. Teenage girls are often difficult in a family because they are ignorant of routine etiquette or because they are not expected to use it. It is easy to become accustomed to bad manners in our families.

The teaching of good manners is a long process best accomplished in discrete steps with constant encouragement for limited progress. Sometimes when a girl begins to move in wider circles, parents become anxious about her clumsiness and attempt to teach her too much too quickly, with a great deal of criticism. The result can be a serious erosion of a youngster's self-esteem and a general resentment of proper social forms. Far better to emphasize that we want a youngster's natural attractiveness to shine through, undimmed by bad form. No matter

---

*Judith Martin, *Miss Manners' Guide to Rearing Perfect Children* (New York: Penguin Books, 1984).

how resistant a girl may seem toward her parents' teachings, what they teach her will be retained.

The single most powerful way to teach courtesy is to behave courteously oneself at all times, even in the heat of provocative behavior or rude treatment. Teens often behave as they are treated, and when we shout, name call, ridicule, or ignore our adolescents, we can expect them to do the same. What's more, when our daughters behave rudely in the community, they portray graphically their families' habits. When a girl is angry and out of control, raising her voice or speaking disrespectfully, courteous but firm reactions can be helpful in restoring her control.

Even polite parental behavior needs power behind it, since modeling alone is insufficient to teach the complex set of skills we call good manners. To help a girl learn the spirit of courtesy, it is important to teach cheerfully, encouragingly, so that she approaches social encounters as an opportunity to learn about others and show her best side, rather than running the gauntlet to avoid social ostracism. To teach with constant criticism suggests that the world is constantly critical.

It is much easier to be encouraging when behavior is discussed *prior* to an event rather than after. Girls are far more receptive to coaching than to post-mortems. When suggestions are made prior to an event, a girl has a chance to try out new behavior and to imagine herself in a new role. Before her overnight guest arrives, for example, we might ask her how she can entertain her friend or help out with homesickness.

Never, under any circumstances, embarrass a girl in public or reprimand her in front of friends. Not only is this bad manners, but it is also poor teaching since her humiliation will block your message. If a girl's behavior needs correcting, ask to speak with her privately, and state your expectations clearly, offering help if she needs it. If behavior continues to be a problem, give polite excuses and end her social contact for the time being.

Encourage a girl to entertain her friends at home, and treat them politely regardless of their manners. Your home is a girl's classroom for social learning and the only place in her life where people will care enough to help her learn courtesy.

When a girl's friends behave impolitely, do not point it out to your daughter. Avoid at all costs direct criticism of her friends since this makes a teenager defensive and closed to your advice. Instead, emphasize and describe courteous behavior:

- "At Beth's house, people leave the table when they're finished eating. At our house, we wait until everyone is done."

- "Chewing gum and cracking it is not for you. It's not good manners to make body noises around other people."

Where possible, take a girl to restaurants, the theater, weddings, and other events requiring formal manners. This supports the precept that civilized manners are important for harmonious living and are not an obscure practice of her bizarre family. It also helps to build her repertoire of social skills.

If family mealtimes become a source of tension because of a girl's unpleasantness, bickering, noisy behavior, or inappropriate personal hygiene or posture, teach the principle that we are all guests at the family table and that no one has the right to participate if it disrupts others' comfort. Have her temporarily eat alone, perhaps at an earlier time, and cheerfully encourage her to practice the behavior necessary for joining the family.

In general, treat a youngster with the courtesy due a well-bred young woman; girls often rise, or sink, to meet our expectations. Telling cute stories about her social flops or angrily criticizing her gracelessness only stir resistance to our teachings about manners.

The next section of this chapter is devoted to suggestions for three periods of adolescence, with social teachings useful for each period.

Eleven–twelve:
1. Physical awkwardness is reaching a peak in these years, so it is important to be patient with spills and breakage. With developing neurological integration, a youngster will be better able to integrate her thoughts, perceptions, and movements. Teach beginning skills of graceful dining, such as using a napkin instead of the tongue to clean fingers and using utensils rather than our fingers to move food around.
2. Develop the art of mealtime conversation by requesting that a youngster look at someone who is speaking and wait

her turn to contribute. Learning to ask polite questions, make tactful remarks, and speak in a well-modulated tone of voice, particularly when feelings run high, is important. Discourage inappropriate subjects, such as the dog's vomiting, dead animals on the road, or what a brother did wrong today.

3. Require that bodily functions be attended to in private, particularly care of the teeth, nails, nose, hair, and ears. Wearing sufficient clothing around the house is also important for a girl of this age.

4. Teach respect for others' property by insisting that permission be sought before borrowing, that items be returned promptly and in good condition (or replaced), and that the privacy of other family members be respected.

5. The elements of having and being a guest can be introduced, with appropriate attention to the needs of others. Proper behavior in public places, good birthday party manners, and behavior required as a spectator or participant at various sports may be discussed. Point out, for example, that yelling encouragement is acceptable at a football game, but not at a spelling bee.

Thirteen–fourteen:

1. Girls at this age begin to be socially involved outside the home, and it is impossible to provide guidance for every contingency that may arise. Better to suggest responding to the social customs of her group with two basic rules: consideration of the feelings of others, and the family's definitions of right and wrong.

2. As a host, emphasize the need to be aware of a guest's comfort, rather than to follow a rigid set of rules. When she is a guest, teach her to observe and follow a family's customs, without making special requests and expecting some inconveniences.

3. Teach proper posture, eye contact, and the use of names when speaking with others.

4. Regardless of her anxiety, ask her to offer help to adult hosts when she is a guest.

5. Insist on personal hygiene routines, which include a daily shower or bath that ends promptly, fresh underwear, well-

manicured hands and feet, removal of bodily hair where required, and appropriate menstrual supplies.

Fifteen–nineteen:
1. In the latter half of adolescence, parents are consultants
more than teachers, available for advice on less common problems. This is an ideal time for teaching the etiquette of the job or
college interview, graduations, and funerals, appropriate manners for those who are hospitalized or grieving, handling the
solo doctor or dentist visit, or dealing with service people in
retail business.
2. As a girl's world widens, she needs help in learning how
to deal with correspondence invitations, condolences, and the
requirements of traveling safely and comfortably.
3. Sensitivity to the rights of others in public is also important. A girl should learn to clean up her own trash, play music
softly or not at all, and leave property in the condition in which
she found it.
4. A girl will benefit from help in learning to deal with her
adult body by moving quietly and gracefully, opening and closing doors without disturbance, learning to say "excuse me"
when she brushes by someone, and moving aside smoothly for
others. These are not pretentious mannerisms of an inferior gender, but rather the social lubrication that allow her to move
easily among others.
5. Teaching conversation that sets others at ease gives a teenage girl a useful tool in relationships. When she speaks of her
interests rather than herself and helps others to share their
thoughts, she is better able to relate in a way that builds her
relationships and her self-esteem.

Friends

SHYNESS AND WITHDRAWAL

Shyness is caused by a lack of social skills; often a girl has no
way to deal with the endless variety of social situations she
begins to encounter in early adolescence. Since training in etiquette was abandoned years ago as sexist and artificial, teens

are often left to their own devices and must invent ways to feel comfortable in social situations. Rarely are they successful, and more often they end up embarrassing everyone.

Shyness is not limited to children, for a substantial proportion of adults see themselves as shy, and often shy parents have shy children. But when teens feel shy, they may cover it up with other behaviors, such as being loud or raucous. Or they may go to the other extreme, becoming engrossed in books or ideas to avoid exchanges with people.

The concern for a shy teenage girl is that she will miss a great deal of social activity and good fun because of her reluctance and hesitation about joining in. She may be left out if she does not take the initiative to join in and may begin to see herself as a social dud.

Shyness is often a way that a psyche protects itself from premature engagement with others, and sometimes a girl is not ready to dive into the social whirl. Shyness is situation specific: a girl who is ill at ease at the school dance may be quite comfortable on the basketball court or talking to small children. When girls feel shy and act shy, it is usually because they have had few successful experiences in the situation at hand.

If a girl wants to have more social contact, which she may not admit, parents can be helpful in teaching the social skills that will ease the way for her. But this must be done delicately so that she doesn't feel that she is being trained in the social graces, which of course she is.

The following will be helpful when a girl is shy:

1. It is easier to be comfortable in any social setting if groundwork has been laid and preparation has been done. It is for this reason that we teach the social forms of staying in touch, such as the social conventions for carrying on telephone conversations, writing notes and letters, remembering friends' birthdays, and attending special celebrations. At the school dance, when no one asks us to dance, we can pass the time by finding an acquaintance and starting a conversation.

2. Watch television with a shy teenager, but turn off the sound and ask her to figure out whose body posture is welcoming and whose says, "Stay away!" If possible, do a videotape of her with other people and then watch it with her. Look at her self-presentation. Does she lean forward, avoid folding her

arms when talking to people, and make eye contact? Does she smile and frown at the appropriate times? Does her voice tone convey friendliness? Sometimes shyness gives the appearance of aloofness or arrogance. What would she like to communicate to people?

3. With her cooperation, tape record her conversation while she is on the telephone, and look at her speech patterns. Does she speak in the patterns of her friends, or is her speech markedly different? How long are her silences? Is she passive or active in conversations? If she is quiet and offers little, others may feel that they have to carry her in exchanges and tire of doing so. Is she hoping that others will make it easier for her, or does she take the responsibility herself?

4. Is she boring? Does she approach social encounters thinking of what she can get from others or what she can offer them? What does she do to make others more comfortable? How can she help another shy girl to be more comfortable in a social situation?

5. Observe the behaviors of other kids who are not shy. What do they do? What does she do differently that causes a problem? How do others make friends? start a conversation? end a conversation? If she is too focused on her own discomfort, she will fail to notice others and will miss the opportunity to learn from others' example.

6. Is she an attractive human being? Does she have characteristics that repel people, such as a shrill voice? Emphasize that she has *choices* about how she wants to appear to others.

7. Ask her to enunciate the rules about how a girl is supposed to behave in social situations, such as in the lunchroom or classroom or on the telephone. Observe for yourself whether they are accurate.

NO BOYFRIEND, WRONG BOYFRIEND, TOO MUCH BOYFRIEND

Between the ages of twelve and sixteen, a major change occurs in a girl's relation to others as she learns to be comfortable with partnerships based on reciprocity. This extends to both girlfriends and boyfriends, even though the latter may occur primarily in fantasy.

By age sixteen, three-quarters of girls are going steady or

have done so at some point, and a majority of girls have had sexual intercourse.* Although sex is not an accurate indicator of the emotional depth of relating, it does point to a change in relationship forms.

Much of a girl's gender relating begins at around age thirteen, when parties begin to include "making out" as part of the entertainment. As girls get closer to age sixteen, exploratory sexual activity becomes private. Awareness of the opposite sex usually starts at an earlier age for girls than for boys, and the first attachment for a boy often is not openly expressed.

An absence of boyfriends or a steady boyfriend does not indicate a problem, although if combined with a general dearth of friends, it may represent a lack of social skills. Young teenage girls often long for a boyfriend as a way to belong and to be included; having a boyfriend provides a girl a conversation focus and a status symbol, even if boy and girl spend little time together.

True emotional relating between a teen boy and girl cannot occur before early adolescence, because a girl is still very much in the late childhood stage and has little room for mature reciprocal relationships.

For some girls, the dependency on parents (particularly a father) that marked late childhood may be transferred to a boy, blocking the development of self-reliance. When asked why she wants a boyfriend, a girl may see all sorts of benefits, but with further probing it becomes clear that these are benefits she feels inadequate to achieve for herself.

The confusion about how to form relationships with others, particularly boys, may lead to an early sexual relationship as a way to create a bond. Rarely is this a bond of strong friendship, and it may produce a superficial but binding relationship between two youngsters.

The following will be helpful when there is no boyfriend:

1. Help a girl to find varied ways to feel special so that she sees herself as having many gifts and does not measure her worth by male attention.

2. Teach relating skills to a girl who seems lacking, begin-

---

*J. Brooks-Gunn and F. Furstenberg, "Adolescent Sexual Behavior," *American Psychologist* 44, no. 2 (February 1989): 249–57.

ning with basic manners. Role play and practice those behaviors that ease social relating, for example, extending, accepting, and declining social invitations.

3. Teach conversation skills, particularly as they apply to teenagers. Help her to develop several areas that she can discuss with her friends, and help her to learn the structure of discourse so that she can be creative in her content, for example, by limiting each participant to three sentences at a turn in a conversation. Teach her to speak with those outside her immediate circle, such as the elderly, foreigners, and others.

4. Explore her understanding of reciprocity and expand her insight into human relationships. "One-way" relationships are characteristic of childhood, when both flexibility and understanding are limited.

A different concern is that presented by the wrong boyfriend, a youngster who is a problem usually because he threatens to involve a girl in undesirable behavior, such as alcohol or drugs, truancy, or sexual activity. The mismatch may be clear to parents, but difficult for a girl to see. Young girls are very much affected by their peers, although they are more influenced by the years of parental teaching. Experimentation with a young man of poor character will generally raise parental alarm.

The following will be helpful when the boyfriend is the wrong choice:

1. Become acquainted with the boy before deciding that he is the wrong boyfriend. He may look dreadful or seem quite unacceptable, but parents occasionally make erroneous judgments.

2. It helps to include a questionable young man in family activities, to allow the contrast between the family's ways and values and his to speak for itself.

3. Be conservative about questioning a daughter's judgment because of a boyfriend. Sometimes girls choose boyfriends for a particular reason that makes sense in context, for example, as a way to be part of a couple, as a future prom date, to ward off more troublesome kids, etc.

4. Instead of railing against a particular boyfriend choice, it is better to focus on behavior by setting limits that are impersonal and clear and that protect a girl, for example, limits on curfews and on places she may go.

5. Arrange trips, visits, and family outings to new settings where a youngster may meet a fresh set of friends. In truly desperate situations, a long visit with a faraway relative may help.

A last concern is the boyfriend who is ever-present, draped on the family sofa at all hours, far too ardent and devoted to a girl, and a general pest. Some families handle this by adopting a boy, treating him like a son in the family, and hoping that this will keep him from getting in the way. In other families, limits are set on how often suitors may visit, and family schedules and privacy are respected.

The following will be helpful with the inescapable boyfriend:

1. Involve other young people in social activities in your home so that the young man and your daughter are not alone.

2. Where appropriate, ask an ever-present young man to help with household chores.

3. Speak clearly with a girl about sexual activity, since proximity in teens always increases the likelihood of sexual experimenting.

4. Explore with a daughter the gains from a relationship that make her willing to give up the opportunity to be with friends. Sometimes a shy girl will hide out by spending all of her time with an attentive boyfriend.

FIGHTS WITH GIRLFRIENDS

When young teen girls have fights with their friends or when girlfriends "break up," it can resemble a romantic conflict because girls become so intensely emotional in their relationships. Some theorists have suggested that there is a natural period of homosexual attachment during puberty in which girls try out relating, in an intimate and nonsexual way, to other girls in preparation for forming more stable, enduring heterosexual partnerships later in youth and adulthood.

Friendships at this age are determined by immediate rewards in ease and fun, rather than by common interests or personalities. Friendships also serve to help a teenage girl to make the many decisions of the age, such as what to wear, what music to like, and how to act socially. It can be misleading to try to conceptualize female adolescent friendships in the same terms as adults friendships, for they are quite different. At sixteen, teen friendships begin to look more like women's friendships, but before this time they may be difficult to understand. In the early teens, almost any friends will do, as long as they don't say they are coming over to "play" and they dress appropriately.

The intensity of a girl's reaction to friendships can be trying for parents who look for serenity for their daughter, because some friends may stir up more upset than others. The worst situation is that in which a girl is the object of others' criticism and scorn, so that she feels as though others are persecuting her. If she has been excluded from a clique of girls who are closely bound and enjoy excluding others, this may be particularly painful. This is likely to be true if a girl says so, and it will only make matters worse if a parent tries to convince her that they don't mean to be cruel, which constitutes inappropriate adult optimism. At times it may be helpful for a teacher or other adult, not a parent, to intervene to make peace among the warring parties or at least to set limits on the feuding.

A different kind of problem is that in which one girl gets angry at another over some real or imagined slight, typically what one said about the other to a third party. This pattern is a form of social relating, and it does foster group solidarity, although without some adult intervention it can quickly get out of hand. The two girls may quickly develop bitter feelings that are shared with others, ending with one girl being ostracized.

These kinds of problems appear because a girl is making a profound shift from being her parents' daughter to belonging to a social group and, as part of a group, learning to have separate and important friendships. Often these groupings form tight cliques; girls find it reassuring to exclude others and thus enhance their sense of belonging. This can be particularly painful for a girl who is rejected. It is worth exploring with her why she feels she belongs with a group with whom she may have nothing in common.

The following will be helpful for a girl who is not getting along with her friends:

1. Listen and sympathize, and accept her feelings, no matter how foolish they sound. Even though an adult would not react

in the same way, her anger, worry, or depression over conflicts with her friends is real and may well be the most important thing in her life. Assume this is a sign of her ability to relate to people in a more than superficial manner.

2. Be very conservative in offering adult advice, much as you would be in offering suggestions for solving a conflict in a foreign country. These are alien cultures, and people may be offended at your assumption that you know more than they do about their home ground. Worse yet, they may take your advice and become even more hostile. What works for adults often does not work for teenagers and may backfire.

3. Teach her how to make peace without denying her own position, a skill she can use all her life. Help her to find a common ground, or to see it her friends' way, or to find a way to give a little, but be careful about suggesting how she should use her skills in the current situation.

4. Help her to enlarge her circle of friends, pointing out that it is a good form of insurance to have various individuals and groups to turn to if she needs a break from a troublesome situation.

5. Keep in mind that sometimes girls fight and argue as a form of practice or to relieve boredom. It gives them training in assertiveness for those days in the future when they will have to defend their ideas or their needs and act according to their own beliefs.

GOES ALONG WITH CROWD, BAD FRIENDS, WRONG CROWD

In any high school, the groupings of youngsters generally follow the broad groups of the larger culture. Some kids are primarily interested in sports, while others are strong academically. Still others may focus on appearance and personal beauty, while others, the "politicos," run for student office. Teenagers who belong to none of these groupings are seen as nerds, geeks, or others on the periphery. Most kids in school are aware of these groups, and by ninth grade they begin to associate with one group or another, although this identification may change. Research indicates that girls who are seen as peripheral early in adolescence will retain this position unless they change schools.

Some high school groups are delinquent, drug oriented, or

geared to academic failure. For a youngster who has difficulty making friends, it can be a great relief when someone is welcoming, even though it may be a group that does not share her values. Sometimes it is difficult for a girl to puzzle out what makes one girl popular, and another not. The presence of the same characteristics as those in adults, i.e., friendliness, intelligence, and caring, make kids attractive to others, but a girl with limited social insight may not be aware of this.

When a teenager is under the influence of other, less wholesome youngsters, it can be difficult for a parent to help get the situation back on track. One of the greatest changes in adolescence is the loss of control parents had in childhood over the social activities of a girl. When a girl is a child, her parents structure or at least supervise all of her social activities, and friends are chosen according a parent's judgment.

When a girl reaches fourteen, she begins to spend more and more time away from the house, at the homes of other kids or in public places, where parents have no control over what is happening. Since she sees friends in school every day, her life is focused on social issues, which are continually at hand. It is not unusual for parents to have no actual contact with some of her friends and to know them only through her comments.

Parents can feel quite excluded when this process begins, and they may even blame her for hiding her relationships or sneaking, for these new social patterns, combined with her new need for privacy, can put parents very much on the outside of a girl's life and can cast a negative light on all of her activities and friendships.

It is worth considering whether the questionable or distasteful friends carry real risk to a daughter. Before judging, it is wise to spend time with the youngsters and talk with other parents or school personnel to get a proper perspective on the friends. It is also worth considering that girls tend to listen to whoever has the best information. Since parents seem well informed about health, college, jobs, and so forth, a girl will probably retain their values. In matters more within the expertise of other teens, for example, clothing styles and music, she is more likely to listen to other kids.

For a girl with difficulty relating to peers, the wrong friends may be better than no friends at all, unless their activities threaten her safety, for at least she is in the stream of learning about relationships. Complete isolation from other youngsters is generally more damaging; it occurs at a time when the self-concept is taking shape and may exert an influence throughout adulthood. She will at least develop a sense of her value to others if she has some friends.

As girls mature, their friendships take a variety of forms, moving from great intensity in the early teen years, to more stylized patterns in the later teen years, friends serving different purposes at each age of development. Early on, friends may help a girl make decisions, but when friends are older, a girl may draw on different friendships for different purposes, drawing on some friends as study partners and others as confidantes.

One of the purposes that friends often serve is to give a girl vicarious information about experiences. A daughter can notice what happens, for example, when a teenage girl gets high grades or shoplifts. When she actually joins in risky behaviors with a friend, the adventuring often cements a friendship. The boldness and daring that a girl can exhibit with a companion allow her to see herself in a new light and to see her life possibilities as far expanded.

Because friendships are so important to a girl's development, it is wise to avoid residential moves during a girl's adolescence and never to change a girl's school as a punishment for bad grades or behavior. Most girls can adjust to one complete change of peer group during adolescence, but rarely more. On the other hand, when things have gone badly for a long time, for example, if a girl feels trapped in a childhood reputation, a new school can mean liberation. But more than one move, and especially more than one change of schools, is dangerous and requires far more skill than most girls have.

Loyalty to friends makes the whole area of bad friends a sensitive one, and it can be puzzling to an adult that a girl will staunchly defend against parental criticism people who are disreputable or unkind to her or whom she barely knows. The reason is that if her peers are invalidated, a teenage girl will feel as though she has lost her foundation for independence and that her only choice is to retreat into childhood and her parent's protection.

The following will be helpful:

1. Be careful not to get into battle position over friends. Generally, teenagers agree with parents when they are reasonable, and if a girl seems to be acting irrationally, consider whether she is in fact dealing with different data than her parents. If her bad friends are the only people who like her, she cannot cut off the relationships. Discuss the *behavior* that you don't like in her friends, rather than the people themselves, and encourage her to try new behavior with them.

2. Consider with a girl why it is difficult for her to have more suitable friends. Instead of forbidding her to associate with one group, require her to be socially active in many directions, for example, joining an extracurricular activity or working to help others in the community.

3. Keep in mind that peer pressure is greatest at the beginning of adolescence, and give her time to catch her balance. In any case, stay away from criticism and encourage the behavior you want to see. Instead of forbidding her to go to a friend's house in the afternoon, help her arrange a baby-sitting job at the same time.

4. Encourage her to have her friends to your home, where at least you can keep an eye on activities and get to know the other youngsters better. This does not encourage her friendships, which grow for other reasons. Be friendly to all kids, ask about school, smile, and offer them something to eat. Let the contrast between your behavior and her friends' make the case.

5. Stay on friendly terms with your daughter. Stay close; be encouraging, friendly, and warm. This makes it difficult for her to reject your influence. Assume you won't like some of her friends at all points in her life, because she is different from you and prefers different people.

6. Recognize and support her attempts to be a friend. Point out where she is skilled and behaves like a good friend, and help to build her confidence in her ability to create and maintain relationships.

PREJUDICE (RACISM, SEXISM, ELITISM)

It is natural for parents to want to raise daughters who respect others and treat people fairly. To have a bigoted or prejudiced daughter is a disappointment, and it is appealing to think of the next generation as furthering whatever progress has been made in developing justice and love.

But teenagers are rarely accepting of the burdens that we attempt to pass down to them, and what to parents seems to be the cutting edge of social progress to a teen girl may seem old-fashioned and out of date. The revolutionaries of one generation become the establishment to their children.

Even more disheartening is the tendency of teenagers to zero in on whatever is a parent's nerve center and choose it as an issue on which to make a stand. If a mother says, "Do anything as long as you keep going to church," a teenage girl will become an atheist.

So it should not be surprising if girls disagree with much of the teaching of values about how to treat others who are of a different gender, race, or economic class. Rather than try to force beliefs upon a girl, it helps to use the opportunity to develop her ability to think and to consider the issue from her perspective.

A girl's experience with society is very different from that of her parents, and she will observe and draw conclusions different from theirs, which can lead to interesting exchanges of ideas.

To share values with a girl the following will be helpful:

1. *Show* what you believe rather than talking about it. If you have to point out what you believe, then you probably don't practice it and a girl won't think you really believe it, or see your values as part of you.

2. Arrange your family's activities in such a way as to support your beliefs, and include her in the activities. If you believe in racial or gender equality, find ways to put your beliefs into practice for the good of your community.

3. Ask about her opinions and experiences, and be prepared to hear different points of view or a plain lack of interest in the whole subject.

4. Emphasize human values rather than singling out any one group to focus on. Teach values that guide her in decisions about how to deal with any human being.

DATING: CLOTHES, CARS, CURFEWS, AND PARTIES

The area of male-female contact is a sensitive one, involving many new feelings for girls. Girls become aware long before boys that relating requires considerable attention, and they think about dating while boys are still acting silly. This can be a frustrating experience for a young girl intent on serious dating activity. But in the early teen years, much of what is called dating is imaginary: two seventh graders who walk from the locker to the lunchroom together on Thursday are said on Friday to be "going out."

This situation is different if an eighth-grade girl spends time with a tenth-grade or eleventh-grade boy, for then the activities are much more like traditional dating and likely to be far beyond her budding social skills. In fact, a girl will find it difficult to find ways to be comfortable with an older boy and to hold her own in social situations, and she may feel inclined to try to demonstrate her maturity in unhealthy ways.

One reason girls like to date or to have boyfriends is not for the entertainment value of a gawky teen boy's company, but rather for the social standing and conversational themes it provides her. If a girl spends one hour with a boy in a week, that generates at least eight hours of conversation with various friends and gives her the appearance of a sought-after belle.

So when a girl decides that she wants to begin dating, this may not be the monumental issue that it seems:

"I'm going out with Joshua, Mom."
"But you never go anywhere."

For real, honest-to-goodness, going-to-the-movies and out-for-a-burger dates, most girls are better off waiting until fourteen in order to be comfortable and have enough skills to handle the experience without undue awkwardness. For unusually self-assured and socially skilled thirteen-year-olds, the time could be moved up, but since her dates would (hopefully) be spent with boys of the same age, we might save her by putting it off.

Clothing choices for dates need to be governed by social understanding of appropriate dress for various occasions. It can be useful to discuss dress and to expose girls to social experiences that have prescribed dress, for example, dinner at a fancy restaurant that requires a dressy dress. In helping a girl decide what to wear for her own social activities, offer wide leeway in choices, setting limits only where a girl would look dirty or obscene. For teenage girls, clothing is indicative of peer-group belonging and signifies far more than personal taste. Where choices look like they might prove embarrassing to a girl, ask her to try them out around the house and provide some back-up when she goes out, for example, have her take along a sweater to cover up.

By the time a girl is fifteen, cars are in use on dates, and it is wise to avoid setting rules for whether or not girls can go in cars, since this is not under a parent's control. Instead, it is wise to teach girls how to choose rides and how to skillfully get out of situations that appear unwholesome. A girl in a car is trapped, and it is worthwhile to discuss with her the kinds of problems that can develop there, all the while encouraging her good judgment and survival instinct.

Often parents feel that setting curfews for girls unduly restricts their freedom. But for a teenage girl the absence of parental guidelines can feel like a lack of interest in her welfare. ("I don't have any curfew — nobody cares what time I come in," one depressed teen said.) It is important for a girl to know that it makes a difference what she does, that people are concerned about where she is, and that she is answerable for her precious person. For without that, it is hard for her to see her choices as important and her welfare as a worthwhile focus.

Parties for young teens need planning, primarily by the party-giver with some parental guidance, and need to involve well-thought-out activities, for example, swimming or bowling. Such activities alleviate the social demands on youngsters, who can concentrate on the activity and work off some of their social tension as well. Parents need to be available, although not in the same room, to insure that things go smoothly and to step in if the hostess feels overwhelmed.

For older teen parties, there should be plenty of food, space, and music, but since social skills have developed much further, teens can take care of themselves. When a girl goes to parties, it is important to ascertain that parents will be there, and that she has transportation home. The easiest way to keep abreast of these events is to make friends with other parents at open school night, sports games, or the PTA, so that you can unobtrusively follow social events. This saves everyone from those situations where a parent threatens to call the parent of a party-giver to make sure that parents will be home, humiliating a daughter and creating a stir.

The following will be helpful in handling a girl's dating activities:

1. An interest in dating offers a fine opportunity to further develop a girl's good manners, which take on new relevance when they promise to show her in a good light. It is useful to remind a girl that good manners are based on sensitivity to the needs of others rather than concern for only our own comfort.

2. Avoid insisting that a girl follow the same patterns that parents knew in their youth. Unless her behavior seems to promise dire consequences, let her make her own choices.

3. Since girls who date early have no more social competence than girls who begin later, it makes sense to let a girl's interest develop on its own, encouraging neither early nor later dating.

4. Remember that dating is also a way for a girl to try out being somebody different from what she has been. If her date choices seem unsuited to her, allow her to expand her self-concept accordingly.

5. Encourage teen girls to be involved in boy-girl activities that allow a great deal of social interaction, such as a school play or student newspaper, but that protect her from too much pressure for social competence.

6. *Do not ever* tease a girl about her dates or her behavior on dates. Play down the importance of how she handles things and remember that she is a learner.

SEXUAL INVOLVEMENT

In the 1970s, the sexual revolution gave rise to the belief that teenagers are likely to have sex and need to be comfortable in doing so. With or without that encouragement, teenagers have begun to have sex increasingly early, so that by age sixteen, half of all girls have had sexual intercourse. The shackles of conventional morality having been thrown off, what has been the impact on teenage girls?

Unfortunately, the consequences for teenage girls have been

disastrous. Even though they may *feel* more comfortable with their sexual identities, there is no evidence that girls who begin to have sex in their teens have better sexual *adjustment* in adulthood. The price seems high for a negligible return.

One in ten teenage girls gets pregnant each year. Eighteen percent of girls using birth control pills get pregnant in the first year of using them. One and a half million teen girls have abortions each year, while many others keep their babies. Only 50 percent of women who have a child at seventeen or younger graduate from high school. As a result of pelvic inflammatory disease, which results from repeated instances of minor sexually transmitted diseases, 35 percent of women having teen sex become infertile, and the prime cause of current infertility rates is early sex with multiple partners.* The risk of AIDS has grown greatly. Sex education appears to have little effect on these figures.

A separate area of consideration is the psychological effect of early sexual relationships. Girls often see sexual relating as indicative of a deep commitment and a lasting relationship, regardless of whether there is a meshing of personalities. They also can feel that other partners would not want them after a sexual relationship. And sex, no matter how much gentleness and consideration is involved, always leaves a girl feeling vulnerable when it is over. Without the security of a mature relationship, it contributes little to a girl's self-esteem. Pleasure does not appear to be a driving force in a teen girl's decision to become sexually involved with a boy; rather girls seem to enter into the relationship as a rite of passage that they must undergo. When a girl says that she feels it's time that she had sex with a boy her decision does not stem from unrestrainable passion. From what is known about women's sexual responsiveness, the early teens are a time of limited sexual response; a woman's response capability tends to build over the early decades of her life and reach a peak in middle age. This is the reverse of male response curves, which peak in early adulthood and decline thereafter. The popular error has been in assuming that female response curves parallel male response curves.

Standards for adult sexual behavior become ludicrous when

*Ellen Hopkins, "Sex Is for Adults," *New York Times*, December 26, 1992, 21.

applied to teens. The expectation that teens discuss their health status or their involvement with other partners — when they are uncomfortable and unfamiliar even with talking on the phone about sex — is an adult exercise in wishful thinking. The data suggest that these are unrealistic expectations and that teenagers are not able, as a rule, to be mature and responsible about sexual relating.

A young teenage girl has neither the wisdom nor the experience to handle the risks of sexual activity, and the statistics bear out the damage done to young females. The foresight, responsibility, and integrity required for responsible sex come only with maturity and cannot be made to develop earlier. Attempts to do so have not changed the vulnerability of teenage girls to pregnancy, disease, or emotional harm. Although early sexual activity may seem liberating to young girls, it is worth noting that in repressive traditional cultures it has been used as a means of dominating and subjugating females.

Many parents will be appalled at the idea of curtailing teen sexual activity, which sounds like a return to sexual repression, and impossible to implement as well. But good ideas sell themselves, and abstinence is good protection for a teenage girl from the dilemmas of early pregnancy, abortion choices, sexually transmitted disease, infertility, dependence on a boyfriend, and other ills. And there is little she stands to gain from premature sexual involvements.

The following may be helpful in restraining a girl from teenage sexual involvement:

1. *Tell her that you don't want her to have sex,* that she's too young, that she's not ready, and that sex is for adults. Tell her you want her to wait until she's older, that she's too valuable to be put at risk for no good reason.

2. Emphasize to her that for a teenage girl, *there is no safe sex,* and that she is far too important to risk.

3. Discuss her level of sexual desire, and ask whether she has had orgasms yet. Ask if unfulfilled sexual arousal is a problem for her daily activities and if it interferes with school or other activities. If so, discuss masturbation, and explain to her that for centuries, women have taken care of sexual arousal without males and that she can too if sexual deprivation is ruining her life.

4. If she feels a need for risky behavior, help her to find adventures that demand courage and boldness, rather than submission, and that promise more than sensual pleasure.

5. Explore her relationship with a boyfriend, if there is one, and ask her if the relationship requires sex and what the consequences are of no sex. Ask her how many sexual partners he's had and whether they've discussed contraception. Teach her about love, that it involves far more than sexual exchange. Deep love is formed of self-sacrifice, courage, and putting oneself aside for the other. Explain to her that when sex is the focus of a relationship, other facets atrophy.

6. Discuss with her the idea of casual sex, i.e., sex without relationship, and ask her how common it is among her friends. Draw a parallel between the recreational use of intravenous drugs and casual sex, and the serious risks of both.

7. Inquire about her plans for an unwanted child and how she and its father would care for it. Also inquire whether she expects you to raise said child.

8. Avoid criticism or condemnation. Remind her repeatedly that you love her and treasure her and want what's best for her.

PETS

With all of the turbulence and discomfort of adolescence, problems sometimes seem to be the major fare for a girl and her parents. There are many ways to help a girl to grow straight and strong, but sometimes comfort is the greatest help. In this realm, the family dog is a powerful therapist for a teenage girl in the throes of teenage girl problems.

A friendly dog offers unconditional approval, warmth, and the simplicity of straightforward adoration. Dogs are enormously reassuring, and often when a girl feels that she can relate to no one, a dog seems to understand.

Curiously enough, dogs seem to help with the development of social skills since they force a person to consider the other's needs in a noncritical way. A dog is also a buffer against loneliness and helps a girl through periods of adolescent emptiness. When a girl sees parents being good to her dog, she is more apt to trust them and to have faith in their goodness.

Teenage girls are not alone in their reaction to dogs, which have psychological value for all humans. In research with patients who had a first heart attack, those who went home to a wagging tail had only one-quarter the occurrence of second heart attacks as those who went home to no dog. In a room that has a friendly dog lying somewhere in sight, children experience a healthy drop in blood pressure and a generalized physiological relaxation. Dogs seem to speed up the process of unwinding in young people.

Human behavior changes in dealing with a dog: we become more attentive, speak more gently, softly, and slowly, with petting and stroking. We have a sense of power with a dog, and we forget ourselves. Defensive behavior seems to drop; we become more at ease, and perhaps more sensitive and sensible, all of which are valuable for a teenage girl.

Competence

LOW GRADES

It is always distressing to see a girl struggle with school, or worse, to see her give up and resign herself to failure. Schools teach to a broad range of abilities, and so any girl theoretically should be able to keep up with a class.

When low grades appear, most parents talk with a daughter to try to determine the source of the difficulties, and they may meet with teachers and guidance counselors as well. All of these folks are likely to have good suggestions. Occasionally a minor problem that has blocked progress will appear, for example, that a girl needs glasses, and with some small changes all will be well.

Much more common is the situation where teachers say that a girl has the ability to do her work, if only she would apply herself, get her homework in, participate in class, and try harder. The girl, tearful, angry, or silent, will say that the work is too hard, that the teacher doesn't tell her what she needs to know, or that she does the work, but it never makes any difference.

To understand how this apparent discrepancy between aptitude and achievement develops, it is important to understand what happens in a teenage girl's life between twelve and fifteen. A girl is changing rapidly in these years, developing new learning abilities and greater intellectual capacity, but emotionally she is less sure of herself, and in some ways more reliant on adults for guidance.

Her educational course changes in these years as well, with school structure radically altered between grades six and eight. A girl typically goes from an elementary school schedule that involves one teacher and one group of kids to a much larger building with a series of teachers during the day and constantly changing groupings of kids, plus a much, much larger student body.

Each teacher in a middle school has his or her own style, expectations, and demands, and there is little of the nurturing atmosphere of the lower school. In addition, the various groupings of kids present many new social opportunities and pressures and a great deal more freedom in how a girl spends her time both in school and out of it. It can be difficult for a girl to cope with changes in her body and her school day at the same time. If there are other changes as well in the same time period, for example, birth of a new baby at home or her father losing his job, the combined effects can cause problems.

In middle school the courses now require a good deal of categorized memorization, for example, in learning foreign language vocabulary. A girl will need the skills of self-discipline and time planning that she has not had to develop heretofore, and she may suddenly feel dumb. The requirements of secondary school are quite different from elementary school, since in the lower school the goal was conceptual understanding of subject matter, but in secondary school, memorization and rote learning by drill become an important part of doing well. For bright kids who have been able to "figure things out," it may seem suddenly much too hard.

As academic problems develop, an adolescent girl may seem to have little concern. She may pay little attention in class, be quickly and happily distracted, and see teachers as mean. Homework may be done in front of television or quickly, in order not to miss television, and term projects are thrown together at the last minute. At school conferences, the teachers' comments can begin to have an irritated edge to them, particularly after the fall and winter have passed. School may be seen by a girl as a headache and an interference with life. But a girl's poor response to academic problems may be a reflection of confusion and a sense of inadequacy.

Perhaps the biggest but least understood change for American schoolchildren is the new student behaviors required in middle school. For an elementary schoolgirl in fifth grade, for example, school is structured to help her achieve: she goes to her classroom in the morning, where yesterday's homework assignment is on the board, and she and the other kids have time to chat or trade homework answers. Books stay in school, in a girl's desk, so that they don't get left at home, and they are not used for homework. There is a library time so that she can get books for a special report. If she has trouble with the math this morning, her teacher, having noticed her distress, will take her aside during recess and clarify the problem. At the end of the day her homework assignment for tonight is on the board, and she writes it down and starts it in the few free minutes before the final bell.

But the same girl in middle school one year later has a very different daily experience. She arrives at school and goes to her homeroom, but since the school is on an eight-day schedule, she isn't sure which class is first. She finds out that it's math from another girl, and arrives late, having left her math book in her homeroom with her homework in it. The teacher has already given out tonight's homework at the start of the class, but she doesn't have anyone's phone number so she can't call to get it. The class goes on, and she is called on, embarrassed, angry and frustrated. The teacher tells her that she'd better "get her act together" for the test on Friday. The demands at this grade level are far more complex that the one-year transition would indicate.

Emotionally, these circumstances can be quite difficult for girls already struggling with the changes of puberty. Some girls believe that academic success is not conducive to social acceptance and feel a need to avoid being conspicuous. These years, in grades seven and eight, are the years of peak social conformity — and also the years when study patterns get set for the years ahead.

After elementary school, school subjects take on new identities, with math and science traditionally seen as nonfemale subjects. Both girls and their parents tend to estimate girls' ability in these areas as below their tested aptitude and to expect that girls will have trouble in these areas. Girls generally estimate their achievement in these areas as lower than that of boys, even when it is the same. Such attitudes reflect cultural stereotypes and affect a girl's energy and optimism in making the transition to secondary school.

Girls do well in math and science when they are encouraged to take risks and when they can participate directly in the learning process, for example, with laboratory work. Adults are often too solicitous of girls, stepping in to help before it is needed or reducing complexity where it might be more fruitful to challenge a girl's intelligence. In most school subjects research has shown that high-achieving boys get the most teacher time in the classroom and well-behaved quiet girls get the least. All children need better elementary school grounding in math and science. A National Center for Education Statistics study, *A Profile of the American Eighth Grader*, found that only 41 percent of them had mastered the math skills necessary to do eighth-grade math.

The following will be helpful for a teenage girl with low grades:

1. Encourage her to take responsibility for her own learning. Reassure her that she has enough brains and that study habits are necessary regardless of genetic potential.

2. Teach study skills, such as carrying and using an assignment pad, preparing a term calendar (for long-term projects and reports), getting student phone numbers to get missed homework assignments, and staying after school to clear up confusion about a subject.

3. React positively to her efforts to participate in class. Encourage her to talk to the teacher, work studiously on homework, and memorize a little each night. Remember that academic growth happens gradually, and not with one resolution to "do better."

4. Teach her how to memorize small groups of facts using practice and drill.

5. Communicate often with faculty, drop in to school unexpectedly, and let your daughter see a close working relationship between you and her teachers, one that you hope she will emu-

late as a way of getting rid of you. Teachers respect parents who care enough about their kids to be involved in school and are always disappointed when less than half of the parents show up for open school nights.

6. Turn off the television, or better yet, exile it to the garage or the repair shop. Instead, sit with her while she works and read a book or a magazine. Bring along a snack for both of you and give her a pat on the back.

7. Help her to find ways to overcome the difficult parts of schoolwork, for example, breaking a large assignment into pieces.

For help with an unmotivated student, the following are useful:

1. Examine your own values. When you get enthused about something at the dinner table, does it show a respect for money, beauty, success, or learning?

2. Are you interested in learning new things? How does it show? Do you seek out community opportunities to develop knowledge and go to museums, plays, and the library?

3. Are you enthusiastic about the new things a daughter learns, and her view of them, or are you bored and waiting for the time to go by when she talks about them?

4. Do you support the demands of teachers and interpret them as part of an overall plan for a girl's future? Do you stress the value of a long-term, enduring commitment to learning and not just passing this test? Do you help a girl to look for ways to learn more about an interesting subject so that she goes beyond the assigned work?

5. Do you get impatient with her learner status and the time that it takes to ask questions, imagine answers, go off on tangents, and think about solutions, and instead gratify yourself by giving her a quick answer rather than having her grow through the experience?

6. Do you read at home as a regular habit?

7. Are you more interested in her grades than in what she has learned and how she has changed?

8. How much do you criticize and how much do you encourage?

ACADEMIC ANXIETY

Some girls have a strong desire to do well in school and may get high grades, but at great cost to themselves. Academic anxiety may take the form of blanking out on tests, panicking when having to give a report before the class, or in other ways having excessive motivation block the goal. All of these are forms of fear of failure, and since the academic arena is one where evaluation is constant, failure and success stand out clearly.

Performance anxiety usually involves a girl's feeling exposed and open to ridicule and attack by others, which causes her performance to suffer and makes her lose self-esteem. It is the *public* nature of the exposure that is most threatening. If a girl is asked a question in class, her thoughts may race; she may sense impending doom, be unable to think straight, and then give a foolish answer. This may also happen if a teacher tries to explain a point to her, and she may be irritated or inattentive to teacher help.

To outsiders, it may seem that a girl is shy or uninterested in work, since she generally does not participate in classroom activities if she can avoid doing so. If new and interesting topics are introduced, she may act bored or clown as a way to avoid dealing with them.

It is the fear of peer reaction to her public performance that strikes terror and freezes a girl. It is a focus on herself rather than on the task at hand that makes her preoccupied.

Test anxiety is a bit different. It occurs in a private situation when a girl is preparing for or taking a test and does not generally involve others, although it may include imagined others in her thinking. Test anxiety develops suddenly, usually in bright, high-achieving girls who feel driven to succeed. They may suddenly develop panicked feelings, be unable to recall any of the material studied, and feel dizzy or faint, with a rapid heartbeat. Such an experience of doing badly on a test can lead a girl to lose faith in her own abilities and be the basis for continuing problems.

Test anxiety is a painful affliction for a secondary school student, the more so if others disregard it or make light of it, for a girl may feel she is losing her mind, both psychologically as well as intellectually.

Both performance anxiety and test anxiety are different from general worries about grades. The former have more to do with overall anxiety level and self-confidence.

The following will be helpful:

1. Be careful about offering a highly anxious girl reassurance and support since this may seem patronizing or belittling. Listen attentively and respectfully to how she feels, and don't attempt to get her to be reasonable.

2. Help her to plan ahead for school requirements so that she can avoid being taken by surprise and can feel well prepared.

3. Ask her to speak privately with her teacher to explain the anxiety problem, and join her if she wishes you to do so. Ask for the teacher's support in reasonable ways to reduce her stress.

4. Help her to gain control over some aspects of the academic situation, for example, choosing which day she will give her report. Establish an escape route for performance situations, so that she can always get out if she feels completely unable to cope. Better she use the escape route, e.g., going to the restroom, than bursting into tears in front of the class.

5. Avoid cues to anxiety, for example, ask if she can give a book report from her seat instead of from the front of the classroom. Role play with her difficult performance situations and imagine the worst that could happen. Generate solutions for catastrophes, and share some of your memories of your own adolescent catastrophes.

6. Reward all mistakes as a form of trying. When a test is failed, use it as a journal entry in a teenager's life.

7. Ask her to help a retarded student with homework as a way of developing her confidence and reducing her self-focus.

8. Keep track of her new learnings rather than her grades. Avoid praise, which draws her attention to herself, and instead offer encouragement, which helps her to look at the task at hand.

9. Teach tolerance for anxiety, which is a part of all life. Keep track of anxiety levels, and ask her how many pounds of anxiety she can press.

MONEY WOES

It takes a great deal of money to raise a teenage girl; the irony of it is that she usually doesn't know how much it takes, and she always needs more. The following illustrates the financial condition of teenage girls:

America's 13.4 million teenagers aged twelve to fifteen spend about $24 per week from allowance and other money from parents. Older teens have an average of $127 weekly discretionary income, and spend an average of $84 per week. College students spend an average of $243 monthly over an eight-month academic year. Among eighteen- and nineteen-year-olds, 74 percent own boom boxes, and 36 percent have cars.*

Girls spend more as they get older, and a teen girl between thirteen and fifteen divides her spending in the following ways:

clothing	32.9%
food & snacks	20.1%
entertainment	10.7%
cosmetics	10.4%
records	4.9%
jewelry	4.6%
savings	10.7%†

What is the effect of these spending patterns? For the American economy, the effect is very positive: teens spend $56 billion annually, and marketing and advertising have paid increasing attention to this new market. For parents, these results may not be quite so beneficial.

The massive media campaign to attract teen dollars leaves most girls feeling chronically in need and underfinanced. Often girls look for a quick way to obtain dollars to make purchases. But the interest in income is a shortsighted one, and there is rarely any interest in saving or in developing one's income-producing abilities. Even lay-away plans in stores have given way to credit purchases. Credit card lenders have seized upon the adolescent interest in instant gratification and have made a

---

*Jonathan Probber, "A Growing Market," *New York Times*, Education Life, April 8, 1990, 54.

†Trish Hall, "Younger Consumers," *New York Times*, August 13, 1990, C1.

strong pitch to young people that they need to "establish credit early" (is buying a house the next step?) and not be left behind. Teenagers with credit lines run up serious debts, which are then absorbed by parents, and the result is a drop in self-esteem for the girl and problems for the family.

It is useful instead to help a girl to develop a budget, even while she is being supported by others, so that she can learn what is required to sustain human life as she knows it. As a teenager becomes more interested in spending money and as she moves further along in high school, budgeting and self-support become less theoretical and more practical. A sample budget for a high school senior is shown here:

JANE'S MONTHLY BUDGET

Housing (parent donation)	$225
Transportation (car payment*)	185
Gas, maintenance, insurance	130
Clothing (averaged over year)	50
Food	200
Entertainment	50
Furnishings	50
Health care (parent donation)	150
Savings	50
Miscellaneous†	80

*car payment for a $6000 car at 10 percent annual interest rate for four years
†includes travel, new stereo, birthday gift for friend, guppy food, haircut, vacation spending, hobbies

Since Jane's monthly expenses come to $1170, she must learn *at least* $14,040 per year (or $8.13 hourly) *after* taxes to follow the lifestyle outlined in her budget. This budgeting exercise provokes many questions that can be a source of fruitful discussion and a way to develop mature judgment. How much support does she want from parents as an adult and how much can they offer? Are there ways she can reduce her expenses? This also helps her to understand the implications of taking a job as a daycare worker that pays $5200 a year, as a sales assistant who earns $17,000, or as a secretary who makes $22,000. It also helps her understand the financial advantages of education: a female high school graduate earns a yearly average of $19,309, while a college graduate earns a yearly average of $33,615.

As you consider her expenses with her, the budget will point out that all most or all of her expenses are currently subsidized by her parents. This suggests that for her to have a self-reliant future, she must be self-supporting as well as self-disciplined.

The following are helpful in dealing with money woes:

1. Develop a realistic list of a girl's expenses and ask her to estimate future expenses.

2. Help her to put together a complete budget for her current living expenses, even though parents are paying for many of these. Project which parts will become her responsibility and when.

3. Consider with her what sorts of jobs she will need to prepare for in order to live in the ways that she prefers. Get information on income levels for various jobs. Ask her to live within her projected budget limits for three months or more, for example, spending only the allotted amount for entertainment, and help her to evaluate the experience.

BOREDOM

- "There's nothing to do"

- "Why can't we ever go anywhere?"

Teenage girls at some point run out of activities and kick around the house complaining that they have little to do. This may be even more pronounced if they have to be home and separated from friends, for example, during a family event. It may occur at other times as well, after school, on weekends, and as a general habit.

Are parents responsible for the entertainment of a teenage girl? When she was smaller, they probably supplied amusements and arranged outings for her, and the carryover into adolescence occurs easily. Boredom is a form of dependency, a passivity in waiting for the environment to generate something interesting, as opposed to creating it oneself. In whining to parents, there is an added sense of entitlement, that a parent *should* keep a girl amused, since she is unable to structure her own time effectively.

But, happily, for any teenage girl of average intelligence there are plenty of opportunities to learn how to arrange her free time in a satisfactory way. Many girls use the free time of the teen years to develop talents or to become involved with other youngsters in extracurricular activities or in community service jobs.

The afterschool events that are most popular with girls are varsity and intramural sports, musical activities (band, chorus, or orchestra), and drama productions. These often provide a chance to be with friends in a comfortable setting, as well as to learn new skills.

Private lessons or clubs that a girl joins to practice a skill often fit into the afterschool hours and offer the chance to learn things that will be useful in adult life. Sometimes girls who complain of boredom want to quit these activities because they feel that they are boring, and a parent must evaluate their utility.

Much depends on whether others are counting on the girl to participate, for example, if she has agreed to be a fourth in learning bridge. If a girl has pursued an activity since childhood, she may want to assert her autonomy by giving up childish activities, for example, playing the piano. Practicing is difficult for many youngsters and may leave them feeling isolated and left out of family activities.

The following may be helpful for dealing with a bored teenage girl:

1. Keep a list of simple household chores that need doing and break large chores into component parts. When a girl complains of boredom or you notice that she is bored, tell her that you need her help and you're glad she's free, and give her a chore to do to help out.

2. If you notice that a teen is consistently complaining of boredom at the same time, for example, on Saturdays, plan with her how she can best use that time to feel satisfied and happy with the outcome.

3. If she is with other youngsters, she is probably not bored: girls invent their own amusements together. Discuss with her how she might arrange to become more socially involved and explore the reasons why she is not.

4. Help her to develop a "wish list" of things that she wishes

that she could do. Break down the wishes into sequential steps, and help her begin to take the first step. If for example, she wishes that she could go sky diving, suggest that the first step is going to the library to learn about the activity.

DRIVING

It often amazes parents that state governments allow teens who can't remember to turn off the haircurler to drive a one-ton vehicle. In most states, girls can begin driving at sixteen, and their reaction to this passage is often mixed. Many girls are not eager to get their driver's license or are actually resistant. They would prefer to ride with friends and assume a passive attitude about getting themselves around.

It seems wise for all girls to learn to drive, and to do so at sixteen, no matter how immature they may seem. Driver education classes at the school or private lessons are helpful, along with a long period of driving with a parent supervising (for example, one year). It seems that the longer a girl drives under parental supervision, the more likely it is that she will develop safe habits and orient herself to the road in the most skilled ways. To teach a girl to drive is not the same thing as subsidizing or encouraging her driving.

Should a girl have her own car? In many high schools, from tenth grade up taking the bus to school is a mark of low social status, and kids try to drive to school in their own cars or with parents. It is embarrassing for some girls to be seen on the school bus, and so kids work hard to avoid riding the bus. A girl may feel that unless she has her own car, she cannot hold up her head in school. But there may be more serious considerations in her wish for her own vehicle, since without a car she is at the mercy of other, perhaps less responsible teen drivers, and she is also a captive in their cars.

But few girls actually *need* a car, although they may feel that it is an absolute necessity. Without a car, a girl could still find ways to get to school — walking is often feasible and a good way to stay healthy to boot. But most girls will see an auto as essential. If she gets a job, she will feel this need more strongly, and so eventually may the parent who transports her.

The difficulty with having a car is the expense, which is considerable, perhaps between $300 and $500 each month, when all costs are considered. How this expense is covered has consequences for her maturity because if parents pay the cost of a car, they have given a very luxurious gift to a youngster, which may affect family finances, particularly if there will be other children who will soon become teens.

If parents do not pay the cost of the car, then a teenage girl needs to do so. In order to work enough low-paid hours to accumulate money, a girl must cut her schedule somewhere, and the most common place is to reduce homework and sleep time.

A car also gives a girl complete freedom over where she goes and cuts off parental guidance. Girls can leave school during a lunch break or they can leave early at the end of the day, so that a car usually works against a commitment to do well in high school.

But what of the concern that other kids may be drinking and driving and having a car saves her from being forced to accept a ride? Thirty-eight percent of tenth graders report riding with a driver under the influence of drugs or alcohol during the two weeks prior to the survey, indicating that driving under the influence continues to be a serious problem.*

Having her own car saves a girl from accepting rides from others, but it does not prevent her from driving irresponsibly herself. A girl may feel compelled to drive when she has been drinking *because she owns the car* and does not want to deal with the consequences of *not* driving because she has been drinking.

Similarly with marijuana. Most teens feel that pot is less dangerous than alcohol because one feels quite confident while high on it. But research shows that pot affects the ability to steer and maintain a course, gauge distance, and brake quickly. A girl may feel more self-confident while she's having an accident if she's under the influence of pot, but she's still more likely to have the accident.

The following should be helpful for a girl who is beginning to drive:

1. Encourage her to learn good driving skills, and be enthusiastic about her developing ability. Avoid making jokes about

_____

National Adolescent Student Health Survey: A Report on the Health of America's Youth (Oakland, Calif.: Third Party Publishing, 1988).

her mistakes, and don't make woman driver jokes. These set up expectations of incompetence that will stay with her throughout her driving career.

2. When you need to correct her, do so gently, with praise for her accomplishments. New drivers need to be calm, serene, and attentive to the road. They cannot maintain their composure while listening to a hysterical parent criticizing mistakes.

3. As a girl begins to use the family car, review the expenses of an automobile with her and ask her to share in them. If you are going to provide her with a car, ask her to take responsibility for part of the expense. Make sure that you are not counting on the car to give her maturity and good judgment. She will be a learner for the first several years of her driving.

4. Discuss the use of alcohol and drugs with her repeatedly, and give her as much information as possible on her vulnerabilities. Imagine problems with her, and help her to figure out solutions.

GIFTED GAL

Our children always seem bright as we watch the miracle of development occur, but gifted youngsters stand out from other kids, which can be a problem for a gifted teenage girl. Often unusual academic ability is hidden by carelessness, underachievement, or lack of interest in school work, and it may be difficult to judge a girl's intellectual competence accurately. Although a girl in this category can keep up with her class with little work, she is not likely to develop study skills or creativity, both of which require immersion in content areas, and does not automatically emerge with high intelligence.

A bright girl is apt to hold a number of misconceptions about her intelligence, including the following:

- Bright girls don't have to study.

- If a bright girl doesn't do well on tests, it's the teacher's fault.

- Whatever a bright girl tries turns out well.

For teenage girls, ability and performance seem to be the same thing, and it is difficult to understand that there is no learning without studying, no originality without preparation, and no uniformity of abilities at any level of mental aptitude. This means that a brilliant teenage girl can flunk a German test if she hasn't memorized the verb tenses, she might need to study many hours to do well in biology, and she may do quite poorly in art.

A more powerful issue is the discrepancy between areas of development: a twelve-year-old girl who thinks at the level of a fifteen-year-old may have the body of a ten-year-old and the emotions of a thirteen-year-old — and feel that she fits nowhere. A girl's reaction to this is often to withdraw from intellectual stimulation and to avoid dealing with academic demands as much as possible. This can be quite confusing for parents, who see only a teenager floundering in academic failure and social incompetence.

The following will help:

1. If aptitude test scores suggest a high intelligence, request a formal psychological evaluation from the school to determine intellectual level and academic needs. Do this in writing to the school principal and indicate that you suspect your daughter is a youngster with special needs who may need a special academic program.

2. Meet with her teachers individually to evaluate her familiarity with their subject and the level of challenge that it represents. Talk with your daughter about what stirs her or gets her working in class.

3. Consider various options for adding more intellectual challenge to her school schedule, including advancing her in courses where she is able to skip classes, enrichment of current classes, honors classes, or working on special projects with interested teachers. Keep in mind that gifted kids do well if they are academically placed well and she is not doomed to be weird or an outcast because of her high intelligence.

4. Expect that most of her education will come from the family's efforts, and gear some of your free time appropriately. Give her a choice of activities, and arrange to introduce her to local museums, colleges, theater groups, and libraries. Assume that you will be the main source of exciting stimulation for her, and be prepared to be excited yourself as you watch her discover the world and herself.

5. Try to get her out of the "good girl" role if she is in it, since gifted girls are often highly cooperative and cause little trouble. Acquaint her with some of the females in history who have had a point of view that has made waves, and help her to develop her own ideas, regardless of how outrageous they might seem.

6. If she has been in a "bad girl" role, channel her boldness to areas that require true courage.

JOB SKILLS

When one sixteen-year-old girl was asked what sort of job she was looking for, she said she'd like a job with an office and a window. Far more common for girls are jobs as salespeople, food servers, or baby-sitters, which generally pay between three and six dollars per hour and don't include an office, much less a window. Most of the jobs available at the low end of the pay scale offer little in the way of advancement or learning of new skills.

Rarely is a teen girl's income used to support herself and buy the necessities for her life. Only a tiny percentage of working girls contribute to the household that supports them. Far more common is for a girl to use her income for nonessential clothing, entertainment, and snacks, with little saving. In a survey of teenagers, 47 percent were found to have televisions, and a large proportion had answering machines, computers, and other expensive appliances.*

The outcome is that a girl sees her income as supplementary to her basic overhead, as though she were already supporting herself. But the luxuries and the immediate gratification of buying them can be so great that a girl will pass up schooling to be able to continue her income, even if it does not represent self-support.

According to current child labor laws, girls younger than fourteen cannot do paid work, and girls under sixteen can work for only three hours a day during the week and no more than eighteen hours per week when school is in session. These are, however, hefty amounts of time, and if a girl works this much,

---

*Jonathan Probber, "A Growing Market," *New York Times,* Education Life, May 8, 1990, 55.

she has little energy or enthusiasm left over for school. If she works in a fast-food restaurant or grocery store, where teenagers use heavy equipment, she is at risk for serious injury as well. There are clearly many drawbacks to demanding employment during the school year, and a girl will need much guidance in integrating work into her weekly schedule. Some work, particularly during summer vacation, will be useful in helping her understand employment, finances, and herself more clearly.

A girl's main concern in considering employment will be whether she can land a job and what she can do with her income. A parent can help her to acquire the skills needed to produce job offers by emphasizing how her attitude shows up in her clothing, her preparation for the job interview, her interest in the workplace as demonstrated by questions, and her eagerness to learn.

There are many skills required for being a good employee, and these can be developed as a girl enters into regular employment.

The following will be helpful:

1. If a girl is to work during high school, it is wise to wait until senior year, although summer work earlier may be appropriate. It is also wise to limit work to weekend days only and to hold the line when pressure builds to increase it.

2. Since the old practice of a girl's wages supporting her household has gone out of style, it will help to insist that she make plans and set goals for the income she will produce, agreeing on the division of her paycheck before the first one arrives.

3. Volunteer jobs often offer far more training and experience than entry-level labor-market jobs. There is apt to be more responsibility as well in community service jobs and the chance to do work that will raise a girl's self-esteem and make her feel of value. Where appropriate paid jobs are not available, a girl can work at volunteer jobs.

4. As a teenage girl tries to adjust to the work environment, ask her to put herself in the manager's or boss's shoes and to imagine what would be required to keep the whole operation running. Support her adult behavior and ignore childish responses as much as possible.

PHYSICAL ILLNESS OR DISABILITY

When a teenage girl takes ill with a lasting ailment or is injured and requires lengthy recuperation, there are psychological consequences as well as physical ones. There are the effects of pain, trauma in the case of accident, and the disruption of normal activities necessary for development. Most important, there is the isolation from peers that occurs as a girl is recovering or dealing with her condition.

Chronic illnesses, such as cancer, diabetes, or asthma, make a girl far more dependent on parents and medical caregivers than others her age. In the teen years this occurs, unfortunately, just as a girl is trying to become independent and self-reliant. Her condition may take on too much importance, so that everything is explained in terms of it and the normal problems of adolescence are masked by the medical focus. Medical treatments instead of too much TV, for example, are blamed for missed homework assignments.

Parental attitudes toward an ill teen girl are different as well. It is usual, for example, for parents of a high school senior to become weary of the noise, activity level, mistakes, and inconsiderate behavior of a daughter. But if the same daughter is ill, she may not receive the tired and irritated responses of parents, who are far more concerned about her health, and so she does not receive enough corrective feedback to change her behavior.

Her need to be separate and self-reliant is also blocked, because the intimate relationship with parents cannot be controlled and limited. Parents must be much more involved in a sick teen's life and will make many important decisions about her care, so that her drive for independence can be thwarted. As a result, a girl may find it difficult to balance her dependency needs with self-reliance.

The following will be helpful:

1. Find ways to help an ill teen girl be powerful. Have her plan her diet or medication schedule wherever possible. Help her to make choices about her medical treatment where feasible, and evaluate her decisions with her after the fact. Encourage her to speak directly with medical caregivers, and allow her some privacy in this relationship if possible.

2. Accept whatever her feelings are without criticism, but in-

sist on proper behavior even though she may feel hostile and angry.

3. When giving her responsibility, give it to her gradually. If she is given too much all at once, it will be distracting for her, and she may feel that her parents don't want to be bothered with her.

4. Accept that her independence may be temporarily delayed because of medical need. The goal of helping her to become a strong, self-reliant woman, however, remains in place. Help her to be creative in finding ways to reach it.

Four

CRISES

I T IS DIFFICULT to see disaster approaching with teenage girls, even for seasoned therapists who have seen hundreds of youngsters. Often teenagers skirt calamity, come to the brink of catastrophe, and veer off at the last moment, like circus daredevils. At other times, small problems suddenly give rise to much more serious difficulties.

Crises in a parent-child relationship usually develop for one of two reasons: because there is prolonged, unabated tension over irritating behavior that causes resentment, or because there is a threat to a youngster's health or safety. Although problems and disagreements are normal in parent-child relations, a surplus of critical issues or crises is usually the forerunner of one or more emergencies.

Constant disagreement between a girl and her parent conditions each to respond angrily and to feel defensive and alienated in the face of any difficulty, even a minor one. Where there have been repeated unhappy parent-daughter confrontations about a girl's skipping chores, discourtesy, or fighting with siblings, it becomes impossible to tune into a girl's worries or sadnesses. Parents become so frustrated that they hear only their own upset and lose a girl's voice in their own feelings. On the other side, an adolescent girl who is used to fighting with her parents can fail to hear the love and wisdom in their words to her. One powerful way to avoid emergencies is to deal productively with crises and resolve them sufficiently so that both parent and daughter can get on with growth.

Crises can develop in a girl's life with no advance warning, and it's not fair to blame them on her lack of foresight or on parents' neglect or insensitivity. To foresee a crisis requires maturity and experience, so adolescence by definition is a period of crisis vulnerability. Communication, open and free-flowing, helps a good deal although kids sometimes resist sharing difficulties with parents because they feel too childish, and all communication falters in turbulent times.

Self-care

BEDWETTING

What may have been an embarrassing problem in childhood is a truly humiliating problem in adolescence, for wetting the bed as a teenager stirs up many painful feelings. There is the discomfort of a wet bed and a disrupted night's sleep, the resistance of an uncooperative body, and the sense of failing at a major life task. It becomes hard for a girl to see herself as capable of much when she can't achieve what others kids did a decade ago. There is additionally the terror of being discovered by other youngsters, who will then see her as weird or childish and never forget, even if she gets over the wetting. When a girl cannot be sure of staying dry at night, other decisions become risky or impossible, including staying at a friend's, having a friend sleep over, going on a class trip, or going away to camp. Girls invent novel ways of dealing with bedwetting, perhaps staying up all night or hiding their wet bed linens. One teenage girl solved the problem at camp by sleeping on the ground and throwing away clothing so that nobody could tell that she was wet in the morning.

Often the efforts to help a girl deal with her enuresis have included all of the typical approaches. There have been long talks about whatever stress she is under; there have been gentle reminders, there have been visits to the pediatrician and the urologist. There have probably been tearful scenes, some shouting matches, and serious things said.

So why can't she stay dry at night, if it's such a big deal to her? About 3 percent of adolescents have problems with bedwetting. There are generally two types of bedwetting that afflict teenage girls. The one is long-term and is the result of failures at early training. There may have been periods of control when a girl has stayed dry, but the problem persists on and off through most of her childhood and adolescence. In the other type, a girl has been trained early on, sometimes with some difficulty, and then there is a disruption, perhaps due to illness, traumatic event, or hospitalization. Often there are other relatives in the family who have difficulties with bedwetting or did in their youth.

What causes one girl to have difficulties in enuresis and not another has to do with personality and experience. It appears that when early efforts to train are not completely successful, that is, when there is dryness for a period and then a lapse, this sets up a pattern in some youngsters. When it is impossible to complete training all at one time, either because the family's patterns are disrupted or because parents are inconsistent or too casual in their attempts, a girl's system does not develop enduring patterns, so they must periodically be implanted again. Bladder control is maintained by that part of the brain that controls other unconscious functions, like avoiding falling out of bed at night. As such, competence in this area requires a different and somewhat tangential approach to develop.

The best way to insure dryness is, paradoxically, a pattern of dryness. For without this, a girl becomes accustomed to a wet bed, her system fails to differentiate predictive urination signals, and she tends to respond in the way that she responded on the last occasion. It sometimes helps to keep a girl up until she urinates and then allow her to sleep no more than three hours, letting her go back to sleep only after she urinates again. Interestingly the ability to make oneself urinate is the same as the ability to withhold urination, so this pattern reinforces control while conditioning her to sleeping dry.

Under no circumstances should a girl be allowed to remain in a wet bed, and alarms or waking her can prevent this. The bedwetting pattern can be deliberately disrupted in a training week in which a girl drinks large quantities of liquids during the afternoon and evening, allows herself to lie down only after urinating, and then is wakened every ninety minutes until her system achieves some control. The critical objective is to condition her system to dryness.

The bigger issue for a teenage girl is how to handle the problem of bedwetting without any further loss of personal power or self-respect. These are the more serious issues, along with social withdrawal and body discomfort. For this reason, a parent's function should be to call attention to the problem, listen sensitively and nonjudgmentally to the distress, and require the girl to work on solving it. She may try many things that don't work before getting to what does, but it is realistic to expect that she will work on it, with a parent's help, until it is solved.

BAD LANGUAGE

"You suck, Mom!"

A pretty girl with a dirty mouth is apt to be called a tramp, a brazen hussy, or something else even less flattering. Why do girls choose to use profanities and vulgarities?

For teenage girls there are many reasons why obscene language is appealing. A girl who wishes to appear strong or to seem masculine may use strong language to strike her stance. Particularly in neighborhoods where girls feel threatened by bullying or fights, obscene language sends a "leave me alone or else" message. Sometimes girls use obscenities to test their own power to intimidate or to influence. Cursing is an adult variation on the temper tantrum, the point of which is to influence somebody to do something that person won't otherwise do.

Since profanity generally violates adult rules, it is a form of distinguishing oneself from both adults and children and of establishing one's identity as a teenager and member of the adolescent culture. The shock value it holds when used around adults can make a teen girl feel like a folk hero to peers. ("She said *that* to the principal?")

Teenage culture has changed along with the wider adult culture, so that taboo words like "asshole" and "suck," are heard not infrequently in films and on television. Teenagers, quick to react to fashion changes, display the changes in the vernacular. The colloquial changes mirror the culture's emphasis on sexual themes and demeaning, depowering references to females have become commonplace, including: "Fuck you," "motherfucker," "cocksucker," "cunt," and so forth. There are relatively few new terms making reference to bowel or bladder functions or religious themes, and "Goddamit" rarely carries much punch anymore. For teenagers, increased sexual interest may take the form of experimenting with new sexual profanities.

The use of bad language usually tapers off as a girl becomes more interested in joining the adult culture and in manipulating it to achieve her goals. Her appearance and overall manners are likely to change at the same time as she trades individuality for power. The following will be useful until nature takes its course:

1. Adults need to remain calm in the face of a girl's cursing and not allow themselves to be provoked to ill-considered action. Sometimes the aim of cursing is to provoke action or create an interesting spectacle, and it is wise for adults to retain control of their own behavior.

2. It will help for adults to examine their language and forms of expression to weed out any obscenities that have crept in. Sometimes obscenity becomes a way to express intense feeling in a family.

3. Keep in mind that language mores have changed and that what was considered unladylike several decades ago is now seen as part of the youth culture.

4. Sort through a girl's obscene vocabulary and ascertain whether she knows the meaning of the words she uses and the subjects she is discussing. If she doesn't want to explain them, define them for her and describe the reference. With words like "cocksucker" and "motherfucker," it might be useful to write out the definitions first and practice explaining them alone before speaking with a teenage girl about them. She is likely to be quite uncomfortable in this sort of discussion, but obscene language is talk about explicit sexual activity.

5. Discuss with a teen girl the ways that a woman can most effectively express angry or intense sentiments. Concentrate on clarity and forcefulness, as well as eloquence of speech. Point out that obscenity is boring and misleading and that it masks direct messages. Consider how well she expresses feelings generally, and whether the household welcomes a free expression of emotion. Does the use of bad language represent a forceful bursting point combined with general inhibition?

6. Consider her ability to fit in with the culture in other ways, i.e., using good manners. Stress the need for consideration for one's listener as well as insisting on the right to express oneself. Suggest that she consider how she wants others to perceive her and that foul language generally suggests a lower

intellectual level, as well as a lower socioeconomic class. Like burping in public, it also indicates underdeveloped self-control and is rarely appealing to others, although it may provoke attention and interest.

SMOKING

It is always a concern to find that a teenage girl is smoking, and a bit of a surprise as well, with all of the negative publicity smoking receives, and the vast numbers of adults who have quit smoking. It is more surprising to find that most girls begin smoking very early in adolescence, usually by about seventh grade, and the habit then becomes more enduring and more likely to persist into adulthood.

If begun early, smoking becomes part of a girl's image of herself and a way to handle stressful social situations as well. It may represent a philosophical as well as a behavioral change. The same girl who begins smoking at twelve may have been one of its most vociferous opponents in childhood, railing against adults who smoke and vowing never to touch cigarettes. In adolescence a girl can become distinctly different from her former childhood self.

Smoking among teen girls frequently reflects socioeconomic class, with much higher high school dropout rates correlated with smoking in girls. Girls who planned to go to college were only half as likely to smoke as those who had no college plans. A surprisingly high percentage of high school seniors, 21 percent, are daily smokers, and girls are more likely than boys to smoke at this age.

What is it that makes smoking appealing to girls? The first cigarette is always unpleasant; it usually hurts a girl's chest and makes her mouth smart and her eyes tear. Why would a girl suffer these effects? It is certainly not from ignorance, because teenagers know the dangers of smoking and are quick to make jokes about "cancer sticks" and "coffin nails," part of bravado and derring-do. To be responsible is not a particularly attractive quality to teens.

More likely is it that smoking helps a girl feel that she fits in with her friends and that she looks sophisticated and fearless. If her parents and older siblings smoke, she is likely to feel this more strongly and the likelihood of her smoking increases. Smoking may also give her something to do with her hands and a posture to hold in social activity.

It also involves certain rituals, such as finding an ashtray, lighting someone's cigarette, "bumming" cigarettes, putting out a cigarette, that are shared with other youngsters. Some girls find it congenial to have a cigarette in the dark with friends while they talk intimately. Girls may smoke to control weight in the belief that smoking inhibits appetite and that if they stop their weight will increase.

Nicotine, a toxic chemical in pure form, is addictive both physically and psychologically; by the time a girl is mature enough to know that there is a problem, she is addicted. This may not seem as serious a problem as drug addiction, but it may encourage other addictive behavior since it diminishes a girl's self-esteem and faith in her ability to direct her own behavior.

The following will be helpful:

1. If you smoke, stop. If others in the family smoke, prevail on them to stop or forbid any smoking inside the house.

2. Deal directly with a girl's smoking and discuss it in depth with her, enlisting the help of friends and the family doctor to speak with her as well. It is unlikely that she will hear anything new, but she will have a clear message of caring and help in avoiding denial of the problem.

3. Point out the immediate rather than the long-term consequences of smoking, that is, the bad breath, the yellow teeth and fingers, the clinging smoke odor in hair and clothes, and how much less attractive she is holding a cigarette. Also mention the shortness of breath, the burning sensation in her chest, the cough, the bitter taste on her tongue, and the worries it introduces. Add up the cost of smoking over a month, over a year, over a lifetime and ask if she wants her money to go "up in smoke."

4. Do not tell her that she's too young to smoke; this suggests that smoking is an adult privilege that she must work for.

5. Teach her how a woman handles a situation in which she has to refuse something, role playing where necessary. Emphasize the need for independence and self-control in quitting, and reassure her that she will have more control of herself as she gets older. For a girl who can't quit on her own, contact

the American Cancer Society for the names of clinics that help people quit smoking.

6. Encourage the local schools to eliminate designated smoking areas. These encourage smokers to give each other peer support and develop a sense of belonging to a smoker's group. Instead, ask the school to present antismoking programs before middle school so that they will have maximum impact.

COMPULSIVE BEHAVIOR

Sometimes parents notice that a girl has some unusual movements or behaviors that defy rational explanation, even for a teenager. It may be that when a girl leaves the house, she goes back in over the threshold and then comes out again, repeating the process several times. Or she may ask repetitive questions about whether she is getting sick. She may need to check to see whether she has turned off the haircurler or the iron or locked the door, and she may repeat these behaviors more than necessary.

The checking behavior, the making sure, is driven by a series of repetitive thoughts that focus on what would happen if the behavior were not done: "What if I didn't turn off the iron? What if I turned it off but the iron was still too hot? What if the wiring was bad so that it didn't go off completely? What if a fire starts and destroys the house? the family?" These are obsessive thoughts usually accompanied by vivid imaginings, and the compulsive behaviors are repeated to try to chase away the frightening mental images.

While most of us occasionally have a stab of worry about whether we have taken care of safety precautions, for a girl with compulsive behavior these anxieties are so distracting that it becomes difficult to go about normal activities. Fear begins to interfere with routine pursuits and requires constant rituals to try to contain it. A girl is intellectually aware that her behavior is unnecessary, but, as she says, she can't seem to stop. She may become panicky as she checks and checks again, but she still cannot contain the anxiety. Her inability to stop the checking behaviors further unnerves her.

Why does this happen to a girl? What is it that leads normal, everyday decisions to become so dangerous in her eyes?

Obsessive-compulsive disorder (OCD) develops in girls who are overly responsible and inclined to behaving well. Sometimes an event that is upsetting, such as a fire or other disaster, particularly if it occurs when a girl is in an anxious state, can trigger such problems, or they may stem from a family setting that is rigid and anxiety-producing.

Obsessive-compulsive problems afflict about 3 percent of the population, and they seem to begin in the adolescent years, although a girl may not have enough objectivity to be aware that her behavior is a problem or she may keep her obsession and compulsion as a shameful secret, believing them a reflection of her character and integrity. Personality structure that is fitted too tightly, when combined with unresolved tensions, can spill over into obsessive thought patterns.

Earlier thinking on this disorder explained it as stemming from difficulty in controlling impulses, so that energy was spent on repressing wish-fulfilling behavior. The weak personality, in this view, was unable to contain basic drives or to find adequate expression for them, and so the drives appeared in conscious thought in the form of obsessions and were controlled by means of compulsive behavior that served to undo the wicked wishes.

A cognitive view would hold that random thoughts, if they produce anxiety, may set in motion a chain of decisions that lead to OCD in the following way: If it randomly occurs to an anxious adolescent girl that she might benefit from the death of her mother, she may immediately try to put the idea out of her thoughts since it is too frightening and guilt-inducing to bear. But thought occurs in a stream, and as she tries not to admit a thought, it becomes stronger, leading to the perception that her thoughts are uncontrollable and that she is crazy or bad. As the thought becomes more and more dominant, her attempts to control it escalate, so that both thought and control simultaneously increase in strength.

At last mental exhaustion and tension spill over into behavior that is also aimed at controlling or undoing the wicked thoughts. The girl may develop a pattern of saying "I'm sorry" to everyone for everything, or especially to her mother, until listeners become aware of something strange about her speech. If the ritual is practiced often enough, it may give the illusion of protecting against the feared outcome, since the feared outcome does not appear while the ritualistic behavior is practiced. In this example, whether a mother dies has no relation to a daughter's thoughts, but the daughter's frantic control of her thoughts may seem to have the magical power to prevent a tragedy. Curiously, these patterns often appear normally in middle childhood, ages seven–eight, and are seen in many children's ditties, such as "Step on a crack, break your mother's back...." For most girls, they disappear spontaneously with the emergence of greater mastery feelings in later childhood and the awareness that events occur without reference to human intention.

For obsessive-compulsive disorders that interfere with daily activity, psychological treatment is necessary. This will probably involve psychotherapy, behavior modification, hypnosis, and perhaps medication if the symptoms are severe. Although OCD is a psychological disorder that must be treated, in mild forms it is often related to high achievement, as it allows the person to focus closely on a task for long periods of time, for example, medical students, researchers, law students.

The following will be helpful at home for a girl who struggles with compulsive behavior:

1. Keep in mind that guidance must be taken from a girl's psychological therapy, and home activity must be within this structure.

2. Avoid suggestions to a girl to "be reasonable" or "show a little self-control," as these will only make her ashamed and alienated. If it were that simple, she would have solved the problem long ago. In this disorder, paradoxically, the more she tries to control it, the worse it gets.

3. It helps to have a free flow of ideas in her surroundings so that she is comfortable with negative feelings and can express them to those who stimulate them.

4. Reasonable risk-taking in pursuit of personal goals needs to be encouraged, so that a girl goes after those things that are important to her and gains a sense of courage and mastery in reaching for them. Where she is too anxious to commit to a course of action, it is helpful to ask her to try something once. It is also worth reiterating that life is full of great risks and that there are no ways to be completely safe.

5. Support the belief that she can make good but not perfect judgments. She can make a reasonable assessment about whether she turned off the lights, and she can rely on that judgment, even though sometimes she will be wrong. Her internal tension and anxiety are not a sign of bad judgment, but only fear of risk.

6. Physical exercise is extremely important for relieving tension and for promoting a sense of relaxation and competence. Aerating exercise, such as running, brisk walking, swimming, or bicycling, which increases the pulse and respiration, will be helpful, especially if sustained for thirty or more minutes four times weekly.

Emotional issues

VIOLENCE THAT THREATENS A GIRL

In schools and other places, girls are victimized by their peers as well as by adults. In a survey of eighth-grade girls by NCES, 22.7 percent of the girls said that someone had threatened to hurt them, and 10.4 percent said they feel unsafe at school.*

In an earlier time, children moved more freely, exploring their communities and seeking out adventures. But now parents are fearful for their children and doors must be double locked. Sometimes daughters must be walked to school, and some youngsters carry beepers to feel safe.

In a time when girls need more protection, how can parents encourage a sense of self-reliance and independence? This is particularly difficult where there are drug dealers, random gunfire, and roving gangs. Even without actual violence, the perception of danger has a psychological impact on girls. A teen girl may be continuously afraid of an attack at school or en route and ashamed at seemingly childish feelings. This may translate to an increase in generalized anxiety and attempts to structure her life protectively, for example, by choosing a boyfriend or group of girlfriends based on safety needs.

---

*National Center for Education Statistics, *A Profile of the American Eighth Grader,* U.S. Department of Education, 1988.

Violence to women occurs most often at home, with 2.1 million incidents of domestic violence each year, more than all the injuries from car accidents, muggings, and rapes. Girls learn to be violent or to be victims of violence at home, and it is here that they are most likely to get hit and hurt. For a teenage girl, the most likely hurting will come from parents or brothers, and if it is framed as sibling bickering, it may not be apparent that a girl is being mistreated.

The following will be helpful when a girl is the target of violence:

1. Listen to her feelings, no matter how irrational or excessive they seem. Feelings alone represent a source of stress, regardless of actual circumstances, and expressing them helps. Listen particularly for those experiences that may have frightened her and made her feel less capable.

2. Support her self-esteem and assure her that you will help her develop ways to deal with the situation. Avoid offering the protection that you would a small child in danger, no matter how upset she is, and always have her take some responsibility for her own safety.

3. Discuss general safety rules, and explore with her how they translate to her environs, for example, where are the safe or the isolated places in her school. Develop survival skills, and talk about your own ways of coping. When you hear news stories of crimes against teens, problem-solve with her to develop effective responses.

4. Talk about when to dispense with good manners, polite responses, and being accommodating, cooperative, and pleasant. Practice tough, nasty, and assertive behavior so that she has more tools in her bag to draw on in a crisis.

5. Consider whether her reactions stem from circumstances or internal tensions and whether her fear of violence represents reality or phobia.

6. Where it is clear that a girl cannot deal with the level of threat, consult with school personnel about a course of action; contact local police if necessary.

7. Accept that life is full of risk and that the greatest risk, as Erica Jong said, is to take no risks at all.

WHEN A GIRL THREATENS VIOLENCE

In an NCES study of eighth-grade girls, 11.3 percent said that they had fought with another student, indicating that girls are a source as well as a target of violence.* Girls learn violence from others and use it when they have no more effective means to accomplish an end. Aggression may be learned from fighting with siblings or friends, or it may be the logical outgrowth of violence in the family. Parents may not be aggressive but may fail to give adequate guidance, feeling that children will grow out of their fighting and that they are best left to themselves to discover more effective ways of coping. If there is a parental pattern of little warmth and much harsh punishment, children are likely to show violent responses to frustration.

Sometimes a teenage girl's violent responses take the form of verbal assaults, with barrages of hostile and derogatory attacks that are psychologically punitive. They may come in response to criticism or implied criticism and may represent impulsive and angry responses to strong feelings.

Girls may react strongly to protect their dignity or freedom, to express their displeasure, or simply because they cannot come up with a better way to get what they want. The excessive responses may become attacks against parents for real or imagined injustices, and they may seem uncontrolled or unprovoked.

The following will be helpful in dealing with a teenage girl's violent behavior:

1. Act immediately to stop violent behavior. Clear the room or the house, close yourself in the bathroom, call the police, or take other action that will interrupt the sequence and the buildup. Be very clear about what is acceptable and what is out of bounds, and act in a way that supports your limits. Letting violent behavior run its course communicates tacit consent.

2. Limit conflicts at home among siblings or marital partners that loosen everybody's controls. Demonstrate and teach negotiating skills: thinking before you act, evaluating consequences, respecting the rights of others. Repeat the same words as a reminder, for example, "Think before you act."

---

*National Center for Education Statistics, *A Profile of the American Eighth Grader*, U.S. Department of Education, 1988.

3. Help a girl to avoid aggressive or poorly controlled peers. Discourage watching violent films and television for entertainment. Instead, encourage and participate in physical activity that works off tension, such as walking, running, or playing ball.

4. Help a girl to express her feelings while they are still of manageable proportions. Teach assertiveness as a way of speaking for herself. Evaluate with her what she is trying to achieve, and help her find satisfying ways to reach her goals.

5. Examine whether her reactions are drug or alcohol induced. Cocaine use in particular is related to violent outbursts.

6. Consider how you set limits for her and whether there is too little approval and too much discipline. Especially consider whether there is a hostile atmosphere toward a girl combined with little real control. It may feel as though parents are submissive, but it may be that she gets little positive attention or kindly help. How much positive reinforcement is there for her behavior?

DESTRUCTIVENESS TO PROPERTY

Teenagers close to puberty are remarkably clumsy, and some will spill a drink while trying to tell time from a wristwatch. The number of objects lost or broken rivals that of childhood, but it is easy to fall victim to high expectations based on a girl's more mature appearance, for she looks like she could be more responsible.

Occasionally it appears that a teenage girl has more than the usual difficulty, and the problem does not coincide with a growth spurt. It may be appropriate to consider medical evaluation for the unlikely possibility of a disease process at work.

It is also helpful to look at the number of frustrations currently active in a girl's life, and whether her reactions represent angry or irritable responses. Contrary to popular belief, the releasing of angry feelings is not cathartic and does not clean out the system. Rather, angry feelings tend to become conditioned, so that the girl who slams doors for occasional irritations is likely to become a chronic door-slammer. Ironically, the habit of angry behavior generally reinforces angry feelings rather than reducing them since the internal response appears along with the behavior, much like the saliva of Pavlov's dogs.

Sometimes a girl's destructiveness or carelessness to things sends a message about herself, that she is powerful and beyond mundane concerns, a grandiose stance that hides painful inferiority feelings. If important objects are broken, such as her boom box or television, she is above caring and may even self-righteously claim to be uninterested. It is worth examining when she is able to feel serenely masterful and composed. More importantly, where is she able to create what she needs and to generate whatever would make her life work better?

If her carelessness extends to the possessions of others, it is worth considering whether she has a clear picture of herself and is able to distinguish how she is different from others, where she stops and where they begin. A strong sense of self always includes a strong sense of others as well, and when she cannot differentiate possessions, it is probable that she has trouble with a clear and dignified view of herself.

Vandalism is in a separate category from the acts described above; it indicates a form of delinquent group behavior that aims at destruction of social objects in order to gain a sense of power, revenge, and group belonging. It is worth considering where a girl belongs, if not with a group of perpetrators, and whether she has alternative peer groups.

A girl's inner monologue is important: it generates her behavior choices and it may underlie destructive responses. When her inner comments are self-righteous, demanding, childish, entitled, and dictatorial, then her behavioral choices will reflect her determination and urgency to control her surroundings for her own gratification. The following will be helpful with a girl who is destructive to objects:

1. Ask her to practice moving slowly and to consider her choices of movement aloud as a way to develop considered rather than impulsive action.

2. Explore with her her overall life satisfaction and her self-rating in important life areas, for example, school, friends, and self-care. Where does she feel masterful in meeting her own goals? Where does she fall short? How can you help her?

3. Ask her to focus on the long term in considering what

happens with objects. Plan with her how objects will be acquired, maintained, and replaced.

4. When she is frustrated or unhappy, help her to focus on how to improve things rather than on her unhappy feelings.

5. Help her to manage her environment to prevent problems from building up and overwhelming her.

6. Limit your exposure and set realistic limits on her access to objects. If she is impulsive and careless, don't let her use your new car and expect her to learn from the experience. *You* will be the one who learns from the experience.

STAYING IN BED

With the onset of adolescence, teenagers' sleep habits generally change. Girls develop an interest in staying up into the small hours and in the events that occur then, including watching late-night television, having intimate telephone conversations, and entertaining overnight guests.

The other side of evening becomes a missing morning; a girl will stay in bed until noon or later and appear when a parent's day is well under way, thus destroying any plans for housework or companionable activities. Parents are usually initially amused and then later annoyed at a girl's failure to follow the regular household schedule. When teen sleep patterns emerge, it can seem decadent to sleep away the morning and stay up into the night. Even though this usually occurs on weekends or vacations, it nonetheless can seem wrong to a more structured generation.

Sometimes sleeping becomes a serious problem. A girl may begin to miss school or important teen events, and her sleeping hours may take more of the day than her waking hours. Although she may have a disease, for example, mononucleosis or chronic fatigue syndrome, more often there is no recognizable physical cause.

Sometimes spending great amounts of time in bed is a way to establish privacy and to withdraw from the family without actually rejecting anyone. A girl may not spend all of the time in her room sleeping, but she is nonetheless isolated from the rest of the family. This may also be a form of defiance of adults, a type of passive resistance that cannot easily be overcome.

Staying in bed seems to follow naturally from leisure-time choices. Americans spend about 33 percent of their leisure time watching television or in other passive activities. Watching videos, eating, drinking, and napping seem to be the great national pastimes, and a teenager's sleep patterns may reflect a parallel passivity.

Withdrawal to her room can be a way for a girl to deal with too much anxiety about changes and about her relationship with her family. Anxiety itself is tiring, and sleep shuts out all incoming stimuli and can give relief. Too much sleeping can mask depression, which involves a slowing down of all processes, and may allow a girl to withdraw into herself. In this case also, a girl may not actually be sleeping, but may be passively lying in bed.

The following will be helpful:

1. Keep track of a girl's sleep patterns, with her cooperation, to ascertain whether there is reason to be concerned. Ask her to help you record her sleep so that you can consider her medical state. Explain your worries and your interest in helping her be her most energetic in pursuit of what she wants. Ask her to estimate how much sleep she needs to feel energized.

2. Examine the quality of her sleep, whether she sleeps through the night (or day), and whether she is wakened by dreams or worries.

3. Discuss with her the current quality of her life and whether there is a basis for her withdrawal. Ask especially about her relations with other teens, since too much sleep cuts her off from her peers. Determine whether there are anxieties operating or whether she is feeling hopeless or helpless.

4. Explore active vs. passive entertainment choices, and ask her to choose how she would like to be active. Sports and physical exercise are particularly helpful for a lethargic girl and should be required as part of the school's schedule. Point out to her that too much sleep and underactivity *increase* anxiety and discomfort.

5. Help her to arrange time with friends and to see them on a regular basis, perhaps by joining a club or other activity.

Family problems

LYING

It is always painful to discover that a beloved child has lied to us with the deliberate intention of deceiving. For a parent, there is a sense of betrayal and a feeling that a girl has tried to exploit our love for her own advantage. When a parent is hard-working and self-sacrificial, this can feel very bad indeed.

But lying for a teenage girl is usually not personally aimed at a parent, although it can be an act of hostility. More commonly, it is a strategy to achieve some end. Lying probably is most frequent where a girl would like to have more control over her choices and is unable to persuade a parent that she is ready for it. So she tells a parent that the boy's parents will be home when she goes to visit or that there was no drinking at the party. To speak the truth in these situations risks a girl's independence, for a parent may take control based on parental prerogative.

A second situation in which a teenage girl is likely to lie is to avoid punishment for misdeeds, especially if she disagrees with the rule violated and it has been unilaterally imposed. When she knows that she will be grounded for poor grades, she will be motivated to lie about warning notices.

Lying can be motivated by a wish to demean others, since deliberately deceiving another insults that person's intelligence and denigrates the value of the relationship. Sometimes teenage girls use lying to express anger or power or to demonstrate to themselves and peers that parents cannot rein them in.

If a girl lies a great deal, a parent may begin to see her as a *pathological liar*, one who cannot distinguish truth from fiction, but this disorder is extraordinarily rare. More commonly, a girl has withdrawn from the relationship with a parent and reflexively lies because it seems futile to be honest. Sensing this, adults may express their frustration and defeat by labeling a girl as disturbed.

Exaggeration is the language of adolescence, and teenage girls generally describe everything, including their feelings, in superlatives:

- Awesome!! Incredible!! Amazing!! Outrageous!!
- Unbelievable!! Far out!! Oh, my God!!

There is rarely any moderation in description, and at some point stretching the truth becomes a deception. But this is a difference that girls recognize, perhaps because they understand that the language is overblown and can be discounted to get at the real meaning.

Lying can be a way to deceive oneself and to avoid the truth, a form of wishful thinking that allows one to be somebody different, and perhaps more intriguing to peers. "I'm going to Europe this summer" is not actually a deception until the summer is over and the data is in, similar to the retroactive "I aced that test!" Can a girl adequately distinguish between these hopeful projections and what is true? It is more difficult when truth refers to events yet to occur.

It is worth considering whether parents want to hear the truth from a teenage girl. In some families there is an implicit understanding that parents will not probe and girls will not tell. So when parents ask what a girl and her boyfriend did at his house, she may say, "Oh, nothing," and parents do not ask further.

The truth about a teenage girl's life is often disturbing to parents because an adult who has information feels obligated to act, which can be intrusive and disturbing to teens. Often girls protect their parents and their own prerogatives by limiting the information that is shared.

Lying may be the only sure way to establish a private life with a parent who is nosy and intrusive. If a parent is accustomed to sharing all of a child's secrets and relating in a close way, the beginning of adolescence can feel like a shutting out. Some parents will try to deal with this by insisting on complete honesty from a girl, which prevents her from growing up, since the caterpillar cannot become a butterfly without a cocoon. A young adolescent determined to grow up has no recourse but lying to maintain her privacy if it is invaded.

Although absolute truthfulness is not always a virtue, the habit of honesty is a good one and well worth encouraging. Honesty is a form of assertiveness, a way of a girl's being whatever she is and standing by it, without backing down, no

matter the consequences. Habitual deception forces her to operate in secret, always checking to make sure that she is not found
out. This drains her energy and flattens her self-esteem, for she
cannot be proud of wearing a mask.

The following are helpful to deal with lying:

1. Examine your habits as an adult. Do you relate stories that
involve cleverly deceiving other people, thereby communicating a value in lying? Or is the courage to be honest described
with admiration? Are you straightforward, or does the family
know that what you are saying is only partially true? How often
do little white lies serve your purposes? Do you lie to a teenage
daughter, telling her, for example, that you can't drive for the
field trip because your car doesn't work well enough, when it
does work well enough to take you shopping?

2. Consider whether her lying is part of a general pattern of
hostility toward parents. Does she often seem hostile and oppositional, ready to argue and fight about trivial matters? Is lying
a way to hold out against parents, to prevent them from taking
control in certain areas? If she often seems angry and negative,
discuss her feelings until you can accurately summarize them
for her.

3. If a girl lies to get attention or to feel importance, examine
whether there are other ways that these are accessible to her.
Can her time be structured to make her feel valuable in other
ways, for example, helping out at the daycare center?

4. Is she protecting her friends by limiting what she reveals about them? Lying sometimes is a way to preserve another's privacy, even when there may be a greater good served
by telling the truth. Teenage loyalty often seems to require
keeping secrets about substance abuse, sexual activities, and
self-destructive impulses.

5. When a girl is discovered in a lie, handle it with the best
good manners you can muster, taking care not to humiliate her
before others. Avoid open criticism, threats, or a forced confes-
sion. Instead, speak to her privately to share her feelings about
the lie and to understand her motivation. Help her to find a better way to achieve whatever her aim was in lying. Be careful
about expressing anger, and focus instead on communicating
distress and disappointment, for the goal here is to teach her
pride and good habits.

6. Help her toward a treasured view of herself, so that she does not pay in self-esteem to get what she wants. Teach her that telling the truth is a good habit, one that simplifies life and decisions and helps her avoid the chaos and tension of deception. Help her to understand that relationships cannot work on the basis of dishonesty and that people get lost from one another when they are not themselves.

7. Let her know that lying always represents an attempt to look better than we are, that she looks good to you as she is, even with lying, and that as she grows older and braver, she will feel less of a need to be other than what she is.

DIVORCE

Divorce is never an easy decision, and even once made, it is fraught with self-doubt and a sense of failure for those involved. In early adolescence, there is a strong sense of losing parents upon whom one depends when they divorce. In later adolescence, although a girl may be more emotionally removed, there is a sense of insecurity and loss and a fear that perhaps a happy family is not a reachable goal in a girl's life.

Marital tension verging on divorce is not uncommon, and it can be difficult to decide which is worse, a cold and unloving relationship or a clear division. For a teenage girl, the answer is usually for parents to remain together unless there is clear injury to family members. Unconcerned about parents' inner hurts or yearnings, a teenage girl finds it far more convenient for her purposes for parents to stay together, preferably but not necessarily amicably.

Since raising adolescents generates conflicts, it is easy for a self-centered teen girl to see parental strife as caused by adolescent issues or behavior, and it can be hard for her to understand that parents have their own needs and difficulties that would persist with or without her. When there is marital tension, girls are likely to see it as their fault, and even if there is no logical connection, they will feel guilty and responsible. This may lead a girl to try to settle parental fights or to respond angrily out of a sense of unfairness at shouldering the blame or responsibility.

The major problem with marital tension for a teenage girl is that it takes parents' time, energy, and judgment, instead of allowing these to focus on a teen girl and her needs. There are enough issues in a girl's life to take up all of a parent's time, and there is very little surplus.

Affairs: Sometimes marital tension is compounded by one parent becoming involved with someone outside the marriage in an enduring relationship. If the relationship persists long enough, there will be telephone calls, meetings, notes or cards, or encounters when a girl is around ("Who is that man, Mom?"). To believe that an important relationship can be kept secret from a teenage girl is an exercise in self-deception and forces a girl to keep to herself and imagine what is occurring.

If affairs cannot be avoided, they can be handled with discretion and self-discipline and will probably be less than satisfying as a result. It will not be possible to have frequent contact with a lover, or to see a lover on holidays, or to make the lover into a part of the family. A parent will often have to choose between the lover and the family — and will, it is to be hoped, choose the latter until children are emancipated. A girl needs an intact family and a dedicated parent, and other commitments must be put aside so that she can have them.

If a girl learns that there is another person, a parent may hope that she will share the giddy feelings and excitement of the new relationship. But a teenager's main reaction is likely to be shame and guilt along with a sense of betrayal for the family. A parent is obligated to keep knowledge of the relationship from a youngster, although this will deepen the rift between parent and child.

Separation: If parents decide to separate, it may seem as if they have found a solution to their problems, but in fact this is illusory. It is, in effect, agreeing not to talk about a problem, rather than solving it. There remain all of the difficulties and disagreements and different needs, which must still be addressed, although now in a more distant fashion. But if both parents love a child, there is never a complete divorce, and parents must continue to work together throughout a girl's youth.

Characteristically in a separation, few decisions are reached beyond the decision to live apart. The matters of financial arrangements, custody, residence, visitation, and shared parental responsibilities are left open, with the hope that solutions will make themselves known over time. Rarely does this happen, and instead teens have a greater say in the arrangements, and hence greater confusion and guilt. After all, if the solution is not obvious to an adult, how easily can a youngster find it? Choices about visitation, for example, may hinge on a girl's reactions, so that if she has little time to see her father, the outcome may be infrequent visitations.

The decision to divorce: When a teenage girl hears that her parents are divorcing, hopefully from both parents at the same time, her reaction is likely to be shock, confusion, anger, anxiety, and fear. The decision represents a major loss to her of an intact family, and no matter how uninterested she may have seemed in her adolescence, it is frightening to find the family disintegrating. There is likely to be remorse as well as sadness and anger at lost opportunities. The strong reactions and disturbance generally last from two to four months, after which there is a gradual readjustment to new circumstances.

It is wise for adults to make decisions together about family arrangements and present them to a girl along with the announcement of divorce. Let her know that she will be taken care of and that her life will continue with most things the same: homework, curfews, clothing, bedroom, etc.

Explain to her why you are divorcing. Do not present it as a mutual decision that is made in friendship and mutual caring, since this is misleading and contradictory. If it is Dad's drinking that Mom can't stand, or Mom's job that Dad won't tolerate, say so. If parents don't give true reasons and sensible explanations, a girl will invent her own, which are far worse ("It must be that I caused trouble"), and will distrust her parents.

It is wise for parents to avoid venting feelings about a spouse to a daughter, although it is important briefly to explain behavior and emotional reactions to her:

- "I'm very angry at Daddy for leaving, and I'm scared of being alone."

instead of

- "He's a no-good bum and I should never have depended on him!"

A teen girl needs some understanding of what is happening and why, but she is far less interested in the subtleties and details of the split than a parent and doesn't need to understand the complexities, even though a parent may feel a need to talk. Criticizing a father stirs a youngster's protective feelings toward him and alienates her from the mother.

Custody: It has always seemed that although parents may feel that they settle custody with their lawyers, in fact it is a teenager who decides on where she will spend most of her time, and generally by fifteen it is her friends who have custody, since most girls prefer not to be with parents for great amounts of time. If arrangements are made for a teen girl that are intolerable for her, she will rearrange custody herself or make her parents so upset that they do so.

It is far wiser to make decisions about where she will live based on what best suits her needs. Her life, with all its demands and activities, goes on regardless of the divorce. She needs to remain in the same school and have transportation to the pediatrician, the allergist, the orthodontist, the ballet teacher, the piano teacher, the hairstylist, the community volunteer activity, extracurricular activities, and her part-time job. She needs to have supervision when she is home and someone to keep in touch with the school to monitor her needs there, as well as someone to be the volunteer parent in her activities. Although many divorces begin with fights over who will get custody, they end up in conflicts over who will give their time for all these needs. Not surprisingly, a girl's major concern is whether anyone will do all of this, particularly if parents are depressed or upset by the divorce. It is wise to make sure these responsibilities are met in the first months of the split so that a girl does not feel abandoned.

When parents try to make decisions about custody and residence, they often neglect these issues and instead focus on how each of them can continue to have time with their daughter. They forget that this may be a priority for them, especially during a lonesome and disrupted time, but it is not a priority for her. Their needs must come second to hers, for if her development is put at risk, neither parent can be happy in the long run.

A girl needs to stay in the same home, school district, and neighborhood, with her siblings, so that as little as possible is changed in her life. It is important to maintain a relationship with both parents, but there must be *one* home base where she sleeps six of seven nights per week. To have her move back and forth between parental homes is a violation of a child's right to a home, and, not surprisingly, in girls who have this pattern forced on them there is an inclination to get far away from both parents at the earliest possible opportunity.

Parents need to consult frequently, particularly on expectations and rules, so that a girl does not opportunistically use the arrangement to escape parental control, leaving for the other parent's house when things get uncomfortable at the primary residence, as, for example, when chores are required.

The majority of fathers do not maintain a relationship with daughters after the first year of divorce and do not financially support them. It is wise to deal forthrightly with a girl's pain and anger when this happens, but to separate it from a mother's.

Dating: Adults will find it easier to adjust to new friends and partners than a girl will after a divorce. For adults, marriage has been only part of their life experience, while for children parents have usually been fixed figures in their life spectrum. Divorce changes little of a girl's feelings for her parents, and dating affects a girl in much the same way it would if her parents were still married.

New people represent the possibility of new, sometimes guilty relationships and elicit the fear of losing a parent to someone more attractive. If a romance ends, it may stir up stronger feelings than the divorce, as second traumas resembling the first often do, and a girl may begin to see romantic involvements as inevitably disappointing. She may also doubt her ability to maintain relationships as an adult and may resolve not to marry.

The following will be helpful:

1. Let a girl have her feelings about a divorce, no matter how much of a burden they seem to you, and empathize with her very different experience. Avoid expecting her to share your feelings or to sympathize with you. A teenage girl cannot be a good friend, a mother, or a supporter.

2. Settle her needs first when deciding on separation, custody, residence, and visitation. Imagine that both parents are missing, and plan an arrangement to suit her needs first irrespective of parental needs. Then add in parental needs in reasonable amounts. It is wise for parents to try out any residence arrangement that they make for a girl, for example, moving between two houses, to develop an understanding of how visitation patterns affect a girl.

3. Support her relationship with the other parent, but don't sugarcoat it or give her overly optimistic explanations of the other's behavior. Point out the she can get along with imperfect or disappointing people.

4. Avoid portraying yourself as a helpless victim, or she will doubt your capacity to take care of her and to make wise judgments. Instead, demonstrate courage and endurance so that she can use these as a model during her life's trying times.

5. Talk over problems directly with the other parent, not through a daughter. Don't ask a daughter to carry messages. Grit your teeth, be polite, and settle your business.

6. Even with the best efforts, marriages sometimes disintegrate. Accept yourself as a limited human being, and forgive yourself for your shortcomings. Forgiving yourself allows you to forgive your partner as well and creates an atmosphere where family members can move on.

7. Keep romance and parenting separate, and give them each their due.

8. *Keep on parenting.* No matter the trauma and disruption in adult lives, there are rides to be provided, teeth to be flossed, and homework to be checked. Don't let routines and care disintegrate, even if a teenage girl seems to welcome the neglect.

STEPDAUGHTERS

Living with a teenage stepdaughter can be doubly trying, for it combines the stress of creating a new family with the turmoil of an adolescent's separating from the original family. If it is difficult to endure the adolescence of a girl we have raised from infancy, it is much more difficult to tolerate a girl with whom we have no intrinsic connection.

Stepdaughters present all of the usual adolescent problems,

but stepparents generally lack the tolerance or acceptance that has been trained into a parent during the first decade of a child's life. On the other hand, stepparents often have more respect for a girl's potential and relate to her in a more adult way than biological parents. A parent and a stepparent together as a team will need to learn cooperation and mutual respect to forge a good working alliance.

A teenage girl who finds herself in the stepdaughter position is in a hard place as well, for if girls have trouble with their families when they go through adolescence, they have much more trouble with a new family that comes about from a remarriage. Girls look for a bland unchanging home life against which to act out the drama of their adolescent lives, and a blended family is far from bland and often vibrates with emotional tension.

Many girls will claim to have no feelings or preferences when it comes to a parent remarrying: "I don't care"; "It doesn't make any difference to me." But in fact a remarriage signals the end of any possibility of a divorce reversal, in which Mom and Dad find a way to come back together and everyone is a family again.

The new family carries its own share of challenges as well, many of which are incidental to a girl's being a stepdaughter. There is likely to be a new residence, with a loss of her old home and her relationship with one single parent, new visiting arrangements, perhaps a new set of stepsiblings who suddenly become her relations with no time for relationships to grow, a new person with whom the old parent is very involved, and perhaps even a new baby, which can be embarrassing and enraging for a teenage girl.

But the most difficult aspect of this family for a teenage girl is the appearance of a stepparent. No matter how long a girl has known Mom's boyfriend or Dad's girlfriend, a remarriage changes everything. Primary among the new issues is the question of where Mom or Dad's primary loyalty now lies. A girl may feel that she is suddenly in second place, particularly if she was close to her parent. If this is a mother, and mother and daughter had a close relationship, it may be quite difficult. A mother in this situation is likely to feel torn between a daughter and a new husband, unable to satisfy either.

When the recently acquired parent is a stepfather, he can be perceived as a new authority in her life, someone from whom she must take direction. Since this is an age when girls typically strain against control, a seemingly disposable authority figure such as a stepparent or substitute teacher is an automatic target. Since there is not likely to be an established emotional tie at the beginning of the relationship, there are fewer restraints. A stepfather who feels like an outsider may attribute a girl's resistance to her being spoiled and attempt to correct her upbringing, further alienating both stepdaughter and wife.

If it is Dad who remarries, there can be a great deal of competition and jostling from a teenage girl who is possessive of her special relationship with her father. A new stepmother, no matter how kind, may often feel excluded or ignored by a ruffled stepdaughter. A father may withdraw from a daughter in an attempt to appease his wife and secure the marriage, provoking more acting up. Or he may protect his daughter but enrage his wife.

To be suddenly assigned a new set of brothers and sisters is a radical change in a girl's life and can mean that she is now dominated by older youngsters or responsible for the care of younger children. These other children will invariably be judged spoiled and as getting everything that they want, and if there is a new baby, the child will be seen as the favorite, perhaps because the baby is the one child that the parents perceive with the same feelings. Rules for each child in the family will differ, and most rules for a teenage girl will be seen as unfair, with the other children having the advantages.

A girl's position in the family changes with the addition of siblings. If she was the oldest, with the prestige of that position, she may lose that advantage (and responsibilities). If she was the baby, with the addition of more children or a new baby this place is now taken by someone else. Her relationship to her natural parent will also change, for she will notice that there are more people between her and her parent, who is also further away emotionally.

When challenged with this sort of assault on its integrity, families tend to close ranks, even if they have fought bitterly before. The two sisters who hated each other will now band together against the bratty stepbrother, and the older kids will see the younger stepsiblings as a pain in the neck. For parents, this means major problems of divided loyalties, accusations of betrayal, and pervasive guilt for abandoning their children.

The following will be helpful:

1. Remind yourself that creating a family, no matter how much tension is involved, is always a gift to a youngster, for it gives her a host of advantages that she cannot have with a single parent. Pause before you decide whether the new family is working. Wait ten years before you see whether it offers children and adults what was hoped.

2. Allow everyone time to adjust to the new family, and let them hang onto their old patterns as new ones take shape. Spend time with a daughter apart from a new spouse. Allow a stepparent to have time alone with a new stepchild, so that they can build a relationship in their own way.

3. Expect little of a stepdaughter except civility. Don't try hard to build a relationship but only to get along. Look for good manners, not love, for she can control her behavior, but not her feelings, which are apt to be quite mixed and uncomfortable.

4. Don't expect yourself to like a stepdaughter, for you didn't choose her, nor did she choose you. Fate threw you together, and love cannot be produced on demand. No matter how hard we may wish for close, well-integrated families, they rarely happen with blended families, and this may leave us feeling as though the family is quite tenuous. But it is commitment and work, not emotions, that hold a family together and enable it to take care of its members.

5. If a stepparent and a stepdaughter have disagreements, it is important that they resolve them alone without help from the other parent, with the understanding that, as in any family, parents must have the final say.

6. Avoid disciplining a stepdaughter until you have lived with her for at least a year, for it will take this long for there to be enough sense of legitimacy in the relationship for your discipline to stick.

ADOPTION

For teenage girls who are adopted, the challenges of approaching adulthood are made more complicated by the missing genealogical lines. In adolescence we are concerned with identifying ourselves and comparing ourselves with relatives serves the purpose of distinguishing family traits from our unique characteristics, and so seeing ourselves more clearly.

For a girl who is adopted, the history and sense of continuity with previous generations are missing, and there is no sense of connection to the broader family group. The family tree and the stories about famous or infamous ancestors leave an adopted teen girl feeling alone and adrift. If she feels capable and secure in the rest of her life, the effect of these experiences is reduced.

As a girl tries to identify what is uniquely herself, there may be confusion about characteristics and personality traits, with the assumption that bad traits come from her biological parents and good traits come from her adoptive parents or vice versa. Sometimes an adopted girl feels that she has questionable genes, ones that she cannot rely on, for who knows what she has inherited from the strangers who are her parents?

A teenage girl may want to search for her biological parents, to learn about her history and the people who came before. This is invariably disappointing, for the parents inevitably turn out to be less than was hoped or imagined, and there is rarely a reason convincing to her for them to have given up their baby. She may have understood from childhood that her biological mother could not take care of a baby and that she was better off in an adopted home, but years later, when she meets her mother, it will appear to her that her mother was not as self-sacrificial as she imagined and could have raised her, had she cared enough. Loyalty to her blood relatives will keep her from disapproving openly, and she will seem to accept the patronizing fiction of the adoption story. This is a private disappointment for girls.

Sometimes a teenage girl's adoptive parents have more concern about the adoption issue than she does. In adolescence, girls begin to break away from parents, and the family seems to be disintegrating, although in fact it is only restructuring itself. Adoptive parents may feel unsure of their connection to an adoptive daughter and less confident of the enduring bond between them as she begins to separate.

The feelings of rejection from a teen girl that parents experience may be attributed to a girl's being adopted and wanting her "own" parents rather than to the natural emotional withdrawal of a teenage girl during adolescence. Estrangement is easier to tolerate if we feel that there is an unbreakable genetic connection, and the physical resemblance of a girl to her parents and female relatives offers a form of reassurance that adoptive parents cannot fall back on.

For an adopted girl who has already been given up once, family ties have proved to be breakable. As a way to deal directly with this threat to the family, adoptive parents may encourage a girl to find her biological parents. If they ask enough times, out of their own anxiety, "Have you been thinking about your real mother?" or "Are you thinking you'd like to find your parents?" a girl will respond appropriately, if she is adventurous, even though she may have no particular interest in this endeavor. Adoptive parents may be projecting their anxieties of loss onto an adopted daughter, and she may then act in a way that increases their anxieties.

The following will be helpful:

1. Assume that a girl's attachment to her adoptive parents is more powerful than their attachment to her, for they are the only parents she has known, but they have known life before her. When adolescence comes, therefore, the bonds will feel much more tenuous to parents than they will to a teen girl.

2. Teenage girls normally withdraw from their parents and respond as though they want nothing to do with them during some parts of adolescence. This is not a condemnation of parents, but only a girl's trying to distance herself from childhood and childish feelings. A girl may go to great lengths to differentiate herself from parents until they begin to feel that they have nothing in common with her. It is wise to endure these reactions and assume that they are part of her efforts to become a woman rather than a reflection on a parent-child relationship.

3. Do not encourage a girl to find her birth parents unless she asks to do so. If it becomes important, it is more likely to be when she is pregnant and about to become a mother herself. Don't imply that she *should* be concerned about her birth parents, for she is at a stage when she is not likely to be concerned about *any* parents.

4. Help her to explore herself, her personality and preferences, by sharing experiences with her and helping her develop new competencies. Describe it as an experiment in self-discovery and share in it.

TEMPER TANTRUMS

To see an angry explosion in a girl who looks like a woman can be an unnerving experience, but such outbursts are usually left-overs from the tantrums of childhood. If a girl often had temper tantrums as a child, they will continue into adolescence. These are most likely to appear in early adolescence and occur sporadically, decreasing in frequency as dignity becomes valued. For some girls, they will not be outgrown and will continue into womanhood.

Some girls have a pattern of rage that includes shouting, cursing, screaming, breaking things, striking people, and running away. They may seem easily provoked or set off by some minor frustration. Often such outbreaks occur in a girl who is restless and moody, with a general air of disgruntlement and unhappiness in the face of routine daily problems. After a temper tantrum, a girl may be quiet, depressed, and withdrawn, but she may resume normal activities after a few hours and act as though nothing had happened, with no remorse.

Generally a girl who has difficulty controlling her temper has been able to win her way in the past through intimidation and explosions. For a variety of reasons, perhaps insecurity, guilt, or fear, parents have been unable to exert their own will, and so a girl's tantrums have dominated.

But at some point, there is a confrontation from which parents cannot withdraw, for the outcome is too important. Then there are usually outsiders involved, and parents are forced to deal directly with a girl's behavior.

The reason a girl uses tantrums is that she has not had to develop other means to get her way. When, for example, she wants a ride to the mall, she might ask nicely, offer to do the dishes for Mom so that Mom has time to drive her, arrange with another girl for one parent to deliver and one to pick up, and so forth. But because tantrums work, these other ways have not been developed.

The following will be helpful for a teenage girl's tantrums:
1. Don't lose your temper when a girl has an explosion, don't give in, don't threaten, and don't argue. Instead, defuse the situation by withdrawing (take a walk or go into the bathroom) and

allow her time to regain her dignity. Put off further discussion until she is back in control.

2. Check her basic reserves: has she had enough sleep and food? Are there pressures outside the discussion that provoke the reaction, for example, time demands or social embarrassment?

3. Set reasonable requirements for her, and wherever possible give her advance notice, so that she has a chance to adjust her expectations. If you can't drive anywhere this weekend or give her any rides, tell her so on Thursday, not when she asks on Saturday evening.

4. Help her to identify when her feelings are getting out of hand, and talk about how you can help her handle them. Teach her to use words to express how she feels, and state back to her what she expresses to you to be sure that you understood.

5. Pay close attention to events that lead to explosions, and monitor how she handles them so that you can step in before she resorts to her childhood habits.

ETERNAL DEPENDENCY

Often teenage girls go to college or get their own apartment after high school, and sometimes they marry. To strike out on their own, however, they must be able to support themselves, both financially and emotionally. It can seem cruel to expect this of a young female, almost as though she were being expelled from the family and abandoned to the larger society. But in the larger society, females are responsible for themselves, and there is little help from family or government, particularly if they need help as mothers.

Many girls seem to want to remain perennial daughters, going home to live if they divorce or lose a job or can't afford a nice apartment and/or want the comforts of home. At times there is a regression from early adulthood back to adolescence, so that a nineteen-year-old is still doing the same things she did at fourteen: sleeping late, using the family car, leaving her room a mess, and asking for money.

A girl may feel that her parents are obligated to continue to support her until she marries, and if she marries, that they are obligated to provide her with a wedding to suit her taste. Such a wedding can fulfill a narcissistic fantasies of being the focus of one's family and friends, while having parents underwrite it.

If a girl is not financially self-sufficient in early adulthood, parents may feel that they are deserting her if they expect her to find her own residence. They may also feel guilty if they are financially comfortable and do not "share" it with her. (We notice that financially comfortable children rarely feel obligated to share their good fortune with their parents.)

To help a girl become strong and self-sufficient, it is important to evaluate the purpose of financial support from parents, for it may prolong a girl's dependency and inadequacy. If support is given as a "capital investment," for example, while she goes to school or makes other serious efforts to become self-sufficient, then financial help is empowering. If financial help serves no more than daily maintenance, it gives credence to the idea that a young woman is a helpless creature who cannot take care of herself.

Sometimes parents are eager to support a daughter because it insures that she will maintain a relationship with them and that she will stay connected. This may lead to parent's being exploited by an immature young woman on whom they feel dependent for emotional support. Money is a form of control, and to offer money to young people is to inject oneself into the power center of their lives.

The following will be helpful with an older adolescent girl who seems to seek eternal dependency:

1. Consider whether your decisions of financial support are saving her from having to test her own abilities and capacity to learn. Ask yourself if her independence means that you lose her as a daughter.

2. If a working daughter lives at home, ask her to pay room and board. Make a contract together as you would with a boarder, one that specifies your expectations and her responsibilities. This saves her sense of independence and dignity and reminds you both that she is not a child.

3. If she plans a wedding, consider what you can afford to give her, and ask her to budget accordingly. Often a wedding consultant (either a professional consultant, grandparent, or family friend) can be helpful in advising her and helping her stay within limits.

4. Consider how long you can reasonably support her, given your own plans for later adulthood. Work out an understanding with her about when support stops, and then taper it off, encouraging her at each step to make decisions that will bring her closer to her goals.

Friends

BRAWLING

Sometimes a girl seems ready to fight with anyone, and fighting itself seems gratifying to her. She may be verbally abusive, engage in physical exchanges, and even be hurt herself, but she may not seem dismayed by physical conflict. Parents will be seriously concerned about this sort of behavior for a number of reasons. It is unsafe, and others may be intentionally or accidentally injured; many will find her behavior repulsive, thus limiting her social experiences.

Those friends who tolerate her behavior may also be combative or belligerent types who are willing to band together temporarily in an unstable alliance. In any case, tough friends will make her tougher. Sometimes others will befriend her to hide behind her bellicosity, especially if they have difficulty taking care of themselves. Worse, some youngsters will spend time with her in order to provoke her to explode and create an interesting spectacle.

A girl may seem masculine in her toughness and may ape the dress of men, with heavy boots, men's clothes, and short boyish haircuts. She may take the male role when with her friends, taking care of them and protecting them. This may be an indication of homosexuality or it may reflect a girl's fashioning her own niche as a female, one that does not carry a pervasive sense of weakness and vulnerability.

When there is a readiness to fight with anyone and an aggressive or vindictive air about a girl, it is worth exploring the underlying hostility. If a girl seems to want to do damage to others and look for opportunities to fight, this indicates a surplus of anger that spills over into neutral situations. The aggressiveness may appear particularly against authority figures, so that a girl seems like a revolutionary or a terrorist and can feel self-righteous and courageous.

When a youngster has a great deal of free-floating rage, it makes sense to look for sources of severe emotional deprivation or provocation. It may be that in the family there are important figures, parents or older siblings, who are violent or abusive to her. More importantly, there is likely to be a disregard of her emotional needs that leaves her continuously struggling to keep herself afloat.

Family violence can sometimes result from discipline that shades over into ridicule and coercion and offers little help in the development of self-control. Harsh punishment may be culturally or generationally rooted, so that families believe that a girl should be severely punished for any perceived misdeeds. Occasionally a parent may suffer from serious psychopathology or may obtain sadistic gratification from violent responses from a teenage girl. More commonly, life stresses may produce low frustration tolerance in otherwise patient parents, and the result may be excessive reactions on all sides.

By the time a girl is an adolescent, behavior patterns have been established and practiced for a long time. A teenage girl who gets into brawls probably has done so since elementary school days and has not learned other effective ways of getting what she wants. Her social skills are clearly limited, and her willingness to cover her defenses and work on a negotiated solution is nonexistent.

A girl may show no insight or self-knowledge in discussing her brawling, and she may insist instead that others provoked her and "made her do it." Insight and self-control develop in tandem, or may fail to develop at all, leaving a girl with little except force to resolve problems. Consequently, there will be little understanding of others, rare empathy, and depression caused by emotional isolation.

The following will be helpful:

1. Examine a girl's circumstances to determine what makes it difficult for her to be restrained in her dealings with others. In particular, look for provocative situations or other youngsters who taunt her or tax her limits in social skill.

2. Explore with her her concept of being female and how

comfortable she is with the variety of feminine behaviors available to her in the culture.

3. Look carefully at the family structure to ascertain what stimulates or maintains her fighting behavior.

4. Consider types of psychological therapy that focus on relationships, for example, family therapy or group therapy. These will help her deal with the realities of her behavior and how others see her rather than the illusions she has about herself. She may believe that acting belligerent and tough produces admiration or respect from others, while in fact, it produces disdain and avoidance. To hear this said, she will need to be in a structured encounter.

BROKEN HEART

A broken heart may not seem like a crisis to an adult, who may feel that disappointment in romance is just one of many problems of the teen years, and not the most important. In fact, an adult may even say, "You'll have another boyfriend before you know it."

But to a teenage girl, the situation is quite different and feels more akin to that of an adult being widowed. In adolescence, the time sense is different, so that time seems to last much longer, particularly when a girl is unhappy and a teenager cannot see the relative significance of youth in the entire lifespan. A boy and girl who have gone steady for a year are often considered married by other teens, and the end of such a relationship can feel like the end of a life. After age fifteen relationships become more adult in structure and tone, and a youngster will feel loss at this age keenly.

If you console a girl by telling her that a breakup is unimportant and insignificant and that in a few years, she won't remember it, you pretend to an inside knowledge of her feelings that is not only presumptuous and demeaning, but may be inaccurate as well. Many of the world's great romantic tragedies involved teenagers, for example, Romeo and Juliet, and there is no greater value to suffering that occurs when we are older.

When we are heartbroken, we learn something about our capacity to love, for the more we are able to love, the more deeply we are hurt when love ends. It helps a girl to understand that in adulthood we create love, we participate in its emergence and do not wait passively for it to be bestowed upon us. It may feel as though we have found the right person when we fall in love, but in fact it is our perception and energy that form the attachment.

If there has been a sexual relationship as part of a teenage girl's romance, a breakup may be more complex and a girl may feel especially bereft and angry. To be involved in an emotionally and physically intimate relationship at an early age can be overwhelming when it disintegrates.

Relationships include some level of dependency, and in adolescence girls sometimes transfer dependency from parents to a boyfriend. A boy may seem parental, protecting a girl, helping her make decisions, and nurturing her. A girl may not work to establish her independence and self-sufficiency and may instead rely on a boy to help her through the transition to adulthood, or do it for her, while she remains childlike. When the relationship collapses, she may feel that she cannot manage alone and may regress to a younger level.

Although parents may encourage a brokenhearted teenage girl to get back into the social swing, she may need to be withdrawn socially for a period to regain her balance. To lose a romance is also a social embarrassment, and she may need time to mend. If her depression and withdrawal are not resolved within a month, she will need outside help in the form of counseling to restructure her life.

Part of being a woman involves learning to be both vulnerable and self-sufficient, so that relating is possible but does not require complete dependence on others. It helps in these circumstances to consider a girl's relationship with people in general and how much self-reliance she maintains in friendships. To depend entirely on one person is risky, and it is more fruitful for her to think about an array of loving friends and how to stay connected to them. This may mean that at times she needs to make an effort to be with long-term friends, but this is part of a mature approach to self-care.

In any relationship love is reciprocal, and although it may be painful to consider whether a relationship was balanced, a broken heart, with all its obsessive soul-searching and morose thinking, presents an excellent opportunity to review one's behavior. It is worth exploring with a girl how she tried to sustain the relationship and whether both she and her boyfriend got what they needed. If she received more than she gave, she may routinely devalue her ability to give and reciprocate. If she gave more than she received, it may be difficult for her to see to her own needs and to realistically evaluate the capacity of others to be part of a relationship. Although it may be uncomfortable to consider these questions, there are learning opportunities in every situation, and this one presents its own.

The following will be helpful:

1. Respect a girl's feelings and do not try to soothe her by belittling or making light of her feelings. Instead, comfort her, empathize, and help her to find consolation in all the time-honored treatments for a broken heart: distraction, good friends, a change of scene, and time. This is a good time to identify with great works of art, music, and literature, for the loss of a loved one is a universal theme and a brokenhearted teenage girl has a unique opportunity to identify with the themes of great art.

2. Consider with her whether the relationship was a balanced one and assess what she gave and what she received.

3. As a girl begins to feel stronger, encourage her to be involved in many types of loving relationships, for example, playing with a lonesome child or visiting an elderly shut-in. Help her to see evidence of her own capacity to generate love and joy in others.

4. If there appears to be regression to a younger level, help a girl to gain a sense of her own power and self-reliance by supporting rather than directing her choices. Ask her what she needs, advise, make suggestions, but leave the decisions to her.

5. Tell her you love her and identify what you love and admire in her.

6. Help her to think about building and maintaining a network of social relationships that can sustain her and meet her needs, rather than finding a new romance.

HOMOSEXUALITY

It is difficult to ascertain how many teenage girls are lesbians, although it appears that it is a fairly small number. One survey indicates that about 1 percent of American females are lesbian.*

Some developmental theories see homosexual attachment as a normal part of the developmental sequence for a girl, so that as she turns away from parents at the end of childhood and looks for relationships in the outside world, her first love objects will be those most similar to her. Young girl friendships have a romantic quality about them, a deep and sensitive attachment in which two girls feel themselves more than sisters.

These friendships may also have a sexual side, and girls sometimes experiment with necking, petting, or genital contact in these early years. In a close friendship, this may take the form of "practicing" sexual maneuvers or sharing fantasies, and often girls will not interpret this as sexual activity, any more than they would see their handholding as sexual.

Best girlfriends may do everything together, sharing adventures and mischief, and they may be quite jealous of third parties who try to intervene. These tight friendships have an excessively emotional quality to them, so that girls respond at a fever pitch to problems and criticisms. They do serve the purpose of providing companionship and experience in relating as girls traverse the tricky divide from childhood to adolescence, and they represent the first powerful attachment outside the family circle.

At the end of this period, girls begin to develop "crushes" on unobtainable figures, including rock stars, teachers, and others who are not likely to respond to a girl's fantasies. This allows relating without risk, so that a girl can try on all of the feelings and perceptions of someone in love without having actually to respond to a real person and the complexities and demands of an ongoing relationship. After this period, girls are likely to experiment with relationships with boys, having honed their skills on girlfriends and fantasy figures.

Many girls will remain in the safe waters of homosexual relationships all their lives and find this a workable arrange-

---

*J.Gordon Muir, "Homosexuals and the 10% Fallacy," *Wall Street Journal*, March 31, 1993, A14.

ment for achieving life goals. Given the number of divorces and the turbulence of heterosexual relationships, it is not always convincing to argue that this is an ill-considered choice. It will be problematical where the accompanying characteristics of the earlier relationships, for example, supersensitivity and exclusiveness, are retained as well.

For a teenage girl who is gay, there is a strong sense of isolation from other teens and from family. A girl feels that no one can understand her and since she is involved in illicit activity as well, feelings of isolation are compounded by fears of rejection. There is a rewarding side to this, since at least a girl knows that she is *something* and does not suffer from the broad anonymity so characteristic of the teen years. There is as well a dramatic sense of being true to oneself, true to one's inner feelings, and it can feel courageous to stand alone and be what one knows is right for oneself. In short, a girl can be the heroine of her own drama.

Beyond this, there is a whole adult subculture made up of lesbian women who seem strong and purposeful and appear to be models worth emulating. They may act self-reliant and independent and may hold out an encouraging image for a girl trying to find her own strength. A girl's first crush may be on an older, much admired woman.

The realization that she is homosexual may be a revelation for a teenage girl, as she has a sudden, overwhelming insight about herself. But true self-knowledge usually comes gradually, in smaller pieces and with many errors, and it is wise to distrust flashes of insight that are all-encompassing. To be a lesbian is to take a stand, and it is comforting to a teenage girl to have a stand to take, knowing that somewhere there are others like her who will respect her. Identity, however, is built over many years, and even with regard to sexual preference, rarely is anyone consistently 100 percent anything. In any case, sexual preferences change over the decades of life, and for a young girl to assert her identity for all time has a distinctly adolescent ring to it.

Often homosexual girls come from families where parents are perceived as repressive, demanding, and stifling. To be homosexual puts a girl beyond their reach and allows her at last to be her own person, albeit alone. She can see herself as different without giving up deep dependency needs and able to establish personality boundaries and have them recognized. Straight parents usually feel alienated from a homosexual daughter because they cannot invoke their wisdom and control, and they certainly can't control her inner yearnings. (It would be an interesting experiment to observe the outcome if parents demanded that their daughters be homosexual; one wonders if there might be a "coming out" of heterosexuals.)

Becoming gay can serve to limit a girl's psychological risk, since other females are more familiar and less challenging than males, and a girl can become independent while not going too far from home. In the process, though, her parents react as though she has done something so unusual, so startling, and so exotic that it puts the family in shock. For her to decide to become a marine drill sergeant, although a much bolder and more radical departure from her youth, would not stir as much of a sensation.

In the popular culture, to be gay puts one in instant relationship with the homosexual community, and there is an assumption of understanding and trust between those of a minority sexual orientation. For a teenage girl, such immediate group acceptance saves the work of building and struggling, and she may feel as if she has found her long-lost family. The "them-against-us" siege mentality, often narcissistic but accurate, allows homosexual girls an instant common bond. In addition, there is a national counterculture with a number of organizations that work for a broad range of human rights, and a sense of the revolutionary, similar to that of the antiwar movement of the 1960s and 1970s. Perhaps the most exciting part for homosexual girls is that the gay rights political movement has at its core a belief in sexual freedom and expression, a heady concept for adolescents.

The following will be helpful:

1. For homosexual or heterosexual girls, sexual activity is unwise, and there is nothing that makes it more compelling or necessary if a girl is gay. A gay teen girl is entitled to her feelings and these must be respected, but her behavior is a different matter. Although the risk of pregnancy is not an issue, the risk of sexually transmitted disease for a sexually active teenager of any preference is high and must be taken seriously. To be gay does not entitle one to sex before one can handle the responsi-

bilities, nor does it cause a greater sexual arousal. For teenage girls of any persuasion, there is no safe sex.

2. As with other issues with a teenage girl, feelings must be accepted and behavior guided. To become gay does not confer instant wisdom, maturity, or access to adult prerogatives. A girl may feel strongly attracted to another girl, but this does not entitle her to disregard her schoolwork, good manners, or community service to spend her time in romantic pursuits.

3. A gay teenager needs help in feeling that she is acceptable as is and that she is distinctly different from her parents. Help her to explore *all* the unique aspects of her personality, since sexual orientation is a relatively minor part of a human being. In particular, help her to form her dreams for the future and to discover how she will use her values and her talents.

4. In any group whose primary interest is sex, a young girl is open to exploitation by those who are older and stronger. Guide a girl to evaluate her vulnerabilities realistically and plan her social relationships with her own interests in mind.

5. Help a girl to develop the concept of a flexible identity in all things, so as to understand that the ways that we see ourselves at fifteen are different at twenty-five and at thirty-five. No matter how dearly we may hold some premises, life and experience change us and broaden us.

6. Keep in mind that love is always a blessing. We must help our children to be loving people and let them love who they will.

SEXUAL RELATIONSHIPS

The teen years are a time for experimenting and exploring sensual and relational capacities. The popular culture promotes teenage sexual experimentation as well, the assumption being that it enhances sexual adjustment, although there is no evidence to support this assumption.

Adults generally consider teenage sex from the viewpoint of middle-age sexual experience, although the two have little in common. Teen girls are far less comfortable in sexual relationships than adults, and although they may have sexual intercourse, they are usually embarrassed to discuss sexual activities or feelings with a boyfriend.

Most teenagers believe that they should have sex when they feel ready for it, although other important undertakings, such as driving, are structured with adult guidance. Rarely do teenage girls develop the wisdom to decide when sexual activity is in their best interest. Unfortunately, many teens discover that they're not ready to have sex after they've had it.

Most teens also believe that as long as they take precautions, using a condom or birth control pills, and act courteously to their partners, they have had sex properly. It may feel like a rite of passage one must experience to bring one up to par with other kids. It is difficult for teen girls to understand why this sort of sexual relationship is disturbing and unfulfilling.

There is little honest talk in the media about sexuality and teenage girls, and societal beliefs in this area obscure a number of basic facts:

1. A teenage girl is not harmed or unduly frustrated if she cannot have sexual relations. Nowhere is it demonstrated that this interferes with her long-term sexual or psychological adjustment. Nor does it block her ability to attend to important concerns such as studies, friends, or self-care. Harsh, repressive criticism of sexual feelings and wishes harm a female adolescent and may interfere with normal sexual development, but gentle, loving guidance helps a girl to make life-enhancing choices about sexual activity.

2. Teenage girls less often seek out sexual relations with boys and are far more likely to respond instead to a boy's overtures out of curiosity, a wish to sustain a relationship, or a wish to be considered adult.

3. Teenage girls who look physically mature are distinctly different from adult women in their bodily needs. In girls, there is still a strong need for privacy and security in physical dealings with others.

How do sexual relationships develop among teenage boys and girls? Most typically from a long-term romance that has taken on the quality of a marriage for the pair. Increasing comfort with each other and growing intimacy lead to physical contact that is exploratory in nature and later develops into a pattern of sexual intimacy. Sometimes sexual experiences happen for teenage girls in less secure settings. A girl may meet a boy at a party or while drinking at someone's house and begin to experiment.

The following will be helpful with a girl who is having a sexual relationship:

1. Explore with her *why* she is involved in the risky behavior of teen sexual relations. Try to get a sense of what motivates her to put so much of her life at risk and what it is that she gains. Since the failure rate of condoms and birth control pills is high and no contraception is foolproof against pregnancy or sexually transmitted disease, explore with her the perceived advantage of a sexual relationship.

2. Consider the broad fabric of her life and what it offers her in the way of opportunities and possibilities. Does she have directions to go, interests to explore, or is the course of her life uninspiring? Are there many challenges that call her, many interesting activities, or is sex her only adventure?

3. Look at her own view of herself and her future. Does she see herself as strong and powerful on her own behalf? Does she have dreams and objectives that she yearns to pursue? Or does she see herself as passive, hoping that something good will come along?

4. Explore with a teenage girl her lover's view of her and why he would put her at risk. How does he show his caring? What do they share besides bodily pleasures? How does the relationship sustain itself?

5. Just as her choice of the most expensive college in the country has serious implications for her parents, her risky sexual behavior entails considerable cost (pregnancy, rearing a child, or having an abortion). Explore with her how these needs would be met if she were surprised with a pregnancy or disease.

Competence

FAILING GRADES

Difficulties with academics usually begin or become more serious at about seventh or eighth grade and rarely improve after that without parental involvement. Often when academic problems develop in middle school, parents hope that there is some temporary problem that will disappear with time or that it is the transition to middle school or junior high school that is at fault and will pass. But this is generally not the case. Unless failing grades are due to an unusual situation in which a girl has a unique problem with one class, the failures are apt to include all or most courses because she has a generic rather than a specific problem.

With the transition from elementary school to middle school, everything changes in a girl's life, and her surroundings become far less supportive and less structured. In the elementary school classroom, she was very familiar to the teacher and well settled in a peer group that remained the same throughout the day.

But in middle school, there is a series of teachers and a changing peer group. Other youngsters may come from many different neighborhoods, and they represent more of a variety of family values and cultures. The same changes will occur again in high school, and these are turbulent experiences for adolescent girls. If the changes are compounded by residential changes, so that a girl changes school districts and neighborhoods, there are likely to be serious problems if a girl's academic skills were limited to begin with.

The secondary school curriculum presents a level of intellectual challenge different from the elementary grades. The material is more complex and extensive, and the standards are much tighter. When teachers teach, their focus is more often on the material than on the youngsters, and they are required to complete an established syllabus. A high school physics teacher expects students to adjust to his or her material, rather than adjusting the material to the students.

This can seem like abandonment to a teenage girl who has grown used to caring teachers helping her in earlier years. Secondary school teachers seem more detached, more academic, and less personal than elementary teachers.

What are the options for a girl who has failed courses and cannot proceed through the regular sequence of high school? Usually courses must be repeated, and if there are enough of them, an entire grade may have to be repeated. This is socially traumatic for a girl and should be avoided at all costs, but sometimes there is no alternative. Summer school can be a choice, but for most courses that have complex content, this does not insure adequate learning to pass in future grades.

Tutoring can be useful if there is still time left to correct the situation, but there must be someone to supervise her work on a daily basis. This serves as a training period to help her develop the organizational and study skills that are necessary in secondary school. Tutoring may be helpful to clear up fine points of course content, for example, how to balance equations or conjugate German verbs, but it will not implant the internal structure necessary for taking responsibility for achievement.

When a girl is failing courses in school, she is usually turned off by the whole concept of learning, and it is worth exploring this with her. Across the situations in her day, how many inspire her to think, analyze, ponder, or speculate? How often does she examine ideas and generate her own outside the academic sphere? Does she know why some girls are more popular than others? Why boys get embarrassed? Helping her to use her mind to unravel interesting mysteries is necessary to become a good learner.

Failing grades create a sense of urgency and emergency; there is a high level of tension and a looking to the next event to spell either disaster or salvation. There are notices home, dire warnings from teachers, serious parent faces, tears, talks around the table, and so forth. Sometimes in this atmosphere a girl is inclined to take precipitous action to relieve the tension.

It is wise to consider the task of passing courses as a long-term issue, much like growing to one's full height, and one that is best accomplished by good daily habits that eventually bear fruit. Long-term goals require bits of work each day and patience to endure the present while working toward a better future. In the meantime, one must live with anxiety and frustration. Don't demand an immediate solution because of your own frustration; instead, teach a teen daughter to work and wait.

She will need to learn to set goals and plan how to reach them. She will have to learn to anticipate problems and develop many ways to solve them, for example, by keeping a dictionary and an encyclopedia handy. She will need to abandon the idea that she cannot do her work without support from others, so that she comes to see that she can achieve even if others are not very cooperative and that she is stronger than she believes.

It is wise for a parent to pay attention to the development of these patterns rather than to the achievement of high grades. Grades will come if the habits are right, but without the habits there can be no real learning.

The following will be helpful:

1. Begin by scheduling a conference with all of her teachers. Ask for a review of her achievement and work habits in each class. Tape record the session or take notes. *Listen carefully and believe what is said.* Although a girl may have a different perception, she is failing to achieve according to the school's evaluation, and that is the only evaluation that counts. If there is disagreement or confusion about her difficulties, request in writing a psychoeducational evaluation from the school or have one done privately. In particular, ask for an evaluation of the school program and its appropriateness for her competencies.

2. Teach her the skills required for doing secondary school work:

- listening in class;

- writing assignments down and bringing books home; planning ahead for long-term assignments;

- estimating the time required to study for tests; drilling, memorizing whatever is necessary;

- asking for special help when there is confusion;

- reading more than is required for the course;

- using tests to correct deficiencies in one's knowledge.

3. Sit with her each evening during a two-hour homework session. Bring a plate of cookies and the newspaper and keep her company. Go over the organization of her evening to help her apportion her time properly, and be positive and encouraging. Point out to her that good grades come from a whole series of such evenings, not from one, and that you have faith in her.

4. Teach her how to memorize and drill so that she can mentally file important information, like math equations. Point out to her that school courses depend more on rote learning as they get more complex, that this is quite difficult and boring, but that it gets easier the more you do it. Also reassure her that no matter how bright a student is, there is no learning

without memorization and photographic memories are a myth. Students may claim that they don't study at all, but this is generally student machismo. Students who do well memorize a great deal.

5. Set a telephone and television time so that she has a clear work period. If there is a television in her room, retire it until the summertime.

6. Stay in contact with the school and monitor her work and her progress. Talk to her about what you hear about her from teachers, and ask for her opinions.

SCHOOL PHOBIA, WITHDRAWAL, ABSENTEEISM

A school phobia usually starts with an illness that doesn't clear up quickly or some other reason to be out of school. A girl returns to school, is there for a few days, and then is out again. After awhile, the problem becomes serious, and she has missed so much that she cannot be said to have completed coursework. Then the choice is more difficult, for it seems as though a girl is in fact withdrawing from school. It is not a deliberate decision and instead has the appearance of a matter of circumstance.

When this is discussed with an adolescent, she may show interest, but little real concern, and no decision to take action, so it may be a parent who carries most of the anxiety in the situation. Parents sometimes become very angry at what they perceive as laziness, and conflicts may develop as a result.

School avoidance usually stems from two difficulties that a girl may experience. The first is seen in a girl who gets poor grades, has little interest in coursework, and has poor learning habits. She has little connection to the school and is not involved in any extracurricular activities. She has no relationships or perhaps only poor ones with teachers. She is very much peripheral to the school, and feels no strong loyalty or kinship. Her friends may come from other schools or may be dropouts, but there is little reason for her to be connected to her school. And her school record demonstrates little connection; she may have a problem with truancy.

A second type of difficulty is seen in a girl who is a strong student, even a top student, and seems to be well organized and effective. When her absenteeism begins, parents are usually confident that she can easily make up her work. But as time passes, it becomes clear that long-term absence is likely to affect her progress through the school curriculum. Teachers send work home, which she does, but she remains out of school.

The cause for her absence is likely to be a legitimate illness, mononucleosis or asthma, for example, which is treated medically, but persists. There is good cause to interpret the reason for her absence as illness. There may be other problems as well: weakness, fatigue, headaches, stomachaches, and sometimes a fever or rash. It is difficult to make a compelling argument for sending a girl back to school in this condition. Friends may stop by or call, and she seems happy to hear from them, but *she is not in school*.

This is a more typical case of school phobia, which is a misleading term for what is more properly called school aversion. School phobia suggests that a girl runs screaming at the sight of a school, while in fact the opposite is true. A school phobic girl may like school, miss it when she's not there, and yearn to go back, but *she is usually not in school*. Although there may be real reasons for her absences, there is also no great striving to get back, and she seems remarkably placid about the enormous loss in her life.

Underneath the calm acceptance of the loss of school and school life, a girl with school phobia generally feels overwhelming social anxiety and conflicts that become far worse the longer she is away from school. After a time, it becomes impossible for her to summon the drive necessary to take herself back to school. The anxiety she feels may not stem from any apparent problem or incident. It is, instead, the reflection of a tight, anxious personality, highly dependent, passive, and eager to please.

In both of these situations, girls cannot deal with their withdrawal alone, and they need adult help to get them back on a fruitful course. The loss to a girl of an education and of peer contact is enormous, and regardless of the current relief that it provides her, she needs guidance and structure to help her get back.

The following will be helpful:

1. Confront a girl directly with the fact of missed school, and point out that whether she intends it or not, she is withdrawing

from school. Discuss with her the motivation that allows this to occur, and frame it as a choice she is making, not a condition she is enduring.

2. Plan a path of reentry into school, beginning with her returning to school immediately, that is, today or tomorrow morning. School anxieties and problems do not clear up with time, and confronting them serves to diminish them. Do not allow time to lapse before returning her to school, since this will only increase her tension.

3. In discussing the problem, avoid anger and frustration. Patience, along with firmness, is the best way to begin a course of action. To insist that she take action immediately and to accompany her in doing so, i.e., to go with her to school the next day and present excuses at the office, will give far more satisfaction than empty railing against her.

4. For a girl who withdraws from school because she is a fringe member of the high school community and has difficulty with academic work, it is worth considering a full psychoeducational workup, with the possibility of transfer to an alternative educational program. Since her connection to the present school is minimal and consists primarily of failure, it is worth finding settings where she can experience success and a sense of belonging.

CHEATING

There is something outrageous and adorable about a little Shirley Temple cheating at a game with us and winning. For a woman-sized girl, cheating is no longer cute. Girls at about age seven cheat or consider cheating at games with others, because they feel entitled to win and have little respect for rules and fair play. But this changes as a girl matures, and her view of cheating changes too. But some girls change more slowly than others.

A fair proportion of teenage girls, perhaps as many as a third, cheat as older adolescents, and many try it at one time or another. Young occasional cheaters are not a reason for concern, but a girl who sees getting through exams as a test of cunning is missing the opportunity for learning that education offers.

Cheating is embarrassing to kids who do not cheat, for they

are faced with the choice of being righteous or being a good friend. Although teenagers accept cheating, it does little to enhance a youngster's standing with other kids

Girls cheat for many reasons. They may find it difficult to accept failure because of pride or a sense of entitlement, particularly if they have been told how bright they are. They may feel that other youngsters have an unfair advantage, or they may have a need to be the highest achiever, generally because parents expect it and may have grown used to it. Underneath a girl may feel insecure and uncertain of her competencies and cheat to check her work.

Sometimes cheating is a good girl's way to rebel and outsmart those on whom she depends for approval. There is boldness in the act, and if she can get away with it, it may draw some admiration, although this is usually reserved for male cheaters. Most often, cheating is simply a practical solution to the problem of how to pass a test for a girl who did not plan better.

Once cheating begins, particularly if there are no consequences, it becomes easier to stifle the conscience and to rationalize behavior. A girl tells herself that "everybody does it," and that the key is to win, to get into college, and it doesn't matter how. She may make jokes about cheating and anxiously mention it to friends with some degree of self-ridicule. But teenagers are all sinners together, and her friends' reaction will be forgiving. The desensitizing process works quickly, and after a period her study habits will be structured around her expectation of cheating. Eventually her plans will go awry and, perhaps after a string of successes, present her with a serious test failure or, worse, she might be publicly accused of cheating.

The major concern with cheating comes from the fear that a girl who cheats is lacking in integrity and trustworthiness. It seems as though this violation of school rules affects everyone because the students who studied hard are deprived of high grades through fraudulent means. A girl who can cheat and pretend to work that is not her own is difficult to trust.

Self-esteem suffers serious damage from cheating, because with each episode and the fear of apprehension that goes with it, a girl develops a view of herself that is progressively more seedy, and therein lies the real damage from cheating.

1. The most powerful way to control cheating is to closely monitor test taking, with an awareness of a girl's tendency to cheat. It is wise to tell a girl of the need for supervision and to make it impossible to cheat. Interestingly, when a girl is watched closely and fails for lack of preparation, cheating loses some of its appeal, because if it cannot be employed, a girl has jumped without a net if she did not prepare adequately for a test.

2. It helps a girl to plan how to prepare for and take tests so that cheating is not useful. Her cheating is based on the assumption that whoever she cheats from knows more than she does. If she is confident in her knowledge, then she risks giving poorer answers if she cheats from others.

3. If she is not sure of her knowledge because she did not prepare adequately, then a grade gotten from cheating is a hollow achievement, and one that means nothing about one's real skill. It is herself that she is cheating, because she did not give herself a chance to master something and show what she could really do. Continually remind her that learning involves effort and risk-taking and that it is well worth the trouble.

4. It helps to talk with her about moral integrity and the sense we have of ourselves as good and decent people. Describe to her how a treasured view of oneself can help her to be strong and self-reliant, can comfort her when friends desert her, can give her faith in her own judgments, can insulate her from others' criticism, and can make her happy in solitude. Ask her if there is any gain for which it is worth risking the precious commodity of self-respect.

5. Encourage her to consider how her peers see her and if cheating raises her friends' opinion of her. Ask her to describe what makes a teenage girl attractive to other teenagers and whether cheating adds to her appeal.

6. Tell her what you value in her and what you find personally appealing. Be imaginative and search your memory, but don't invent things. If you like her boldness or her casual approach to things, say so. Make it clear that you will always care for the person that she is, but that you have a higher opinion of her than she has of herself. Let her know that in time she will come to see the truth of your view of her.

7. Let her know that you will stop her cheating, in cooperation with her teachers, because she is far too important to

disregard. Make contact with her teachers to alert them to the problem and ask that they supervise her test-taking carefully if she cannot prevent her own cheating.

FIRED FROM A JOB

There is a relationship in adolescence between employment and identity, and the problem with losing a job is that it may strike at a girl's sense of who she is. It may be that a job is the first occasion for a girl to be treated like an adult. It is a heady experience, after so much yearning, to be treated like a full-fledged grown-up, although it has its price.

Girls usually take part-time jobs to afford all of the things that are considered luxuries by adults and necessities by teens: makeup, clothes, snacks, etc. When a girl loses her job, she also loses all of these things that she provides for herself. If her job has been important to her, she may very well have been less involved in school, taking easier courses, and skipping extracurricular activities to have time to work.

Working also takes a girl out of the family and makes her less reliant on her family for transportation and money. She may form relationships with older teens who work at her place of employment and offer her advice and help, making her more dependent on them than on herself. But in general girls become less reliant on their families through working.

So losing a job is more complex than it might seem because it involves a regression to previous and quite different circumstances in which a girl has little money, more free time, and much more contact with her family.

There are many circumstances that can lead to being fired from a job:

She does not do the job well. For a girl who is immature, it may be too difficult to understand the attitudes and habits required to be a good worker. She must be able to put aside her own needs and preferences and try to please a boss, who may not be fair or skilled. She must also put aside her own judgment about how to do the job and do it the way someone else thinks is the right way. For a girl just discovering her own style, this can be especially trying.

She doesn't learn quickly or she is oppositional. A resistant teenage girl will oppose attempts to change her way of doing things, preferring to argue or debate rather than to do as she is told to do. She may have trouble understanding how to do a task, but not take the initiative in ascertaining what is required.

Her personal presentation is wrong. If she appears at work looking weird, sexy, or disheveled, she is appropriately dressed for a teenager, but she is not prepared to work for an employer. Employers want teenage employees to look more like adults than teenagers. She needs to have neatly combed and styled hair and to avoid habits like gum chewing, belching, and doing one's nails at work.

The business isn't doing well. Part of the reality of being in the labor market is that workers are subject to changes in the economy. If the business where she works is not prospering, then there will be a cutback in jobs, usually beginning with the least skilled.

The following will be helpful:

1. Consider a girl's behavior at home and evaluate whether you would hire her as a worker if she were a stranger to you. If you notice that she does the bare minimum, complains a good deal, and watches the clock, ask if those are her practices at work. Ask her to think about how she would see them if she were the boss.

2. Suggest that she ask for a job evaluation from her work supervisor and, if possible, get it in writing. This will give her a chance to examine her work coolly and to consider making improvements where they seem to be needed.

3. Talk with her about finding another job and whether she thinks this is wise for her. Encourage her to create her own jobs by baby-sitting, starting a small business, or being a maid at neighborhood parties. Consider especially whether another job will cut into her school work. Suggest that she arrange some job interviews to keep her skills in shape.

4. Teach her the relationship between job skills and wages. Help her to understand why a receptionist makes $15,000 a year, while a high school teacher makes twice as much, and an attorney makes four times as much. Ask her to project how she would fare in any of these careers.

5. When a girl loses a job, support her self-esteem and support her growth as she goes through this difficult experience.

Five

EMERGENCIES

A LTHOUGH ALL TEENAGE GIRLS experience problems and difficulties in the decade of adolescence, most of these will resolve themselves without adult intervention. But sometimes the problems are truly disasters and a girl cannot extricate herself. The major concern, as with all adolescent difficulties, is the long-term effect on a girl's growth and development. Emergencies have the capacity to alter permanently the course of a youngster's life, and so adult help becomes critical.

What can adults do to help in an emergency? In general, they can support a girl's developing competence, even when it appears that she has little of it. When she has been a victim, the need is to help her regain her balance and her strength. When a problem becomes an emergency, adult judgment is needed, which may mean overriding a girl's decisions, even while teaching her about decision-making and problem-solving.

Sometimes the youthful perspective of a teenage girl makes her oblivious to the seriousness of her predicament. To reassure herself, a girl may minimize the impact of an event and make light of it, an exercise in bluster and bravado more than an indication of irresponsibility. In these circumstances, it helps to give a girl tasks to do as part of reaching a resolution so that she can feel some sense of mastery over events.

As the emergency is met, there must be calm discussion of choices, with an eye to the future and some optimism that there will be better days ahead. The first goal in an emergency is always to protect a girl from further damage and to limit the impact of catastrophic events. Her life goes on, and there are still many competencies that she must develop in the teen years.

There is more drama in a young woman's life even without emergencies, as a result of the new experiences and challenges of her age. A teenage girl has many simple and complex skills to learn, and adults sometimes believe that girls should have all this under control and behave like adults. Adults, however, also get into serious difficulties, but because they are older, they are rarely chastised or shamed. Girls must feel their way and make many mistakes in the process.

Girls who take high risks are sometimes adventurous and daring, and hence more likely to get into trouble. Their experiments become problems when decisions have grave or irreversible consequences. Ours is a society that takes a dim view of risk-taking and treasures protection in general. Seat belts, bike helmets, product safety, and smoking bans are all meant to protect people from themselves. For a teenage girl, there are few opportunities for courage and daring.

A young female with a bold and adventurous spirit will find ways to test her mettle. Far better she take risks to develop her character and talents that can offer the promise of increased strength and self-confidence. For without many challenges, a teenage girl can become passive and vulnerable, or she may take risks that are self-destructive.

Encouraging risk-taking to avoid adolescent emergencies may seem paradoxical, but trying to keep a girl safe rarely makes her strong. Far better to encourage the development of values and judgment by helping her to develop courage.

An emergency sometimes represents a spirit straining to move. When Mary Victor Bruce was arrested in New York City for testing her newly acquired pilot's license by flying around the Empire State Building, it was said that she flew such tight circles around the structure that the typists inside could see the color of her eyes. "Going slow," said Mary, "always makes me tired." Later she would break the world record for the longest solo flight and create an air ferry service across the English Channel. She never wore overalls or slacks, preferring a blouse and skirt and pearls, and she refused to be called a "women's libber." At eighty-one she made a spectacular comeback as a pilot, flying a loop-the-loop in a two-seater plane. "What a lark," she said leaving the field. She lived to be ninety-four. Without appropriate outlets, what happens to an adventurous spirit?

How can a girl's bold and decisive action be kept within

fruitful bounds? Sometimes it can't, but it helps to anticipate problems that will develop. How can we help her to be strong and courageous after a tragedy like rape or school failure? By continuing to build, slowly and bit by bit, an image of herself as competent, resourceful, and brave.

The emphasis in American media on short, intensely stimulating news stories has led to sensationalistic portrayals of many teen issues as emergencies, so that it appears that teenage girls confront dramatic, life-threatening dilemmas at each moment. In fact, most teenage girls pass through adolescence without profound problems and without any real challenges that help them grow and mature. Headlines may lead us to believe that teenage girls are fragile and vulnerable to a succession of disasters, when in fact they are resourceful and durable, but usually untested.

Sometimes a girl is suddenly challenged by events or conditions that test the limits of her endurance and creativity. The effect of any individual event varies according to a girl's life circumstances, but some events, particularly assault or rape, will always be catastrophic.

Psychological treatment will usually be necessary when events have reached the level of an emergency. Counseling and related psychological help need to help her resolve the difficulties and resume her developmental course. When the emergency is over, it is important to survey a girl's life and to evaluate the course of her development. There are many forms of psychological treatment that a trained professional has at his or her disposal to help a girl. They will not be reviewed here, for they must be planned individually with a therapist to be appropriate for a particular situation. Do all emergencies require psychological intervention? Probably, for whether problems are the result of her choices or circumstances, she will need help to get back on track.

This manual is not intended as a substitute for professional help. Neither is it intended to show a parent how to offer psychological intervention. Rather, it offers parents ways to help a girl in an emergency and to act effectively as parents in helping her.

Antisocial behavior

STEALING

Stealing first occurs in girls at age six or seven when they are learning to distinguish what is theirs from what belongs to others. ("It was yours," one seven-year-old said, "before it turned into mine.") At this age, conscience is developing, and stealing diminishes as girls begin to construct a differentiated view of themselves.

When stealing continues into adolescence or emerges anew, it often represents a problem in defining personal boundaries. To a small child, everything is one mass, and when a girl takes money from her father's dresser, she will say quite innocently that she found it. But the shaping of personality proceeds with the years, and as a girl takes form, a form that includes possessions, she becomes aware that others are separate from her and so are their possessions. When teen girls tape signs on walls and doors, defining their space and themselves, they are supporting an emerging sense of self.

In these years a girl also develops a clear view of her own behavior and the moral structure to evaluate it. She knows when she is bad and good. If self-restraint does not develop as part of this structure, she may instead use denial to avoid seeing her own behavior clearly, and will interpret her stealing as borrowing.

In childhood, girls are entitled to care and nurturing, so that adults give a child what she needs, sometimes depriving themselves. When a teenage girl takes her mother's best clothes without asking, she is reflecting the same relationship as she had when she was small and the same belief that she must be provided for and is not expected to do for herself.

Sometimes a girl steals as part of a compulsive habit. She is likely to steal the same things each time, and to have little use for the item, which may have some childish appeal. Encountering the item provokes the stealing; a girl may feel powerless to resist the urge, and ashamed of her behavior. Called kleptomania in earlier times, the compulsion to steal seems to be a manifestation of a rigid personality, incessant guilt, low self-esteem, and impulsive behavior.

Shoplifting is a crime more common in females than males and may involve several girls stealing together. It is a disorder of impulse control, with the primary targets items like makeup, underwear, and bathing suits, which are expensive and easily concealed. Shoplifting provides a girl a sense of excitement, courage, and accomplishment. Underlying the impulsive behavior are often feelings of loss and yearning, along with a demand for nurturing. The sense of personal power that comes from stealing is a strong antidote for these helpless feelings.

Parents have their own view of antisocial behavior, and many parents have grown up in an age where defiance of the law in areas like the draft or civil rights represented a higher moral good. For girls growing up decades later, the philosophy may be interpreted to mean that anything that "beats the system" is admirable. The antisocial behavior may also connect a girl with others who also steal, for example, friends or an older sibling, and may help her feel that she belongs or has gained the others' admiration.

The secret aspect of a girl's stealing suggests an alienation from parents, because the secret is too terrible to confess or because there is some subtle gratification in violating a parent's trust. Sometimes when a girl steals, there is found to be little or no communication with parents. If a girl steals from parents, it may be a way of symbolically taking for herself what is not available emotionally. Parents who are cold and critical and offer little real help with self-control, may be the objects of a girl's thievery.

The following will be helpful:

1. Immediately respond to the stealing by confronting it. Require that the girl make recompense and take her to the store to do so if the stealing has occurred there. Require that she assume responsibility for correcting the deed and insure that this occurs quickly.

2. Have a brief but direct discussion about stealing. Point out that stealing is morally wrong; it is illegal; it destroys relationships, trust, and self-respect; it is unfair to others; and it will make her unpopular.

3. Examine your own feelings about the behavior and consider whether in the past you have ignored similar behavior out of embarrassment or inadequacy. Examine angry feelings and

consider whether they have made you overlook a girl's deeper needs. Explore whether you offer a girl warmth and kindness along with clear moral guidance that make her feel wanted and valued.

4. Structure situations so that a girl is likely to be caught stealing. If you work during the day and she is alone, find someone to supervise her behavior. Periodically inspect her things for new acquisitions so that you can establish that she is not stealing. If stealing has involved others, for example, at school, speak with school personnel about monitoring her behavior.

5. Try to determine through conversation or counseling the motivation for the stealing, and whether it constitutes compulsive behavior. Look at other behavior to ascertain whether there are cleaning rituals, difficulty in departures, and generalized anxiety. Obsessive-compulsive disorder is a disorder that includes persistent, intrusive, and irrelevant thoughts along with repetitive and useless acts, and can manifest itself in stealing useless items.

6. Evaluate a girl's overall self-control to determine if there are other areas where she has trouble regulating herself, for example, in weight control, study habits, or spending. Does she have difficulty with planning adequately for her own needs and structuring her surroundings appropriately? Is there enough supervision and guidance in her life to help her gain success in what she wants?

7. Consider what a girl needs and how she is to finance it. Arrange an allowance or job to generate enough income to help her. Consider her expenditures, with an awareness that high expenses often indicate drug dependency and may be a motivation for stealing.

DELINQUENCY

Antisocial acts that cross the boundary into illegal acts make a girl a juvenile delinquent and involve her with the law. Sometimes delinquent behavior is spontaneous and prankish, occurring in the context of a generally successful teen life. More ominously, illegal behavior is internally driven in a girl who has trouble with school, family, and peers.

Delinquent behavior is *criminal* behavior, and at some point is bound to involve confrontation with the law. The most common crimes for female juvenile offenders are running away, substance abuse or dealing, vandalism, and disorderly conduct. Among the more serious criminal offenses, stealing and assault are most common for girls.

Families of delinquent girls are usually characterized by weakened parental authority, sometimes because parents offer much criticism but little effective help with self-control, or because parental control is too harsh and overloads a girl with anger and turmoil. When parents expect adult judgment and control from a girl who is struggling to control her life and self, she usually fails. A family that is generally adequate may break down under external stresses such as unemployment, illness, or marital discord, for these drain adult energies and creativity and limit help to daughters.

All girls need teaching in the early years to learn self-control. Learning to fly a plane, a task almost as dangerous as learning to be a woman, a student is given increasing latitude as she develops skill, and while the instructor prevents her from making serious mistakes. To hope that a girl will "learn from experience" or "learn for herself" as a pilot or a woman puts her in a deadly situation. A family that is generally adequate may break down under external stresses such as unemployment or marital discord or illness, for these drain adult energies and creativity.

The pattern of hard-core delinquency is generally highly predictable and begins early in a girl's life. A small child's behavior, naturally obnoxious and antisocial, is met with excessive or unpredictable parental responses, and since a parent in these circumstances has limited emotional connection to a girl, he or she offers no practical guidance for her activities, instead making increasingly forceful attempts to control behavior, with little success.

In school, the immaturity and disruptiveness of an untamed girl meet with teacher disapproval and scorn from other children, with poor learning skills the result. A girl has trouble staying in her seat, doing her work, and listening. In fact, through childhood she may remain at a toddler level in competency. When other kids are unfriendly, she acts out more and comes to be seen as peripheral or bad. In fact, bad girls are often childish girls whose social skills are retarded and who meet constant rejection from other kids.

Given her loneliness and isolation, a girl becomes vulnerable to any overtures, even those from older boys or from exploitative adults. Other kids who get in trouble or don't fit in are a better alternative than no friends and so she is further affected by friends who behave poorly. Through all of this, parents offer little real help and do not recognize the child's growing ostracism.

As a girl enters adolescence, already on the fringe of social groupings, hopelessness is a constant companion and receptivity to deviant standards is immediate. A delinquent peer group will offer the training in social skills that has been lacking, as well as a strong sense of belonging and personal achievement. Being good, getting good grades, getting along with parents, and dressing acceptably will now offer her little, and she may get disapproval from friends if she is to behave well. The circle is now complete: *At last she has a family and the help she needs to feel like a person.*

If a girl gets involved in illegal behavior that tarnishes her future and provokes legal action, the effects will pursue her throughout her life. If she manages to avoid permanent damage, then delinquency can provide a temporary vehicle for personality integration and the development of a sense of personal power that if taken in healthier directions, can become the basis of a powerful adulthood. When a girl grows up in a dysfunctional family, adapting, accommodating, and coping well can prevent her from developing the self-reliance or the energy to create a new life and may keep her mired in the conflicts of the original family.

By the time a girl has reached the status of a juvenile offender she needs help from beyond the family. The current philosophy of juvenile justice systems is diversion and decarceration, i.e., to remove kids from the justice system, particularly the prison system, and to offer a nonpunitive treatment approach. These approaches are most often used where there are minor noncriminal, or first-time offenses, which are distinctly different from adult crimes. When a girl commits repeated offenses her violations are felonies, and incarceration in secure juvenile facilities is more likely. Increasingly, in response to public pressure, teenage girls are denied juvenile offender status where serious crimes are involved.

State laws on juvenile status vary and may offer this designation at sixteen, seventeen, or eighteen. Status offenses are violations that would not be crimes for adults, for example, curfew violations, but that are seen as such because of a girl's age. These are problematical and highly subjective evaluations, for what is "running away" or "unmanageable behavior" depends on the eye of the beholder. In most states, status offenders are separated from criminal offenders and delinquents.

Much of the justice system's involvement with juveniles reflects discretionary justice, an area between morals and law where the judgment of the relevant authorities operates more freely than in adult courts. Discretion replaces statute, with the result that similar cases may be treated quite differently. About 50 percent of youthful offenders are involved only with this level of the justice system and have no contact with higher levels. The critical factor here is the seriousness of a girl's crime, her prior record, her behavior, the type of community, police department policies, the availability of alternatives to court action, and the willingness of parents to cooperate in a fruitful solution.

The following will be helpful:

1. If you first are alerted to a daughter's delinquent acts by a call from the police, do the following:

- Get as much information as you can and draw no conclusions. Keep your head and avoid excessive emotional reactions.

- Hire an attorney to represent your daughter and protect her rights. According to the Miranda decision, juveniles have the right to remain silent and the right to counsel but any statements they make may be used against them.

- Arrange bail and have her released as soon as possible. Be concerned about the danger of suicide, rape, or physical attack for a girl in jail. Be aware that if a judge finds her to be dangerous to herself or others, she can be detained before trial with no bail. Assume that if an offense is serious, involving crime against person or property, she will be referred to court. If the infraction involves fights between teens, complaints of a nonserious nature, shoplifting, or running away, court action is less likely and the contact will be with a juvenile police officer or probation officer.

• Get professional help for a girl to deal with her experience and to plan productively for her future.

2. Use family counseling to explore the nature of the family and how it can support a girl's development. Pay particular attention to the teaching techniques used to help her learn what she needs to know. Consider the level of valuing and warmth in the family and how conflicts are settled.

3. Examine how a girl makes herself feel powerful, important, and valuable in her life. Identify how she perceives sources of achievement and accomplishment.

4. Do everything possible to cooperate with police in getting a girl back on track, but acknowledge to yourself that you don't have either complete control or complete responsibility for a girl's behavior.

5. If a girl is institutionalized, develop the skills of an advocate to provide educational and vocational training for her. Keep in mind that institutions often promote a highly traditional view of acceptable female behavior and rarely give much reinforcement for achievement-oriented behavior, for example, boldness, ambition, or creativity.

RUNNING AWAY

There are runaways, throwaways, and system kids, the last being older teens who have been in a variety of social service placements and are too difficult for an overburdened social services system to track. It is estimated that there are 1.5 million runaway youths each year in the United States, with 21 percent not allowed to return by their parents. Among twelve- to seventeen-year-old girls, 8.7 percent run away from home and plan to stay away.* In the 1960s and 1970s, the same group would have been seen as hippies or cultural dropouts. Often teens who run away live a nomadic existence, staying at friends'

---

*M. J. Rotheram-Borus, C. Koopman, and A. Ehrhardt, "Homeless Youths and HIV Infection," *American Psychologist*, November 1991, 1188–97.

homes or sleeping in cars, stealing what they need, and getting food through deception.

When a youngster runs away, the assumption is that her home life was intolerable, forcing flight as an act of self-preservation. While this is sometimes true, when a girl becomes a runaway, she radically alters control within the family. The power balance at home previously favored parents, who provide all of a youngster's support and necessities. Running away forces parents to recognize a girl's ability to act autonomously. If parents feel angry, guilty, or frightened for a girl's sake, they may become helpless and subservient to her.

Running away may be a girl's solution to escaping abuse, an unloving family, or problems that she has created, but regardless of the immediate cause, the result of running away is that she gains a great deal of power. Some girls live in truly ghastly situations, and it is only their spunk and courage that allows them to survive.

Girls are more likely to run away from changing families. Twenty-one percent of homeless youths have new stepparents, 62 percent have moved at least once in the three months before becoming homeless, and 43 percent have entered a new school.* When parents' residential arrangements are undependable, a teen girl may be left stranded or may opportunistically strike out on her own. If a mother moves in with a boyfriend, a teen girl may move in with a friend.

When there is a pattern of changes, a girl's ties to her family can be weakened. She may have frequent changes of home or apartment, with related school changes, which force premature independence and self-reliance, offer freedom from rules and supervision, and make it difficult for her to reintegrate into the household.

Some girls live in families where adolescence descends on them before they are developed enough to leave childhood and therefore behave like adult-sized children, with temper tantrums, narcissism, and poor judgment. A girl who is highly impulsive and looks for instant gratification and solutions to problems is likely to use avoidance when problems develop.

---

*Rotheram-Borus, Koopman, and Ehrhardt, "Homeless Youths and HIV Infection," 1188–97.

For parents whose daughter has run away, there is likely to be anger, frustration, fear, and worry that she will run away again and perhaps disappear completely. Often there is a sense of guilty relief that the tension in the household is alleviated. There also may be a perception of having been deserted by part of one's family, and a parent may feel quite forlorn. There may be a sense of panic at what may happen to the girl and what the adult has caused by his or her behavior.

Sometimes girls run away to the house of a friend, a grand-parent, or the noncustodial parent, or, if they are older, they may run away to dreams of glamour and glory in the city. A teenage girl who runs away from home with no other home to go to is likely to end up on a big-city porno strip, involved in prostitu-tion, with exposure to pregnancy, disease, street crime, drugs, violence, and the loss of all of the advantages of a home with parents, albeit imperfect parents.

A New York City study of homeless youth showed that one-sixth had been physically assaulted on the streets, one-fifth had been raped or sexually assaulted, and one-fifth had been robbed. Between 50 percent and 71 percent of street youths have a sexually transmitted disease, and one-quarter of homeless youths report trading sex for money or drugs.* Unless a girl's life or sanity is at risk, it is difficult to view running away as a viable solution to her problems. It would seem to result in far worse conditions than even the most dreadful home situations.

The outlook is more optimistic where girls run away to live somewhere else. A new home, if there is adult supervision, probably has requirements similar to the old home (Get up for school, come in on time, do your homework), and because a girl cannot feel completely secure as a house guest, she may be forced to draw on her reserves of adult behavior to do well, especially since she has an interest in proving that she can suc-cessfully leave home, thus exonerating herself in her running away ("All I needed was a good home to get my life together!")

Most teenage girls will accept parental supervision and not rebel too strongly if there is a loving bond and a belief that a parent, no matter how misguided, has their best interests at

*Rotheram-Borus, Koopman, and Ehrhardt, "Homeless Youths and HIV Infection," 1188–97.

heart. Girls will submit to a parent's requirements, or at least give the appearance of doing so, without trying to escape. But without a sense of warmth, a girl may feel overpowered by a parent and unable to hold her own in the face of parental coercion. In these circumstances leaving the house does not entail as great a loss as it would if she and the parents were close.

Prostitution: The great majority of adolescent female prostitutes are girls who have run away from home because of family conflicts or physical abuse. The descent into prostitution is not direct; runaways often stay first with friends, then with strangers, and finally live on the streets. The average age for running away in these circumstances is fourteen, although it may be considerably younger.

The adolescent prostitute is isolated and has few social supports other than her pimp. Suicide attempts are frequent, and adolescent prostitutes are far more ignorant than the nonprostitute population about sexuality. Girls "in the life" experience high rates of physical abuse, violent rape, robbery, and economic exploitation by pimps.

The motivation for first engaging in prostitution is often to provide means of self support. Although girls often become involved in prostitution as an act of defiance, they are tightly controlled by pimps, customers, and police, and generally feel trapped. They are introduced to the life, or "turned out," by a friend, or sometimes by a pimp.

The family backgrounds of young prostitutes are usually troubled, with one or both parents absent early in childhood. Relationships with parents are poor, particularly with the father, if he is present, and many girls in this category have no close relationships with adults at all during childhood. Sexual abuse in childhood is common, and physical abuse is also frequent.

The following will be helpful:

1. When a girl runs away, react directly and immediately. Call the police and the school, and ask for all available help.

2. Evaluate a girl's situation with her to determine what is unbearable. Pay particular attention to the possibility of physical or sexual abuse, her relationship with other teens, her

success in teen activities, and her strength as a problem-solver. Evaluate the possibility of substance abuse.

3. Consider carefully whether your daughter belongs in your home. Since she is expressing her inability to deal productively with her residential arrangement, both the home and the girl need to change. Family counseling is particularly useful for evaluating what is needed in both areas. Make a plan that considers her needs and how best to meet them, along with the needs of the family. A teenage girl needs a structured and supportive setting and parents need protection from the strain of threatened departure and helplessness. Transitional living arrangements that help a girl develop adult competencies are particularly worth considering.

4. Consult with an attorney about the advisability of having a girl declared a ward of the court, which may be termed "status offender," "incorrigible," "person in need of supervision" (PINS), or other. This involves the legal system and social service agencies in a girl's care, giving them power to require behavior of her and to take corrective action where appropriate.

5. If a girl has run away to an unwholesome situation, consider asking the police to investigate or bring charges against older youngsters or adults who may be involving her in unhealthy activity.

6. In dealing with unrelated runaway youngsters who seek refuge in your home, consider carefully your contribution to their future. Contact emergency services to check out charges of abuse, sexual exploitation, or neglect. Offer help but don't encourage avoidance of problems that need settling.

7. Keep in mind that there are good kids who run away and there are bad kids who run away, but that avoidance is essentially childish behavior meant to deal with inadequacy.

8. Many teen girls use brief periods away from home to escape parental supervision and guidance, and these are usually the girls who most need it. Sometimes a girl leaves home after a parental fight and coincidentally just before a dance or rock concert and then returns home after it is over, escaping curfew and parental supervision. Staying at a friend's house for the weekend can be a means of avoidance of the home situation and often avoidance of parental control.

9. Where a girl is involved in prostitution, she will need

extensive help to change her lifestyle and relationships. Institutionalization can be powerful in breaking the hold of old patterns, although most adolescent prostitutes, if arrested, avoid juvenile offender status, since adult criminal status allows them to be released immediately.

ASSAULTIVE BEHAVIOR

Girls are responsible for far fewer assaultive crimes than teenage boys, but they are sometimes violently assaultive. Fistfights, muggings, and other demonstrations of power are all forms of female adolescent violence.

Girls who hurt others usually come from violent families, which makes the problem easier to understand and harder to solve. Family violence seems to originate in too much stress and too little warmth, with relational patterns that frustrate family members and lead to more violence. At the core of the family is often a marital alliance that is ineffective in creating a workable partnership.

When girls are exposed to emotional confusion at home and excessive physical aggression, it is difficult to learn self-control and to develop the skills needed to negotiate with others to get what they need. Girls sometimes unconsciously learn the behavior of a violent parent or copy an older brother or sister.

There are other factors that can lead to violent behavior in a girl, including the use of drugs, especially cocaine, crack, basuco, and freebase, chronic delinquency with escalating aggressiveness, gang membership, and personality disorders, particularly psychopathic or borderline personality disorder or schizophrenia.

Girls learn aggression early in childhood, when children use it to achieve their ends. Often when a little girl wants to dominate others, she uses spitting, biting, pushing, kicking, slapping, or throwing things to get her way. She may also use verbal assaults, name calling, teasing, belittling, quarreling, and threatening.

Without appropriate adult guidance, girls do not outgrow these behaviors, and, if effective, they may be reinforced. These behavioral patterns also lower frustration tolerance and increase irritability as they raise the overall level of tension. By age six or seven, most girls have learned to substitute other, nonviolent behaviors to get what they want, and by age nine, aggressiveness in girls is rare. But when it does exist, it tends to be a serious problem. It develops often from a responsive environment, for example, adults or siblings who are submissive when the girl becomes violent or, at the other extreme, who treat her violently.

Interestingly, girls who respond violently are often unable to deal with others assertively, supporting the theory that "all bullies are cowards." Assertive behavior involves speaking clearly for one's own needs and insisting on a solution that offers some satisfaction while respecting others' needs as well. Aggressive behavior intends to damage the other.

Assertiveness will not be an attractive behavior choice where the aim of the assaultive behavior is to instill fear and compliance in the other and to establish a dominant-submissive relationship. Girls who seek these relationships generally take the submissive part when they meet powerful others whom they cannot defeat, suggesting that they may be able to relate to others only as the dominant or submissive partner. The presence of assaultive behavior usually suggests a high level of anger and a need for power. Usually, these develop if a girl has been severely threatened and overwhelmed.

Spiritual issues are particularly important in assaultive behavior, for they indicate a despair about the potential of human relationships, and girls who become violent generally see little promise in emotional relating. There is often a pattern of repeated failures of nurturing relationships, so that the universe seems like a cold and rejecting place that must be forced to provide for one's needs.

Girls who engage in violent behavior often have great difficulty being tender and loving, and they are uncomfortable in situations where nurturing or altruistic responses are called for, probably because these awaken the needy side of themselves.

The following will be helpful:

1. Examine the context of a girl's life to look at what supports violent behavior particularly in parent and sibling relations, and in peer friendship patterns.

2. Consider whether violence is necessary for a girl in her neighborhood and school and whether it protects her.

3. Examine the adult relationships around a girl for excessive conflict and aggression. What is the tone of the household, and is it conducive to violent exchanges?

4. Consider a teen girl's relationship with other teens and whether she belongs to a subculture of violence. In particular, look at the possibility of teenage gang membership, which has spread to suburbs and towns in recent years.

5. Think about whether a girl has enough of the basics without fighting, for example, enough privacy, enough respect, enough warmth. Where does she find approval? Who likes her?

6. Look for sources of anger and denigration in a girl's life and at ways to construct sources of nurturing and power. Help her to develop patterns to share and resolve anger without demeaning herself.

7. To control assaultive behavior, there must be external structure and restraint. Consequences that are memorable are important, and supervision and guidance that help a girl to control herself are necessary. Punishment for assaultive behavior should *never* be physical and should involve restitution in a real or symbolic way.

8. An overall treatment strategy that involves individual psychotherapy, group or family therapy, and spiritual training within the family or the girl's religious tradition is advisable.

GANG MEMBERSHIP

Even though it is easy to romanticize teenage gangs, they are generally poorly organized and unstable in their structure, with a small core group that maintains the gang and a shifting membership. Leadership is apt to be disturbed and erratic, fluctuating with the personal characteristics of the girl in charge.

Girl gangs have increased over the past decade and now account for 10 percent of gang membership. It is estimated that there are six hundred gangs in Los Angeles alone, with seventy thousand members. Girl gangs usually function as the "ladies auxiliaries" of boy gangs, and these groups are often much smaller than the larger male gang. There appears to be a social hierarchy of gangs, with girl gangs on the lowest rung of the ladder, boy gangs one step up, and adult gangs on the top level. Gangs are most common in urban areas and among low-income groups, although gang activity has moved to smaller cities and outlying areas in recent years.

Sometimes girl gangs fight each other, but these "catfights" do not often include weapons and may involve charging two girls to represent their respective gangs. There may be physical fights between gang members over boys, possessions, or insults. All gangs promote delinquent activity, sometimes as part of their rituals and often for material gain. Sometimes gangs focus primarily on violent behavior, accumulating weapons and planning neighborhood wars, while others engage in criminal activity for profit.

Drugs have changed the nature of gangs, and this lucrative business has given kids a valued place in the criminal structure as runners, distributors, and vendors. When the employment options for teens are minimum-wage jobs with adult supervision, dealing drugs is far more appealing, particularly if a girl is a user, and a gang can be a training ground for introduction into the drug trade. The flow of large amounts of money in the drug business encourages greater organization, and the availability of weapons makes the whole business more attractive.

From a larger perspective, gangs are often a poor girl's sorority, serving the purpose of helping her to make a transition to a new and more demanding life stage that requires greater interpersonal skills. Gangs represent a way for kids to raise themselves when adult parenting is not effective enough to teach them to reach their goals in mainstream American culture.

Even though they are poorly organized and have shifting membership and norms, gangs offer the illusion of stable life patterns, and there may be more stability here than in a girl's family life. There are rites of passage, ways for girls to protect honor, and help for each other out on the streets. There is also uniqueness for each girl, reflected in the practice of taking a gang name on initiation and in the use of special, secret signs to one another.

Although girls may feel protected and connected in belonging to a gang, the reality for girls is early pregnancy, drug addiction, run-ins with the law, and physical harm, the side-effects of gang membership.

The following will be helpful:

1. Speak to local juvenile police officers to learn about the

presence and criminal record of gangs in your locale. Evaluate a girl's safety and need for protection and whether she perceives gang membership as necessary.

2. Explore opportunities in the community for girl organizations and activities and become actively involved in supporting them. Bring your daughter with you and teach her how to belong.

3. Investigate thoroughly before sending a girl to another town to get her away from gangs and gang membership, for many gangs have branches and affiliations in other geographical areas.

4. Evaluate whether a girl is using drugs or alcohol, which would pull her into gang membership to support her habit.

5. Get to know a girl's friends and have them at your house. Listen to their conversation without judging them or disapproving, share their concerns, and help them to be creative in figuring out how to get more of what they want. Encourage them to increase their self-respect, raise their aspirations, and demand more from life than safety and satisfaction on the streets.

RELIGIOUS CULTS

Organized religious affiliation is productive for teenage girls, since it generally raises their self-esteem, teaches them to relate to others, and challenges their minds to explore issues beyond themselves. Participation in messianic or radical fringe religious movements, however, can endanger a teenage girl's psychological health.

Religious cults share many of the characteristics of gangs, since they are based on fear, self-righteousness, and a yearning to belong. In religious cults, however, recruitment begins by attacking a girl's good view of herself, inducing doubt and shame. This is followed by an introduction that disorients a girl's thinking and offers highly suggestive messages, making it difficult for her to think critically about what is being presented.

In order to build a girl's dependence on the religious cult, her personal identity, her education, and her relationships, which may have formed the basis of her self-confidence and her resilience, will be portrayed as sinful, illusory, and self-indulgent, so that she is forced to look elsewhere for psychological security. As she begins to crumble under this emotional onslaught, the cult offers her refuge and salvation in return for personal sacrifice, self-erasure, and financial contribution.

Painful self-disclosures and intimate confessions are often demanded as part of the process of attaching her to the group, so that she feels deeply bound to other members. Her intellect and common sense will be attacked as signs of self-deception and failures of faith. Societal beliefs, for example, in freedom of speech, will be seen as failures of will.

Depending on the style and approach of the particular cult, there may be rewards and punishments to speed up her conversion and obedience to the judgment of the leaders, with good things happening when she performs to expectation and punishment if she does not, mostly in the form of peer disapproval but sometimes involving physical discomfort. As a girl conforms, her self-esteem will be restored and there will be a sense of having seen the light, being transformed, being one with the universe, and being at peace. Her newfound feelings of inner peace will be difficult to sustain away from the group, and so the group will limit her exposure to nonmembers. She will feel increasingly less comfortable around others, particularly questioning parents.

Girls who have been brought into cults will resist any attempts to disrupt their participation and will self-righteously criticize others who can't see the light. There is likely to be some paranoid ideation as well, which can be dangerous, as witnessed by the disasters at Jonestown and Waco.

The basis of religious cults is the breakdown/buildup approach, which initially stirs shame and self-doubt and then offers an emotionally compelling solution to a vulnerable personality. Much of a girl's vulnerability to this approach will depend on how steady her self-image and confidence are to begin with and how much she has practiced relying on her judgment as she grows up.

The following will be helpful:

1. Consult with local or regional police and established religious leaders about the religious group in question, to gain information about the practices and history of the group. If

a girl is under seventeen, consider legal action to end her involvement.

2. Psychological treatment is important to help a girl deal with the guilt, shame, lost self-esteem, lost faith in her judgment, and loss of the group after she leaves a cult. Often this treatment will not be effective until she has been away from the group for a period, but it is important to begin early to offset the shock and loss of cult membership.

3. Help a girl to comprehend how she gradually gave up herself and surrendered not only her good view of herself but her good judgment as well in joining a religious cult. Share the sadness with her of the things she gave up and sympathize with how hard it is to get what we want. Consider her goals and her strivings, and help her build other ways to reach what she wants.

4. Help her to understand that the warm feeling of surrendering oneself to a greater good and merging with others must always be balanced with her own good judgment and that transformational experiences are rarely a replacement for hard work, patience, and courage.

4. Develop contacts with others who have been through cult experiences and have successfully withdrawn, and offer help from your own experience and your daughter's.

Failure to mature

SCHOOL DROPOUT

Although many of the other problems in this section have the urgent and heart-stopping characteristics of emergencies, dropping out of school may seem less dramatic, but in fact it has far-reaching consequences that can handicap a girl for the rest of her life. When girls give up on school, it is usually with the stated intention of returning, but this becomes increasingly difficult as time passes. Without adult intervention and help, it is practically impossible for a girl to return to school once she has left the normal educational sequence.

What is the effect of an incomplete high school education on a girl's life? Most immediately, it takes her out of the mainstream of youth and puts her into a category of youngsters who develop alternative means of gratification and success. It separates her from her peers, demonstrating that she does not belong and cannot master life skills that other youngsters handle competently. So at the outset of adulthood she is likely to perceive herself as far behind others.

For this reason, peer acceptance becomes much more critical to a dropout, because it offsets a girl's sense of herself as a loser. If only somebody likes her or finds her worthwhile, she can feel that all is not lost. But the other young people who offer this acceptance are unlikely to inspire her to higher goals and may encourage her to aim lower. If a girl dropped out of school to keep company with a group of ambitious, adventurous young people, parents might feel reassured. But along with dropping out of school comes dropping out of a school-oriented peer group.

The alternative to attending school is to work, but younger teens will have few employment options, and older teens will be considerably limited by the absence of a complete education. There will be real limits on earning power, but these will not initially be felt since a girl earning minimum wage will feel very wealthy, particularly if she is working full-time.

The most drastic effects of dropping out of high school will be over the long term and will coincide with the increasing difficulty of returning to school. A woman's earning power is affected far more by the lack of a high school education than is a man's, and a girl will be restricted to minimum-wage jobs with little if any chance for advancement. Her dependency on others for financial support may take the form of remaining at home with parents or marrying to gain a means of support. If she has children, she will be stymied in helping them to achieve academically or occupationally.

Although it may seem that a girl makes a sudden and dramatic decision to give up on school, in fact the process is much more gradual and involves withdrawing from other kids as much as from academics. In the year before a girl quits school, there are likely to have been changes that disconnected her from the school scene and led her to feel that she was not an integral part of school. The change from junior high school to high school is a difficult one for most girls, coming with the major physical changes of puberty and the drop in self-esteem and sense of personal strength that characterize this period.

Academic achievement suffers when a girl's setting changes, and high school requires new skills that may not have been mastered previously. High school presents many new challenges and choices, and there is greater access to substances, more potential for involvement in delinquency, and more opportunities for trouble.

These pressures occur at a time when a girl is least skilled in dealing with her environment and the pressures in it. She may be further hampered by unique factors in her situation, for example, if she has a poor academic record, has had several school changes prior to the transition, is slow to develop, or is part of a minority or disadvantaged population.

As she gets into high school, new pressures make themselves felt and tax a girl's resources and problem-solving skills. The high school setting makes far more demands on her and forces her to choose among courses, friends, and recreational activities, with far less adult guidance than before. She is also of an age to hold a job, which may seem more rewarding than school, pulling her away from school.

There will be many adjustments to be made in high school, the most important being a new school schedule. Many high schools have an eight-day-week, in which the schedule is different each day, and although a girl may be able to arrive at the right class each morning, the mental structuring required to remember when homework and reports are due can be beyond her emotional capacity.

Friendships and connections also change in the transition to high school, and a girl must locate or create a new set of friends for support and sharing. If she finds high school confusing and overwhelming, she is likely to attach to other youngsters who feel the same, sharing failures and finding alternative gratifications, for example, drugs or delinquency.

Schools differ in the climates that they offer. High schools that are poorly administered, with frequent changes of faculty and high levels of staff dissatisfaction, or schools with large numbers of problem youngsters, high crime levels, or many school dropouts can offer little help to a girl who is floundering. The best teachers and administrators will be neutralized by a school setting that cannot support the best efforts of teachers.

In an effort to prevent students from dropping out, school districts often encourage attendance at any price, with the result that there are students who come to school with no intention to participate, disrupting classes and engaging teachers in constant struggles. This is more of a problem in the early grades of secondary school, where attendance is mandatory, than in the later grades, where many of these youngsters have left.

Dropping out is usually a gradual process that takes a girl from full attendance and belonging to a peer group through gradual stages of leaving school. The process may be marked by a girl's leaving school early or arriving late, cutting classes, taking the minimum number of courses, avoiding involvement with teachers or extracurricular activities, or being frequently absent or truant.

Concomitant with these changes are falling and failing grades and isolation from other kids who attend school. Friendships fall away and more time is spent in the streets or in other activities, such as a job.

Usually girls would like to return to school and often vow that they will do so after something else occurs — after this job ends, after they can afford clothes, or whatever. But in reality there are usually solid factors that block them: a bad reputation with teachers and administrators, alienation from other youngsters, and personal problems such as substance abuse, or family or legal difficulties.

The following will be helpful:

1. Massive adult help is necessary in getting a female high school dropout to complete her education. This will involve arranging services of many sorts for her and supervising and encouraging her to make sure that she remains with them. Perhaps the most critical element here is an adult who *cares* enough about her to insist on working with her to provide for her future.

2. An educational program must be designed that will meet a girl's needs and compensate for her weaknesses. To begin with, a psychoeducational assessment must be arranged that will provide a complete survey of deficits and learning levels, and this is usually available at no charge through any public

school district in the U.S. This is followed by an individual plan for a girl's education that is made by a team of specialists and that may include special programs or special schools.

3. Under Public Law 94-142, the Education of All Handicapped Children Act of 1975, all American students must be provided with free public education suitable to their needs, including special education and supportive services. A program that helps a girl to remain in school and graduate is such a form of special education and must be available or created.

4. The main thrust of a special education program for a girl who has dropped out should be to reduce the academic and social confusion in her surroundings to give her whatever support is needed. It helps to have few changes of rooms or teachers during the day, with counseling to help a girl develop effective work habits. Teacher-student ratios need to be low, with one teacher supervising and keeping an eye on her overall progress.

5. A girl needs to have a small peer group, preferably the same group in all of her classes, so that she can develop a sense of belonging and avoid isolation. She should have little contact with older students or those in the larger high school and social activities need to be limited to her classmates.

6. Parent involvement and encouragement are critical, and a girl will be unable to maintain her energy and hope if parents do not actively support her efforts with their enthusiasm, optimism, and presence.

UNEMPLOYABLE

When a girl has finished school, be it high school, college, or graduate school, her focus turns to employment. She may have worked during her educational years, and most girls will have gained experience and maturity from the experience, but some will have experienced disappointment and failure.

A girl may be temporarily unemployable, i.e., unable to hold a job, or she may be unprepared to do anything at all for pay. In a more traditional era, ladies were not supposed to be qualified for work, and it was considered unfeminine to toil. Nonetheless, women and children toiled in great numbers, in dangerous conditions, until new labor laws and rising male incomes made it possible for women and children to remain at home.

Currently, women are employed in great numbers, and their dependency on men has decreased, not always by their choice. Since women spend an average of sixteen years living without a mate and half of all marriages end in divorce, most of them without child support, it is reasonable to assume that if a woman is unemployable, then she will probably live with inadequate income, at best.

So if a girl begins womanhood without being able to support herself, it is an ominous sign. It is also a puzzling sign, because childhood and adolescence are a time of preparing, mastering, and becoming competent, so we might initially wonder how her time has been spent.

There are two sources of problems that may make a girl temporarily or permanently unemployable. The first is a general immaturity, in which she lacks the worker skills necessary to get and keep a job. The second is a pervasive disorder, such as substance abuse, depression, or school failure. If a girl is only immature, then she will have trouble getting and keeping jobs until she grows and learns. A major psychological problem, however, will block her progress toward self-reliance.

General immaturity stems from a home and school situation where a girl has remained a child and does not have the esteem that comes from meeting age-appropriate demands and expectations. This can occur because a girl is the youngest in a large family or an only child, or because parents or siblings have wanted to shield her from pressure.

The result is apt to be a girl who has little experience with the reciprocal nature of relationships and who sees her position as one who is nurtured and cared for by others. If she has difficulty in holding a job, she is likely to blame the employer as unfair or too demanding rather than taking the responsibility for evaluating her work skills. In short, she will feel entitled to a job and unable to develop whatever skills are required. Jobs are for adults, practical adults, who understand that the exchange is pay for effort and production. In a child's world, pay or care come automatically, while in the adult world, reciprocal exchanges do not balance on caring, but rather on self-respect. Even though a girl gives up nurturing in a reciprocal adult relationship, she gains self-esteem and personal power.

In the more serious case of an unemployable girl, there are

likely to be other problems in addition to general immaturity. If a girl struggles with alcohol or drug abuse, delinquency, or school failure, her energy will be drained off in trying to deal with the consequences of these problems. The problems themselves indicate an overall difficulty in life management, and rarely does job proficiency develop independently of the rest of a girl's personality.

The following will be helpful:

1. In helping a girl to become responsible enough to work, begin with counseling that aims at helping her to analyze her predicament and plan a constructive solution. If a girl is unwilling to become involved in counseling, parents need to pursue family counseling, since her inability to be self-supporting has serious consequences for their lives.

2. Where there are longstanding and powerful personal problems, such as delinquency, emotional difficulties, or anorexia, it is important to locate programs to help her restructure her life and her behavior, since these cannot be dealt with by psychological counseling alone.

3. Job training programs through the school district, aiming at youth who are difficult to employ, should be considered if a girl is seventeen or older. Many of these programs are offered in conjunction with local businesses and offer counseling. Job training opportunities with the armed services can be helpful, and the structure of a "total environment" can sometimes be therapeutic.

4. Discourage marriage and motherhood as an alternative to employment; these require more skill than employment does, not less.

5. Begin to teach self-reliance by having a girl over nineteen live independently of her parents. This may be more costly, but it reinforces the image of an adult rather than a child.

Personal safety and welfare

SUICIDE THREATS AND ATTEMPTED SUICIDE

American society today fosters a great deal of loneliness among teenagers. The high divorce rate, the need for parents to work outside the home, and missing connections with other family members often mean that adolescents are home alone, bombarded by media images of what they should be. The guidance of loving adults is often in short supply, and there are few powerful alternatives to offer structure to teens who experience turmoil and confusion.

What makes a teenage girl desperate enough to want to die? Three-quarters of suicide attempters are women; most of completed suicides are male. Sleeping pills, poison, or gas are most often used by girls, and precipitating factors are most commonly romantic problems and family problems. Teen suicide is generally more common in the spring and around Christmas. When media stories about a teen suicide appear, these can provoke other attempts. Suicide attempts are more likely among teens who are jailed or are lesbian.

News of a girl's threatened suicide usually comes indirectly to parents through school staff, friends, or other sources. Sometimes accidents are suicides or suicide attempts in disguised form. A teenage girl's behavior may be inherently self-destructive, for example, if she shares needles with other intravenous drug users or drives after drinking. Given the widespread informational campaigns, these behavioral choices cannot be seen as unintentional.

When there is everything to live for, why does a young girl try to die? The reasons are complex and unique to each individual, but they generally involve a sense of despair and exhaustion, a belief that things are bad and that they won't get better. These feelings are very different from the passing episodes of the blues, for they are persistent, sometimes at an unconscious level.

Depressed kids often don't seem unhappy, and the clinical term doesn't refer so much to emotional tone as to guiding life beliefs. In severe depression the motivating precept is one of personal helplessness, a conviction that one is not powerful enough, smart enough, brave enough, or good enough to find one's way to whatever is seen as the good life. A pervasive pessimism leads a youngster alternatively to wallow in and struggle with problems, but the results seem always to be failure. For teen girls, the recurrent themes in depression involve a lack of personal attractiveness or adequacy, an absence of peer group membership and belonging, and an inability to gain sufficient approval.

In recent years, suicidal teens have been idealized and romanticized by the media and often portrayed as misunderstood and deprived. But becoming suicidal does not automatically convey legitimacy on one's demands; rather it indicates a paucity of alternative routes to one's goals and a childish demand that the world conform to one's wishes.

Teen thinking about suicide is usually based on movies or novels or reports of the deaths of other adolescents. Fantasies surrounding suicide include "going to sleep and never waking up" and other similarly serene images. There is the belief that after a funeral, a dramatic event at which the youngster imagines herself memorialized and revered, there is also likely to be improvement of some sort in the world. Rarely does a teenage girl see her death forgotten after the funeral. If youngsters in her peer group have died, she may be impressed by the focus and drama of a funeral.

Fantasies of suicide are often deeply satisfying since a girl can feel released from repressed anger and sadness and in control of her life through one powerful act. In imagining her own death, she can gain stature, influence, and position, and she cannot be criticized, controlled, or disappointed. Girls sometimes picture death as a soundproof glass room in the sky from which they can observe events invisibly.

An acceptance of death as a final, terminal act after which the body has no feeling or response takes many years. For many teens, suicide is seen as a partial death, final but not complete, and rarely do girls see it as total removal and separation from all that occurs around them, with most of life going on as before. Having little understanding of biology and limited experience with their own bodies, teenage girls do not grasp the organic survival drive that causes most young bodies to violently oppose death. Dying is rarely peaceful or pleasant in young people, and often only parts of the body are destroyed, leaving a youngster handicapped or maimed.

The long-term characteristics that indicate a downward progression of a teenage girl toward suicide include angry hopelessness as well as depression. Problem-solving deficiencies, impulsiveness, and unrealistic thinking can be long-term indicators of suicide attempts. Problems with drug and alcohol abuse are related to suicide attempts and are in themselves self-destructive forms of behavior. Previous suicide attempts or verbal indications like "Life doesn't seem worth it" are predictive, as are death of a loved one, especially through suicide, or divorce in the family.

The signs of an impending suicide attempt include any of the following: a serious loss, for example, when a family member or pet dies or a romance breaks up, isolation from other kids (especially missing school), drug or alcohol binges, giving away one's things or planning for one's death, and making comments about one's death, even in jest. Alcoholism in particular is closely related to suicide attempts. There are also forms of behavior that suggest that a girl is self-destructive and perhaps inviting injury or death. When, for example, a teenage girl hitchhikes on a dark road, or when she rides public transportation while drunk, she is literally casting her fate to the wind, and it is worth inquiring why she is so careless with her own welfare.

The following are helpful:

1. Ask a girl directly, "Do you feel like life isn't worth living?" "Are you thinking about dying?" *Always* take talk or mention of suicide seriously and pursue it.

2. Tell a girl what her death would mean to you: a shattered life, an inability to ever enjoy anything again, an overwhelming sense of failure, and the loss of her unique person, her laughter, and her tears.

3. Tell her that suicide is painful, unlike the movies, and that often it doesn't work and leaves a girl disfigured, brain damaged, or crippled for life, imprisoned by her own body. Work against a romantic view of death as being beautiful and serene. Point out how a young body struggles hard before dying, and how it is a grisly, painful, slow experience.

4. Don't leave a girl alone if you suspect suicide. Form a relationship and share her feelings. *Listen* to her with compassion and a wish to understand. Be aware that you may feel inadequate, frightened, and overwhelmed as you try to help. Don't try to talk her out of it or gloss over her despair. Don't be quick to assume the crisis is over because she changes her mind.

5. Find a professional person to help her: psychologist, social worker, clergy. Find her a safe setting where she can be

cared for. Interestingly, most initial suicide attempts do not lead to long-term psychotherapy, because families fail to realize the seriousness of the attempt. Tell everyone who loves her of the danger and ask for their help. Diffuse the responsibility so that you are not alone in handling it.

6. Don't trivialize. See things from a youngster's perspective without melodrama. She is different from you. To lose a first boyfriend can feel like the end of the world when you're fourteen.

When a suicide occurs, the following may help:

1. Save those who are left. Suicide often takes more than the original victim in its wake. Devote all of your energy to salvaging what can be saved.

2. Deal with the social stigma and draw friends around you to help. Don't expect feelings to follow a prescribed format, and expect shock, denial, and embarrassment. If you feel that you are losing your mind, let those who love you support you, and seek additional help.

3. Be prepared for thoughts of your own death and physical symptoms that may occur after the suicide of a teen. It may be difficult to think clearly about anything after a young person's suicide.

4. Have a public funeral, and let others help you and grieve with you. Avoid isolation at all costs: families need contact and communication under these circumstances, no matter how painful.

5. Allow yourself a long, long time to recuperate from the death of a child, and lean heavily on friends and loved ones for help. Stoicism and forced cheerfulness are dangerous to all.

CAR ACCIDENT

A car accident is an emergency because a girl's life is immediately in peril and because the consequences of injury are serious for her development. It is also of concern because it is often symptomatic of deeper emotional problems.

Driving is a risky activity and requires judgment and skill. Teenagers often have little of either when they begin to drive, and therefore they are at high risk. Sometimes accidents result from being too careful or too cautious. This is reflected in the

EMERGENCIES 271

statistics. In Canada, young people between sixteen and twenty-
one have 58 percent of all traffic accidents, even though they are
only 21 percent of the licensed drivers.*

American adults generally see themselves as safer, more
skillful drivers than the rest of the population, and adolescents
share this view of themselves. It seems that there is a national
optimism about driving that makes it difficult to take risks
seriously.

Why do teenagers continue to drink and drive or to ride
with someone who has been drinking? Despite all of the education, warnings, no-questions rides home, and designated
drivers, accident rates continue to show that teenagers mix
alcohol and driving.

The answer is often that teenagers have little basis on which
to evaluate driver competency or alcohol ingestion. In the few
minutes it takes to pile into a car, a girl must evaluate whether
the driver is sober and safe, and not surprisingly she is often
wrong. But sober is often a matter of degree, and it is difficult
to object to a driver who says he had only one beer. In any case,
by the time she has had an adequate sampling of his driving
proficiency, she is already in too deep for extraction.

To refuse to ride with another teen drive requires superb
social skills to avoid the social consequences of open criticism of another teen. Consequently, most teens do not refuse,
particularly if the driver is not obviously drunk.

How skilled is a girl at estimating her own driving proficiency? Her skill is apt to be quite limited, since it depends on
road experience for development. Often when a girl learns that
her skills are inadequate, she is already in trouble.

Sometimes the reasons for a car accident are not so much
limited driving skill, but rather a deficiency in related skills
that are required in driving. A girl may be inaccurate in judging travel time and distance, so that she is pressured to speed,
or she may be unfamiliar with geography and find herself on
roads that are beyond her skill or into neighborhoods where
she is not prepared for challenges. It may be that a girl takes
too many passengers or that they are rowdy and distract her,

*National Center for Health Statistics, Public Health Service, DHHS Publication
No. PHS85-1232 (Washington D.C.: U.S. Government Printing Office, 1984).

but she hasn't the social skills to handle the situation. She may drive when she is too tired or when road conditions are more than she can handle.

A girl may have been drinking and then had an accident, which will cause her legal difficulties of greater or lesser degree, depending on her blood alcohol level. It is important to determine whether she has a problem with alcohol and how drinking affects other parts of her life. Clearly, alcohol has obscured her judgment in driving.

If a girl is injured, the situation becomes more complex, since teenage girls are only just beginning to develop confidence and ease with their new bodies. Hospitalization, in particular, is a serious disruption of adolescence, since a girl is forced to be in a passive, helpless position and there may be regression to earlier ages as a result.

The greatest anxiety for a girl who is injured is that she will lose those skills that she has mastered and that she will lose her friends as well. To be incapacitated causes a narcissistic focus, which may be difficult to change as a girl improves. Sometimes when girls survive serious car accidents, they begin to see themselves as charmed and beyond the reach of tragedy.

Occasionally an accident is an indication of suicidal ideation. Research shows that the incidence of suicide is twelve times greater among teens who had previously been hospitalized for injuries, suggesting a link between accidents and suicide.* This is a plausible connection, since suicidal youngsters pay less attention to remaining safe and are more likely to takes risks. The number of car accidents related to levels of depression and past suicidal motivation suggests that many teens kill themselves and disguise the act as an accident.

Car maintenance has generally been seen as a male activity, and most girls know little or nothing about car care. It is fruitful for girls to learn, perhaps through continuing education courses, how to check the gas, oil, water, and brakes on a car, and how to do basic repairs such as changing a flat tire. This saves her from being stranded in a disabled vehicle.

The following will be helpful:

1. After her health and safety are established or restored,

---

*Jane Brody, "Teenage Accidents and Suicide," *New York Times*, March 24, 1993, C13.

discuss the accident with her nonjudgmentally and ascertain what happened, using toy cars to simulate it. Read the police report to verify driver impressions. Discuss with her what she has learned from the accident and how it could have been avoided.

2. Avoid too much reassurance, since a car accident is extremely serious and must be treated as such. Let her shock wear off over a few days and then deal with the realities, including injury to herself and others, property damage, changed insurance rates, and legal vulnerability. Reassure her that she is loved, but let her feel the responsibility for the accident, for it belongs with the drivers, and the experience can help her in the future.

3. Drive with her for a period after the accident to add your reassuring presence. Help her to become readjusted to driving and to develop good self-monitoring skills.

4. Consider whether there are other places where she puts herself in danger, for example, by drinking or using drugs, and whether she is able to take *reasonable, healthy* risks in service of her goals.

RAPE AND SEXUAL ABUSE

Rape is always a sad crime, for it is a betrayal of youth and trust, and its effects are irreversible. All sexual abuse, be it incest, sibling abuse, or child molesting, is rape, because it involves a child in behavior to which she cannot give informed consent and over which she has no control.

Forcible rape: Sexual assault on teenage girls is a depressingly common occurrence, with girls frequently refusing to report their victimization. Of the female rape victims who do report the crime, one-sixth are girls between twelve and fifteen. For one-third of girls the first sexual experience will involve forced sexual activity, and the likelihood of a second sexual assault is statistically higher after a first.

Only a small percentage of girls (between 20 and 35 percent) tell their parents of these experiences, and so there is often no treatment or retribution for the crime. The majority of these rapes are spontaneous, involving verbal threat, drugs, or alcohol, and are associated with other delinquent behavior.

Rape is a violent offense, with the object being more than sexual satisfaction. In a large number of cases, rapists have an accomplice or operate in groups, so that there is a multiple rape, which serves the purpose of group bonding or male rite of passage. Sometimes there is defiling or humiliation of the girl as well.

Rapes are more common on weekends, at night, and in warm weather, and most often occur in the victim's house, a car, or a deserted location. The most common age group for rapists is between fifteen and nineteen.

Runaway girls are the most vulnerable to rape, which serves as a means of subjugation and domination on the streets. It can be a pimp's way of recruiting prostitutes and may follow friendly overtures. Urban prostitution is a big business, annually generating $400 million in Los Angeles alone, one-third of it from children under eighteen. Certainly a lurid life, it nonetheless looks better to a girl than sleeping in doorways and garbage dumpsters.*

Sometimes rape is the manifestation of psychotic processes, as with the serial rapist who unconsciously acts out early traumas. A portrait of the serial rapist includes this chilling picture:

> [He] appears to be relatively normal, coming from an average or disadvantaged home, well groomed, intelligent, employed and living in a family.... In most cases, the serial rapist had been institutionalized during adolescence and reported sexual abuse as a child or adolescent; [he does not stalk] a particular woman, rather [his] choice of victim depends on proximity to her and access to her residence.†

There is only a small chance that a rapist, if caught and convicted, will be imprisoned; 82 percent of convicted rapists spend no time in prison for their offense.

College campuses are not immune to predation and with their free and easy atmosphere often seem to be an easy target for rapists. The open residence halls, the unlocked bedroom doors in deserted dormitories, and the passivity of students

---

*Gerard Whittemore, *Street Wisdom for Women: A Handbook for Urban Survival* (Boston: Quinlan Press, 1986), 152.
†*New York Times*, June 19, 1980.

all combine to make it easier for a girl to be trapped and assaulted. Most rapes on campus involve young people from the surrounding area who are repeat offenders.

The following are helpful in preventing rape:

1. Develop the habit of planning ahead, so that a girl's activities can be as safe and as enjoyable as possible. When she is out in public, she needs to be clear about where she is going, to stay with people, and to avoid becoming isolated. If she is bothered, she needs to be rude and assertive, and if need be to yell, scream, and make a ruckus.

2. A girl should be guarded about sharing personal information such as details of her life or schedule, which should not be released to strangers, either in person or over the telephone.

3. If a girl has contact with strangers, it should be in public places, and she should always have an escape route in mind.

4. When a girl is at home, she should develop the habit of locking the doors and admitting no one.

5. On public transportation, a girl needs to be sober and informed of her route. She should not sleep or read and should stay with other people, avoiding public restrooms and isolated areas.

6. A girl needs to learn good car safety, which involves locking doors and windows and *never* picking up hitchhikers, even other girls. She needs to know her way around and how to find the police station. She should be able to deal with basic car problems.

7. When traveling, a girl should be aware that tourists often feel a false sense of security in attractive foreign places, where they are easy targets for rapists.

What happens when a girl is raped? Generally, the initial reaction is terror, panic, humiliation, and a variety of other responses depending on the characteristics of the attack and her level of injury. Over the first few days following the rape, there are likely to be periods of upset that involve fear and crying. Her initial reaction to the experience is the best indicator of its overall effect on her, but if there is no reaction at all, this is a cause for serious concern. Over the weeks after the experience, there may be fear of being alone, nightmares, panic attacks, disturbed bodily cycles, and avoidance of others.

What makes a difference in how well a girl recovers from a rape? The characteristics of the episode are most important, and the effects will be worst when there are high levels of terror, injury, or mutilation. A girl's life circumstances may help her recovery, for example, if there are few other disturbances in her life, if she is close to her family, and if there are males who are loving and trustworthy.

Acquaintance rape: When rape occurs between two people who have a friendly relationship, it may be called date rape, but it still is forcible sexual intercourse. It can involve some flirtatious or romantic activity, but it becomes coercive when a girl refuses and cannot control the outcome.

This sort of rape constitutes 70–80 percent of rapes and results from a male's deliberate or unintentional failure to read a girl's message of refusal, and a girl's lack of clarity and decisiveness about her sexual preferences. When both of the young people have been using drugs or alcohol, the situation becomes even more complicated to interpret.

The male role of seducer of young females, the conqueror, is often a factor in date rapes, and there is adequate evidence that young males have a vested interest in misunderstanding the refusals of young females. Teenage girls, who often have mixed feelings about sexual activity, may communicate ambiguity rather than a decisive message. Often the situation becomes coercive or violent as a power struggle ensues and positions become clear, but by then it is too late.

Date rape has lasting effects for teenage girls and is often followed by fear of being alone and depression over the years following the event. In addition, because girls often keep the experience secret, they have no access to help in dealing with it.

The following will be helpful:

1. Girls should be self-protective in *all* circumstances, but particularly where their companion is not thoroughly familiar to them. They should arrange settings with protection and escape as well as entertainment in mind. They can choose, for example, to double date, to go to busy places, and to have access to independent transportation.

2. It is helpful to discuss female signals and to sort out which indicate a wish for sexual involvement and which send

a message of refusal. Insist that girls avoid jokes or levity in discussing rape or forced sex.

3. Practice assertive behavior with a girl so that she can feel well-mannered and expressive and can set clear limits:

- "No, thanks. Walks on the beach aren't for me! We can see the stars from inside the restaurant here."

4. Teach a girl to fight an attacker and to use whatever is available to protect herself. Also teach a girl to say: "This is rape and I will go to the police."

5. Communicate in every way possible that if a girl is raped, you want to know and you will not blame her.

Incest and child abuse: When young girls are sexually molested, it is commonly between seven and eleven, a time when most girls are just beginning puberty and dealing with the beginnings of womanhood. Sexual abuse may begin much earlier, sometimes in infancy, and may continue much later, and is almost invariably perpetrated by older adult males. The person who abuses a girl may be a father, stepfather, mother's boyfriend, storekeeper, janitor, paperboy, grandfather, landlord, or baby-sitter, but the abuse is rarely more than just one episode.

Most sexual abuse begins with attention and kindness, with an adult talking to a girl or taking an interest in her, often an adult so loving that he seems too good to be true. Physical contact begins with hugging, holding, or touching, and a girl becomes aware that something forbidden is occurring, but is afraid to voice her objections, since nothing clearly wrong has happened and the person seems loving and kind. By the time there is more flagrant sexual activity, a girl is likely to feel a party to the crime and frightened at what may happen. When the police are finally involved, some girls think that they are being arrested.

Sexual involvement with a child is always a form of rape, since informed consent to sexual activity is possible only for an adult. Eighty-five percent of child molesters are known acquaintances or friends of the family and are often those who are seen as particularly good to children: camp counselors, teachers, or anyone with an unsupervised relationship with children. Often the adult gives a child presents, wants to spend time alone with her, or wants to take her photograph. The wish to believe that adults are decent and kind and that children are safe often leads parents to trust exploitative adults with their children.

When sexual abuse happens within a family, it is more difficult for a youngster, since a child cannot easily distinguish father and abuser. In fact, parental rapists show no difference from other criminals in personality profiles and incest is often only one part of their criminal activity.

A child who reveals the incest may feel that she is betraying a relationship with a father or an older brother, and this raises the possibility of rejection from other family members, most notably the mother, who may not believe the girl or may hold her responsible. A girl may feel that it is her fault that the events occurred, and experienced child molesters are able to stir up a child's guilt to keep her in the relationship. For this reason, 98 percent of the victims of child sexual assault do not report the offense when the offender is a relative.

Some adults naively expect a young teen to come sobbing home to Mom with proof of molesting and perhaps a few witnesses or photographic evidence, as well as accounts of heroic attempts to fight off the predator. But the sequence of events is usually quite different. A parent is approached by a hesitant, anxious child who seems guilty and ambiguous about "things that happened with the minister," an uncle, or a teen cousin. When a parent probes, the girl may become more distressed, contradict herself, get confused, and change her story or retract it entirely. At this point, the girl may withdraw psychologically, with a profound sense of helplessness and self-doubt. Rage toward the disbelieving parent is often the predominant trauma, with consequent damage to the girl.

Beyond the genital damage and exposure of an immature human to a painful experience, there is far greater psychological trauma in sexual abuse. To be drawn into an evil secret that one keeps out of fear teaches a warped view of intimacy as shameful and dangerous. The average sexually abused child never tells, afraid that she would be blamed or that the perpetrator would take vengeance. Sexual predation often begins at an early age and continues into adolescence to a point where a girl feels strong enough to resist escape or sometimes expose the abuser. He is most typically a relative, with 10 percent of adult women reporting sexual molesting as children by an adult relative, almost half of those fathers or father figures.

The following will be helpful:

1. Communicate to a girl repeatedly that she is your first priority because of her youth and your love and that you will always help her with problems, even if she feels they are her fault, and that you are her best ally.

2. If you hear her tell of abuse or inappropriate behavior by others to her, tape it or write it down so that she doesn't have to keep repeating it and ask for as many details as possible. *Believe it*, since she can't describe Paris if she hasn't been there. The vast majority of kids are far too embarrassed to say anything at all about sex or their genitals, and if she mentions such an incident, she trusts you.

3. Call the local child abuse hot line and discuss the situation, and ask for help in the form of referrals and guidelines.

4. Separate the girl from whoever is the perpetrator, and do not allow him to speak with her or see her *under any circumstances.*

5. If the abuse involves an older sibling, assume that the perpetrator had been abused somewhere in development and explore this possibility.

•

In any of the forms of sexual abuse described in this section, the following will be helpful:

1. Contact the nearest rape crisis center for consultation and services. When a girl is being attended to, stay with her and make her as comfortable as possible.

2. Get medical care immediately. In the case of assaultive rape, don't wash, comb, brush, put on clean clothes, or make any changes. Bring all surrounding items along and save everything. Medical attention should focus on injury, possible pregnancy, and risks of infection.

3. Contact the police. Medical personnel will not report rape unless requested. If the decision is made not to report the crime and bring charges, an anonymous third party report can be made which alerts the police and offers evidence of the crime but does not involve the girl in a legal proceeding.

4. Immediately after a sexual assault, a girl should talk with a caring person and describe the attack in as much detail as possible, no matter how unimportant the details seem. Memory is sometimes obliterated by shock, and it is important to have basic data for latter clarification and decisions, as well as for her long-term psychological welfare.

5. A girl will need constant companionship after sexual assault for reassurance and protection. Be sure to clarify that your angry reactions are toward the perpetrator or event, not to her. Be nonjudgmental no matter how you see causation. Sexual assault and coercion are never justifiable, regardless of a girl's behavior or appearance.

6. Insist on long-term counseling, for sexual trauma always has long-term effects.

7. If necessary, prepare a girl for dealing with the legal system by arranging for her to have an attorney to represent her interests. Make sure that in legal dealings she always has a supportive person with her, that her privacy is preserved as much as possible, that procedures and questions are explained to her, and that a written account of her comments is kept for her.

8. In all activities, help her to reestablish the development of independence and strength. Reassure her that she can survive and that the same good and strong person lives inside her and will prevail as she recovers.

REPEATED PERSONAL INJURIES

Most parents focus closely on a girl's safety and are often concerned about whether they overprotect or underprotect. The need for a girl to be free and to handle simple dealings like visiting friends can become especially challenging, particularly in high-crime areas where a girl must take subways, elevators, and so forth.

Injuries that result from accidents and misfortunes are less of a concern, but can multiply to a point where it seems that a girl is constantly being physically hurt. There may be small bruises or cuts on her legs, arms, neck, or face, and there may occasionally be more serious injuries. When asked, a girl may treat these quite casually and say only that she bumped herself.

The first concern is always for a girl's health. A girl whose balance, judgment, or other central nervous system functions are disturbed will have great difficulty in navigating smoothly. If there are such difficulties, it may be hard for her to notice them since she may not perceive the change in her coordination. In the same vein, unexplainable black and blue marks must be medically evaluated.

Sometimes repeated personal injuries are a means of obtaining nurturing and parental care when a girl feels too defensive to express needs clearly, either because she risks her independence or because she would need to explain her neediness. To be injured gives a youngster a great deal of control and entitlement without having to reciprocate, as in an adult relationship. The complaints represent a form of blackmail; the implication that the parent should take care of her suffering. A girl may feel that she can't risk more direct communication or she doesn't know how to use it and still maintain her independence.

A girl may develop a pattern of injury that makes no medical sense but does make psychological sense, for example, if she is always injured the night before a test. Insist that she meet legitimate responsibilities even if injured, and find ways that she can creatively overcome her obstacles.

Another source of repeated injury is physical abuse by a parent, older sibling, or other adult. Families are sometimes violent settings, and because she is not always as strong as other members, a girl may be a target. But such treatment is likely to be hidden in the family, and a girl may be reluctant to tell because she fears worse treatment or because she believes she deserves it.

Another source of injury is an abusive boyfriend, who may be physically as well as emotionally abusive to a girl. There may be additional ways that he puts a girl at risk, for example, by drinking or by driving dangerously. For girls, involvement in this sort of relationship is invariably a sign of low self-esteem, for they feel that no one else wants them.

Even when others try to point out the liabilities of such a relationship, a girl may try to demonstrate her strength by staying in the relationship, or she may continue to suffer as a way to punish parents and make them focus on her. There is real cause for concern, however, since one-third of female homicide victims are killed by their husbands or boyfriends.

The following will be helpful:

1. Arrange a full medical exam, and write a note to the doctor before arriving that describes the symptoms and your concerns. Be sure to mention how long the problem has existed; it should be more than two months.

2. Explore with a girl how she is injuring herself, and keep a record of your understanding of what is happening to her body. Discuss this with her to try to help her find common pitfalls and to avoid further injuries.

3. Examine the gains a girl received from her injuries, which may include attention and caring, and assess whether she has other ways to achieve these gains. Also consider whether a girl is able to ask for caring without a clear justification, such as an injury.

4. Ask a girl directly if someone is hurting her, and discuss her relationships with her father, brother, and boyfriend. Ask about how anger gets expressed in these relationships.

5. If she appears to be involved in an abusive romance, arrange counseling and insist that she participate.

Self-regulation

DRUNKENNESS, ALCOHOLISM

Alcohol dependency and addiction are the greatest substance abuse problem for American teens and far outpace drug abuse. Over three million teenagers have been treated for alcoholism, and estimates are that 5 percent of adolescents drink daily. Alcohol abuse among teens may have received less than its share of attention because many adults are uneasy with their own alcohol consumption patterns. Eleven million adults are currently in treatment for alcoholism.

Even with all of the educational efforts, teenagers are not particularly responsible in their alcohol use. In one study 17 percent of high school students reported using alcohol or drugs while swimming or boating, and 38 percent of tenth graders reported driving in the past two weeks with a peer who had been drinking.*

Experimentation is normal in adolescence, and in this country young people learn through the media and from others that drinking is a sign of maturity and strength. Beer commercials talk about gusto and living life in a joyful, daring way, while alcohol advertisements present an image of tough, sensuous femininity.

Young people look forward to the age when they can drink legally, a sign of "coming of age." But long before that time, they are exposed to beer and wine at parties and at their friends' houses. Often there is pressure from other youngsters to try alcohol, with the question of whether a youngster is "cool" enough to do it. Sometimes alcohol is used to ease the tension of sexual experimentation.

A teenage girl may use alcohol for one or several reasons, but she is most easily influenced when it is offered by friends. For many girls with limited social poise, alcohol is a way to ease entry into social groups. A girl may feel less conspicuous if she holds a beer can, even if she doesn't drink from it, and it is a sign that she is part of the group and belongs.

Sometimes the pressure for early sexual activity may lead a girl to alcohol as a way to feel more feminine and to hide or still her own vulnerable feelings. In an age when television videos present pictures of interpersonal exchanges involving insensitivity and brutality, particularly among rock group members, a young girl may use alcohol to feel stronger, less vulnerable, and more aggressive. Some teenagers do become more belligerent with alcohol use.

Almost all kids try drinking, and many get drunk at some point. Adolescence is a time of experimenting, learning, and sometimes making mistakes. But adolescent alcoholism involves far more than experimenting. Youngsters can gradually become physically dependent on and psychologically addicted to alcohol. Over a few months' time a youngster's relationship to herself and the world can change as she enters the early stages of the disease.

National Adolescent Student Health Survey: A Report on the Health of America's Youth (Oakland, Calif.: Third Party Publishing, 1988).

The problem is far more widespread than might be apparent, and alcohol, although popular, is a dangerous drug. The statistics on teenage suicides and fatal accidents, which often overlap, indicate alcohol as a primary causal factor.

Drinking for teenagers as well as for adults is a socially sanctioned aspect of group activities. It can be difficult to identify alcohol as a source of trouble in a girl's life, for often she hides it well from everyone, even herself. A simple measure is that if a girl would be better off without alcohol in her life but can't give it up, then drinking is a problem. The difference between drinking and alcoholism involves the level of dependency and individual control. An alcoholic cannot face the prospect of life without drinking, while a drinker feels merely disappointed. An alcoholic's life is frequently disrupted or made worse by alcohol, while alcohol has little effect on someone who drinks occasionally.

Alcoholism involves alcohol as the central motivator of many aspects of life. Everything becomes an excuse to drink, and settings are constantly sought that facilitate drinking. Life without alcohol is too dull, and other kinds of entertainment are ridiculed. Relationships, particularly with nonalcoholics, become confused and painful.

For teenagers, however, the pattern is somewhat different than for adults since alcohol addiction develops more rapidly and may take more varied forms. A girl may drink only occasionally, but when she does, she drinks excessively and seems unable to use her normal good judgment. This may occur at parties or as part of a sexual relationship, but the excessive drinking is confined to particular settings.

Another type of alcohol abuse occurs at particular times. A teenager may drink with friends on Fridays and continue at some level of intoxication through the weekend, but remain sober all week. Most alcoholics have predictable periods of sobriety and abstinence, and these periods lead others to believe that alcohol is not really a problem. When a teenage girl's problems continually have alcohol as a component, alcohol addiction should be suspected.

It can be difficult to recognize alcohol abuse when it is developing, because many of the symptoms are an excessive form of the normal signs of adolescence. A girl may become moody and irritable and seemingly nervous all the time. It may be that she can't settle down and stay with something, which shows up particularly in school work. She may often seem on the defensive and ready to argue.

As alcohol consumption increases, motivation for good grades is lost, attendance at classes becomes unreliable, homework assignments are ignored, and conflicts with teachers and school staff develop. Alternatively, a teenage girl may become increasingly quiet and withdrawn while using alcohol, preferring solitude to human contact. Depression is at the core of these behaviors, and past or present problems may take on great importance. There may be a concomitant loss of physical energy and pep with little enthusiasm for anything.

In the family of a teenage drinker, there are usually certain patterns that develop that have to do with avoiding awareness of feelings. Alcoholism develops when a girl wants to ignore her feelings and when there is complicity in this effort from those around her. Often parents are afraid to hear a girl's feelings, and apprehensive about how they will feel if confronted by them.

The following will be helpful:

1. Learn everything that you can about teenage alcoholism. Begin with the local library and develop an understanding of adolescent drinking patterns and why girls drink.

2. Begin to list your concerns about your daughter's behavior as it occurs, for example, when she misses her curfew and smells like beer, when she is picked up at school and smells heavily of perfume.

3. Put away mental attempts to soothe yourself by saying it's not really the drinking that is the problem and it's not really her fault that she's drinking. Drinking that repeatedly interferes with a youngster's life constitutes alcoholism. For alcoholism to be controlled, others must require the drinker to be responsible for her choice to drink and to accept the consequences.

4. Look at drinking and talking patterns in the family. How much do adults drink and how often? Are there also concerns about adult drinking? How do family members talk about their feelings and how often? Are love, anger, humor, sadness, and dependency freely expressed? Do fights get settled or do they drag on?

5. Discuss with an alcoholism counselor the utility of treat-

ment programs for your daughter and accept that treatment may require disruption of her life to improve it. Halfway houses and residential treatment facilities usually free a girl from her old patterns of drinking and help her to understand her own needs and meet them. In choosing any treatment plan, make sure that there is *understanding and experience in working with alcoholics and with adolescents*. Consider treatment help for the rest of the family, because everyone is affected when one person in a family is alcoholic.

6. See an alcoholism counselor *yourself* without your daughter, to evaluate whether there is a problem and to determine the effects of her behavior on *your* life. When one person in a family is alcoholic, the needs of the other members are often ignored.

7. It is important to have relationships and connections outside the family to distract and support you, so that only part of your attention is tied up with a teen girl's problems. Avoid social isolation, initiate new relationships, and revive old ones.

8. While caring deeply for a daughter's welfare, it is still possible to draw a line between where she begins and you end. Remember that all you really control is yourself; you can take good care of yourself, expending your energy on her behalf selectively and avoiding being used up by her problems.

9. Alcoholics Anonymous is a powerful source of information and help; there are branches of this organization in every community. Contact the local group and ask for help.

DRUG DEPENDENCY

Children encounter drugs in many places before they reach adolescence. Parents take medications for stress, depression, illness, and headaches; a girl may have been given medication for illness or psychological problems; television continuously touts pharmaceutical remedies; caffeine, nicotine, and alcohol are all widely available. The medical profession increasingly relies on chemical treatments for a wide range of ills, and by the time a girl reaches adolescence, the use of chemicals to solve problems is accepted as normal.

The assumption of drug education has been that if teenagers were provided adequate information about illicit drugs they would choose not to use them. The results of drug education programs have generally been disappointing because teenagers rarely use drugs out of ignorance.

Societal norms about responsible substance usage are difficult to identify, since many adults in our culture abuse drugs and deal irresponsibly with alcohol, even with full knowledge of the risks. New research shows that adults as well as adolescents can overestimate their ability to deal with drugs and that both are vulnerable to seeing themselves as invulnerable.

Estimates of drug usage by teens in America vary, but most experts assume that about four million American teenagers use drugs routinely, beginning in sixth or seventh grades. Often a chemical addiction is hidden by other problems that are more easily recognized or accepted, such as depression, eating disorders, learning disabilities, delinquency, or family problems.

All kinds of adolescents get involved with drugs, not just antisocial kids. An introduction to drug use can begin casually, frequently at a party and without a great deal of soul-searching or decision-making, where a youngster sips a little beer and tries pot because the other kids are watching. Teen girls often use drugs with alcohol, to ease social situations, and to be more comfortable with other teens, the same reasons that adults use these substances.

Since the signs of drug abuse are also the signs of other adolescent problems, it is unwise to conclude that a girl is involved with drugs if she begins to act differently and to accuse her. Far better to talk and listen at length and to become familiar with her life and feelings before making any assumptions.

It is wise to learn about drugs from talking with a daughter. What does she notice about drug usage in our culture? Why are some drugs more popular than others? How can schools help teens avoid drug addiction? Don't grill or cross-examine her, but show interest as an outsider in her age group and its practices.

Ask for her opinions and judgments. Should pot be legalized? Is it harmful? Is there a difference between those who use drugs socially and those who are dependent? Listen to the values being expressed and ask about her reasoning. Is she parroting what you want to hear, or is she speaking provocatively to "get your goat"? How does she feel about teens who do drugs? By accepting the fact that your daughter is exposed to drugs and can obtain them if she wishes, you can change the nature of the problem. It is no longer an issue of who is more powerful, but rather who is most wise in the decisions that affect her life.

It is important *briefly* to get across your own values and concerns. Teenage girls can rarely listen to more than three sentences in one hearing, so it is best to offer your wisdom sparingly. Otherwise, it is speech for your own ears. A powerful technique to use with a girl is to choose a sentence that will be influential both because it says something good about her, and because it shows some insight into her workings and to use it in many conversations, for example:

- "You're far too classy for drugs."

- "You're too much on the ball to let drugs take you down."

- "There are great things ahead for you."

Avoid talking about your own youth. Teenage girls want to feel special and unique, not a dull repetition of a parent. Most adolescent girls are primarily interested in themselves and bored with tales of a parent's youth. A wiser parent acts ignorant of all teen practices and continually asks for enlightenment. Better to point to what you know about her and what you see rather than trying to draw tedious parallels with your own life.

Seventeen percent of high school seniors have tried cocaine, and one in twenty-five report smoking marijuana every day. The use of marijuana, cocaine, and other drugs, however, has declined markedly for high school seniors over the past years, from a high in 1978 to a low in 1992. Drug usage for younger adolescents, while generally following the same patterns, shows more fluctuation.*

Using less dangerous drugs, such as beer or cigarettes, does not guarantee that a girl will move on to cocaine and liquor, but when girls use hard drugs, they usually begin with less potent substances. More commonly, drug use is part of a larger picture of peer dependence on substances for escape, entertainment, and bonding. Many girls will be able to be involved in

---

Monitoring the Future (Ann Arbor: University of Michigan, Institute for Social Research, 1986).

social usage with minimal effects, but some girls will become addicted and unable to control their consumption. The reasons why girls use drugs and why girls become addicted to drugs are distinctly different. Using drugs seems to be part of a pattern of social acceptance, in which youngsters participate in group rituals. In contrast, drug abuse results from a girl needing to numb herself against emotional upset. As she does so, she increasingly loses contact with the original peer group and moves deeper into the drug culture.

Adolescence, particularly for girls, is a difficult time. It is painful to agonize over acceptance from other kids, one's attractiveness, the yearning to belong and to feel a part of something, fears about one's future, tensions and problems within the family, school difficulties and failure, and the need for excitement and adventure. Sometimes a pill or joint offers an immediate solution and blots out anxiety and anguish.

Unfortunately, by blotting out the anguish, a girl is also blotting out the productive experimenting and searching for solutions that come from discomfort and that precede learning and growth. Studies of adults who used drugs heavily as adolescents show major gaps in the development of social competencies and life skills in this most formative time.

The most common drug for girls to abuse is nicotine. Forty-five percent of high school students smoke, the majority of them girls. Girls are also far more likely to use amphetamines, with urban usage rates generally higher than in rural areas. Both nicotine and the other amphetamines stimulate the central nervous system and produce feelings of energy and confidence. Their particular appeal for girls is that they initially decrease appetite and fatigue, but gaining this effect requires increasing dosages over time. When this use is abruptly discontinued, fatigue and depression (called "crashing") set in.

There are two types of drug usage, one that involves moderate or occasional use, and the other involving dependency and/or addiction. Unfortunately, most substance abuse prevention programs have assumed these were the same, failing to help the addicted and alienating the moderate users.

When a girl is unable to deal with her substance abuse, it can be useful to become involved in family counseling to discuss overall concerns and reach a consensus with a counselor.

Parents cannot hold themselves solely responsible for diagnosis and treatment decisions regarding substance abuse.

The following will help:

1. Start with yourself and other adults in the family, and consider how often you use chemicals to deal with problems. Drinks before dinner, aspirin or other painkillers once a week, and coffee, tea, or diet soda are all chemical solutions to problems of living. Consider life without pharmacological support and whether it would be livable.

American advertising routinely encourages chemical use as a way of improving the quality of life, and the enormous funds in the advertising industry produce irresistible appeals. Alcohol is still the most widely used drug, and for young people alcohol abuse and drug abuse are usually connected. Learning alcohol abuse at home through adult modeling often increases vulnerability to drug usage.

It is useful to examine the picture of life presented to youngsters, i.e., we work, love, play, rest, and attack problems, or we struggle through life's burdens and relieve ourselves by numbing or flying. A family may be full of natural highs or chronic lows, and parents vary in their capacity for creating healthy families. It will help to consider the rules in a family for coping with strong feelings and practical problems.

2. Drug abuse sometimes fills a spiritual need: a girl might be seeking for something outside her own experience that is uplifting, transcendent, and inspiring. Involve her in the family's traditional religious activities, or choose a spiritual outlet that suits current needs. Join in yourself.

3. Drug prevention programs that provide factual information about drugs or that attempt to frighten youngsters seem to have a great impact on adults, but relatively little influence on teenagers. Programs that teach social skills, particularly assertiveness with other kids, decision-making, anxiety reduction, and dealing with relationships show more promise in helping kids avoid drugs.

4. Distasteful as it may be, make a distinction between drug usage and drug abuse in conversations with a teenage girl. She surely knows the difference, as do her friends, and to fail to distinguish these two alienates her. To control drug use, it is important to teach and rehearse social skills and assertiveness so

that a girl can control the frequency and circumstances under which she chooses to use drugs, if at all. To refuse to share a marijuana joint at a fraternity party, for example, is particularly wise, given the statistics on acquaintance rape, but it may require some rehearsal for a girl to do so without self-consciousness. To teach a girl these skills and then to show strong confidence in her developing good judgment are very different from teaching her to "just say no," for it recognizes the social complexity of her situation.

5. For girls at risk for drug abuse, consider the broader spectrum of their psychological development and look at the sources of misery and hopelessness in their lives. Counseling is particularly important for a girl who is not happy to begin with. Address these problems before she begins to do her own form of therapy.

6. Avoid the twin perils of denial and hysteria in evaluating a teenage girl's involvement with drugs. For drug addicts it is common for families to refuse to recognize the seriousness of the problem and to reassure themselves with denial. The pattern of denial is part of a girl's illness since she fails to recognize that she no longer controls her use of drugs. For parents to acknowledge her loss of control and take action takes great courage. For those girls who use drugs but are not addicted to them, the approach needs to be distinguished from addiction treatment.

The growth of the drug abuser treatment industry has made help available to many who need it, but it has also led to errors in diagnosis and the lumping of addicts with users. Girls who use drugs and have problems need psychological treatment. Girls who are addicted or drug dependent require therapy with a specific substance abuse focus. To place a girl in a drug treatment program when she is not drug dependent or addicted is extremely risky; it can do incalculable damage to her developing self-esteem, judgment, peer relations, and family trust.

7. When treatment is required for drug addiction or dependency, longer treatment programs that involve families tend to have higher success rates. It is critical that a girl's schooling continue uninterrupted and that she remain with her peer group, unless there is no way for her to do so and remain drug free.

When teenage girls become involved with drug abuse, they are far more likely to shorten their adolescence by marriage, child-bearing, working, and generally cutting short their preparation for adult life, so it is important to enlarge their opportunity to develop life skills.

8. Areas of life outside drug dependency need attention in treating a youthful addict. Drug-free living is important, but it is not a goal in itself, and there must be much beyond to lure a girl into life. It is important to add dimensions to a girl's experiences that offer the chance for growth, adventure, and creativity and to provide highs that are addictive, as she discovers who she is and what she can offer, for drug abuse is always a retreat from the world.

EATING DISORDERS

All eating disorders, including anorexia nervosa, bulimia, and compulsive overeating, stem from psychological sources. They are caused by an obsessive concern with the self, with taking care of the self, with satisfying the self, thus leaving little energy for reciprocal relationships with others.

Social deficits are characteristic of teen girls who eat too much or too little, and eating disorders lead to further withdrawal from social contact. Because there is no one else to talk to, eating-disordered girls become increasingly isolated with their own thoughts, reducing life's complexity to what they eat and how they look.

The self-image of eating-disordered girls is usually one-dimensional and stereotyped, so that girls yearn for a generic rather than a unique identity. There is little room for individual personality, and there is a general belief that if the weight is right, there are no other problems in life. Correct weight means approval and being nurtured, a child's motivation that avoids all the complexity of adulthood. To be a woman in this view means to be taken care of extremely well, even luxuriously, rather than to be powerful and generative. Even if a girl is active in preparing for a job or career, her fantasy is still likely to be one of complete care by a parental partner. Anorexia, bulimia, and compulsive overeating share basic characteristics, although each has distinct manifestations in thought patterns and behavioral habits.

With eating disorders there may be other compulsive behaviors as well, for example, smoking, overspending, alcohol or other substance abuse. Because compulsive disorders generally disorganize thinking patterns as well as behavior, it becomes extremely difficult to persuade a girl to cooperate with treatment until she has reached levels of acute suffering, and even then she may stay in treatment only briefly.

Eating disorders constitute a form of pathological behavior, which cannot be changed merely by providing information. Eating-disordered teenage girls can usually recognize good nutrition and know what is required for weight control and health, but are unable to make it happen. The eating disorder produces behavior that is highly narcissistic, passive, socially isolated, and based on the belief that appearance and sensate pleasure constitute life satisfaction.

All eating disorders, including anorexia, bulimia, obesity, and mixed diagnoses, require professional intervention. Intervention typically involves a team of professionals including a physician, psychologist, nutritionist, and others, and treatment must be long-term. The beginning of the solution starts when a girl and her family accept that the eating disorder is more powerful than the girl and that a solution must begin outside of the family.

Eating disorders confine a girl to a life of emptiness, loneliness, and despair, and a parent's insistence on a solution is often the beginning of a way out for her.

Anorexia: The starvation disorder usually develops over three to six months as a girl gets hooked on denying herself and on the good feelings she has when denying the bad feelings. It is not the initial weight that constitutes the disorder, but rather the compulsive nature of weight loss and the obsessive focus on self-denial. Girls deny that they are too thin, no longer pretty, deprived of nutrients, weak, hungry, and obsessed with food. Anorexia fits in the larger category of obsessive-compulsive disorders with its rituals, repetitive thought patterns, and high anxiety levels.

Anorexia involves a difficulty in establishing independence

from the family. The language of the family tends to focus on food and appearance, with little discussion of feelings. Anorexic girls, having too much of a good thing (thinness), see themselves as special and unique because they have been able to achieve something that other girls only dream of and as a result can feel powerful and unique within the family.

Self-esteem is vested almost completely in appearance, and how a girl looks outweighs any other characteristics. The rest of the personality and character remain childlike and underdeveloped. The appearance of an anorexic is also rather childlike; she begins to look like a preadolescent girl, as her weight drops and curves disappear. A girl's talents and abilities are neglected since she is obsessed by how others see her.

The following will be helpful:

1. Consider whether a girl's way of talking about herself has changed since girlhood and whether she now speaks like a woman or a child. Examine the family's expectations for increasing self-reliance. In particular, notice whether she speaks for her own needs or depends on others to express her feelings.

2. Consider how a girl disagrees with the family and how frequently. As she develops her own personality, she is likely to have ideas sharply different from her family, which need to be expressed, but her habitual focus may instead be on attempting to please others.

3. Explore whether a girl clearly expresses her emotions or rather expects others to speak for her or know what she is feeling. It is normal for teenage girls to feel that no one understands them, but eating disorders are characterized by passivity rather than emotional activity in expressing oneself.

4. Seize the initiative and change the family language by talking about feelings, and in particular your feelings about her eating patterns.

5. Begin to think of a girl as responsible for herself and encourage responsible risk-taking.

Bulimia: A bulimic girl controls her impulsive urges to eat by acting on them compulsively and then reversing them by vomiting. This pattern creates increasing excesses; there is a joyless, compulsive binge and a penitent and releasing purge. Binging can be set off by any emotional discomfort, but after a time it takes on a life of its own, and a girl needs no reason to binge.

It is difficult for a person who eats normally to imagine the extent of a binge; listed below are the foods that one girl consumed twice daily in a binge (with some variation):

8 Twinkies	1 pint chocolate marshmallow ice cream
8 oz. cream cheese	4 bagels
6 eclairs	1 lb. chocolate chip cookies
8 slices toast	1 cup peanut butter
6 waffles	2 cups maple syrup

The pattern requires considerable vomiting (or laxatives, diuretics, exercise, or fasting) to clear the digestive tract and results in dental damage, damage to the esophagus, low potassium levels, electrolytic imbalance, cardiac arrhythmias, and a hunger level that requires increasingly larger meals to be satisfied. In addition, there is a gradual upward climb in weight.

Thinking patterns characteristic of both anorexia and bulimia involve dichotomous categories; things are either perfect or terrible, black or white. Compromise positions and moderate solutions are not acceptable, and there is much lurching between excesses, with constant attempts to regain balance. Decision-making is extremely difficult and often shows itself in endless procrastination.

The following will be helpful:

1. Be aware of a girl's eating patterns, particularly if they involve long stretches in the bathroom after large meals. The use of laxatives, diuretics, diet pills, emetics, or other medications for digestion should also be of concern. Sudden changes in dental health or the disappearance of large amounts of food from the kitchen should also raise questions.

2. Consider whether talk about food, weight, and appearance dominate the family language and how feelings like anger, resentment, sadness, guilt, anxiety, and fear are expressed.

3. Encourage moderation in solutions to problems and consider solutions as experiments that will be modified with new information.

4. Be prepared to change your relationship with a girl as she begins to move forward out of an eating disorder into more

adult thinking and behavior. Change your expectations of her, and recast your parental role to one of consultant rather than caretaker.

Obesity: Girls who are extremely overweight and whose weight handicaps their physical, emotional, and intellectual development are compulsive eaters. They are unable to regulate their nutritional intake and use food to numb feelings rather than to nourish the body. Similar to the anorexic, compulsive overeaters have an obsessive focus on self-gratification, with food and the good feelings associated with it used to avoid thinking about bad feelings. The disorder brings a sense of powerlessness and worthlessness and makes a girl feel that she must depend on others to identify her needs and to take care of her.

Family eating patterns often contribute to a girl's disorder, so that obese parents tend to have obese daughters. Disturbed feeding patterns in small girls are often accompanied by extreme dependency on parents, with overfeeding as a way to deal with difficult relationships. Hunger, tension, discomfort, and other feelings are not differentiated as a girl grows toward adolescence, and she does not learn to understand her own needs.

There is overprotection as well, with a failure to encourage boldness and adventure because of fear of what might befall a girl. Occasionally a traumatic event that restricts a girl, such as an accident or surgery, begins a pattern of disturbed eating and weight gain that may continue after the crisis abates. Childhood obesity often leads to even larger weight gains in adolescence, which are seen as indicating a lack of self-control.

Unfortunately, obesity meets with a great deal of social disapproval, and a girl who is noticeably overweight encounters painful social consequences. Sixteen percent of adolescents are obese and suffer socially and internally as a result. Body weight is predictive of adult status for girls, and girls who are thin are likely to raise their socioeconomic level, while girls who become heavy are likely to fall into a lower socioeconomic class.

In social settings overweight girls avoid activities that might focus on their weight, which are often those most important for controlling weight and appetite: swimming, running, and other sports. An overweight teenage girl is apt to dress in dark, baggy clothes, hoping to forget her shape, and to interpret reactions from others as rejection based on her appearance, which is sometimes accurate. In general she is likely to avoid active or daring pastimes in favor of passive and solitary activities.

Depression, accompanied by a high level of self-pity, grandiosity, or a sense of entitlement, is not uncommon with obese girls, making their social relationships even more troubled. The shame at lack of control over eating stirs guilt, remorse, and further preoccupation with food, along with the fantasy that she will "take off the weight" tomorrow.

1. When a girl begins to diet, be reserved in enthusiasm and help her to set realistic long- and short-term goals. Consider especially whether she is getting enough sleep, exercise, and help in changing old habits.

2. Explore with a girl what thinness would offer in the way of more friends, more romance, a better job, and better grades, and help her to move toward these goals now rather than at some future date. Avoid "If only..." thinking. Help a girl to give voice to her dreams and goals and to set ways to move toward them, no matter how small.

3. Support good health care, but avoid encouraging or supporting self-abuse or inadequate care in the form of poor nutrition, fasting, or unhealthy diets. Avoid fad diets or diets that rely on special food substances. Encourage instead those programs that focus on changes in thinking patterns and behavioral choices and that aim for gradual, long-term change.

4. Consider the family nutritional patterns and whether they support healthy nutrition or impulsive eating. Examine what in the surroundings supports or discourages good nutrition. Also examine activity patterns in the family, as well as styles of relating and exchanging conversation. Begin to change a girl's life by changing your life, in particular your eating, activity, and sleep patterns. If television is on for more than one hour daily, consider retiring all television sets to the basement for six months and interest yourself in more active pursuits.

5. Explore with an obese teenage girl what will give her a sense of power and competence in her daily activities. In particular, discuss with her the things she would like to try but is afraid to, for example, joining the ski club, running for class office, or looking for a job.

PREGNANCY

Attitudes toward teenage pregnancy have changed in recent decades, from the 1950s, when it was considered a social disgrace, to the 1980s, when it came to be seen as the result of a woman's choice to have a child as a single parent. About one million teenage girls between fifteen and nineteen — about one in ten — get pregnant each year, and half of these keep their babies. In earlier decades, if a girl became pregnant, she usually married the father, but teenage boys are not likely to marry a pregnant girlfriend in the 1990s.

What happens to the teen girls who have babies? When a girl gives birth in her teen years and raises her child, she is likely to become a high school dropout and end up on welfare.* She is also likely to have another child before age twenty. A teenage girl's decision about becoming a mother affects others as well as herself, most dramatically her parents, who become not only grandparents but also substitute parents.

Pregnancy itself is problematic for a girl. The discovery that she is pregnant is usually traumatic, and rarely her own choice. She is likely to feel frightened, overwhelmed, ashamed, and guilty, although her feelings will be powerfully affected by the reaction of her peer group. Half of all pregnancies occur in the first six months after a girl first has intercourse, and 20 percent occur as a result of the first experience. Girls become pregnant because they choose not to use birth control, and about half of all teens do not use contraceptives the first time they have sex.† Girls' reluctance to use contraceptives stems from spontaneous decisions to have sex, avoidance of responsibility, misunderstanding of fertility cycles, and fear of parental disapproval.

The changes in the body during early pregnancy can be unnerving to a girl who is just getting accustomed to a woman's body. Thoughts about gaining weight, looking pregnant, and labor and delivery usually frighten a teenage girl, who rarely has any understanding or preparation for these events. Girls rarely

---

*G. J. Duncan, *Years of Poverty, Years of Plenty* (Ann Arbor: University of Michigan, Institute for Social Research, 1984).

†J. Brooks-Gunn and F. Furstenberg, "Adolescent Sexual Behavior," *American Psychologist* 44, no. 2 (February 1989): 249–57.

understand the endless work and cumulative stress that go with mothering and the complex needs of young children.

The major anxiety for a pregnant teen is telling parents that she is pregnant. Some teenagers hide their pregnancy, relying on peers or a boyfriend for help and support. Parents may be aware that something disturbing is occurring in a girl's life, but she may make decisions without adult support or intervention.

Upon hearing that a daughter is pregnant, parents generally experience a range of reactions. They may be shocked that a daughter is old enough to conceive and carry a child, as well as surprised to realize that their child is sexually active. They may be angry at her for becoming pregnant, at the boy for his part in it, or at each other for inadequate parenting. There may also be guilt and shame at what they see as failure in their role as parents.

Pregnancy requires decisions and planning, which will be overwhelming for a teenager. It will be less profound for a very young teenage girl, who will have little understanding of the impact of her decisions and whose parents may dominate the process. For older girls, the responsibility will feel heavier since there is more cognizance of the long-term consequences.

The options in pregnancy are three: (1) to carry the child to term and raise it, either as a single parent or in a marriage, living with parents or on one's own; (2) to give the child up for adoption; or (3) to have an abortion. All of these choices involve stress and trauma, and there is no way to arrange an alternative that returns a girl to her original girlhood state.

Keeping the baby: In this pattern, a girl carries a child to term and gives birth, usually with the help of parents. If she remains single, the father of the baby may help out, both financially and emotionally, or he may withdraw. Parental help will be more critical if she is younger, and at very young ages, thirteen and fourteen, it is the grandmother who will provide the mothering to both a girl and her baby.

The drawbacks to this arrangement are the medical risks of early pregnancy and the stressing of an immature system, as well as the increased risk of birth defects. The baby enters a chaotic family system, with a mother who has not completed her own development, a grandmother in an ambiguous role, and no father.

For a teenage girl this is the least promising arrangement since the likelihood of her completing her education is small, the possibility for higher education is extremely limited, and her ability to support herself and her child is nonexistent. The likelihood of additional pregnancies also increases: in a recent study of teenage girls who gave birth, almost half were pregnant again within eighteen months of the birth.

Perhaps most significantly, a girl takes on a woman's responsibilities long before she has had time to grow and develop the skills that she needs to do so. For girls who have gone this route, there is often a chronic sense of inadequacy and guilt over not being able to meet standards that the society sets for mothers and women. Early childbearing is a strong predictor of long-term welfare dependency as well.

If a girl decides to raise a child while she is still a dependent, she is usually adding a child to her parent's household, since they will absorb most of the responsibility for supporting and caring for the youngster. This cannot be a decision that she makes alone because she is in effect laying out the course of their lives for several decades.

If a teenage girl marries, she gains some emotional and financial help, but not without costs. A young man who becomes a husband and father at the same time is not in a strong position to support emotionally and financially a wife and family since he has not had time to grow and prepare for adulthood. Marriage and parenting are demanding and require wisdom and maturity. By adding marriage to the demands on young people, their resources are stretched very thin.

Adoption: In this arrangement, a girl carries a child to term and then gives the child up when he or she is born, usually in the hospital. The baby is typically placed with a waiting couple, and the girl has no further contact. The drawbacks of this arrangement are that a girl often becomes attached to a baby during pregnancy and experiences a loss when she gives up the child. For the parents of a teenage girl as well, giving up a grandchild for adoption can be a traumatic experience. Adoption is currently not as popular an option as abortion or keeping a baby, but there are sometimes informal kin adoptions that keep the child in the same family while freeing the girl to continue with her development.

It is wise to outline with a girl what is required in the way of parenting to raise a healthy human being. A new mother needs financial, emotional, and other kinds of support, as does a child. If a mother is to work, she will need a good income to cover child care and a flexible job that will allow her to be with her child often, but particularly when he is sick. Parents need to be ready to give up financial freedom, social interests, schooling, romance, travel, and hobbies to minister to the needs of their child. In evaluating potential adoptive parents, adoption agencies expect such commitments. It is worthwhile to ask a girl to rate herself as a parent and to consider whether she would qualify as an adoptive parent.

Since there is no contact with the adopted baby after birth, a girl cannot be certain that her child will receive good care. Over the years this gives rise to fantasies that can be upsetting. Sometimes girls attribute depression or disappointment in later years to the decision to give up a baby and imagine that if they had not done so, then life would be much better. The decision becomes more important when a girl later marries and gives birth to children and experiences a fuller emotional response to motherhood.

Abortion: There are two types of abortions usually performed to terminate a pregnancy. In the first three months of pregnancy, the vacuum aspiration method is used, in which the uterus is emptied by a pump. In the fourth and fifth months, a dilation and evacuation procedure uses the same process but with larger instruments, general anesthesia, and hospitalization. Although abortion procedures are safe when performed by trained professionals, they are not without medical risk. Abortions after the fifth month are difficult to arrange and sometimes illegal. About 40 percent of teen pregnancies end in abortions.

Teens have more than one-quarter of the abortions performed in the U.S., and girls who choose abortion are generally educationally ambitious, high academic achievers, of higher socioeconomic status, and of limited religious affiliation. Recent research suggests that girls who choose abortion to terminate a pregnancy fare better than those who give birth.*

Although abortion is widespread, it can be a traumatic experience for a young girl. Emotional support, reassurance, and help are critically important.

The following will be helpful to a teenage girl making decisions about pregnancy:

1. Arrange for a standard laboratory pregnancy test to confirm a pregnancy, followed by a visit with an obstetrician. In a three-way meeting, discuss with the physician the girl's needs for medical care and the available options. Provide her as much information as possible about what is happening to her body, and work to dispel fearful misunderstandings.

2. Be supportive and reassure a girl that you love her and will help her. This is not a time to ask her to deal with your feelings or to help you feel better, no matter how strongly you might feel.

3. If a girl is considering raising the baby herself, arrange for her to baby-sit a friend's baby for a weekend, and spend the time with her, instructing her on how to care for the child. After the baby-sitting ends, set up a daily schedule with her that includes caring for the baby, school, work, and free time. Contrast this schedule with her current schedule. Figure out the cost of caring for a youngster and how much she will need to earn. Help her to lay out her plans for her life and examine where a baby fits into them.

4. Be *extremely realistic and clear* about what help you are able and willing to offer for the care of a daughter's child. Consider the question in the same way that you would if you were adopting a child from an agency.

5. If a girl is considering adoption, provide her as much information as possible about the process and care of the children involved. If possible, arrange for her to speak with adults who were raised by adoptive parents.

6. If a girl chooses abortion to terminate a pregnancy, make

---

*Steven A. Holmes, "Teen Age Study Hints Gains for Those Having Abortions," *New York Times*, January 25, 1990, C18.

sure that she has a thorough understanding of the procedure
and stay with her throughout.

7. Even though it may seem too late to be concerned about
teenage pregnancy, it is important to discuss carefully with a
girl her plans for future self-care, for a girl who has become
pregnant once as a teenager is likely to become pregnant again.

SEXUALLY TRANSMITTED DISEASE

Although education has been seen as the solution for most adolescent problems, the results of education about sexually transmitted disease have been disappointing. Teenage girls have the
highest national rates of gonorrhea, cyomegalovirus, chlamydia
cervicitis, and pelvic inflammatory disease of any age group,
excluding prostitutes and homosexuals.

Clearly, teaching about "safe sex" and "responsible sex" has
had about the same effect as teaching girls about the need to
clean their bedrooms. Most teenagers do not use condoms for
protection from disease, and since there are often no symptoms of sexually transmitted infections, many operate under the
assumption that they are disease-free and tell their partners so.

The problem lies partly in the increase in rates of sexual activity. In 1950, about 7 percent of females had intercourse by age
sixteen, a figure is now closer to 50 percent.* Girls generally experience early sex as part of social emergence rather than as part
of a passionate relationship. To a large extent, the norms of the
peer group determine a girl's involvement in sex.

It is estimated that one in seven teenagers has a sexually
transmitted disease†, and in the past three decades the incidence of gonorrhea has quadrupled among ten- to fourteen-
year-olds.‡ Because many sexually transmitted diseases go un-
diagnosed in girls until adulthood and because teens are often
reluctant to admit they are infected, teenage girls generally
assume that they and their partner are disease-free.

AIDS is the most feared of the sexually transmitted diseases

---

*Brooks-Gunn and Furstenberg, "Adolescent Sexual Behavior," 249–57.
†M. B. Sunnenblick, *The AIDS Epidemic: Sexual Behavior of Adolescents*, Smith College
Studies in Social Work 59, no. 1, 21–37.
‡National Center for Education in Maternal and Child Health, *The Health of
American Youth*, 1990.

and for good reason: there is no cure, there are no symptoms or external evidence in the early stages, and the progress of the disease is slow and painful. AIDS can be spread through deep kissing, oral sex, anal sex, intercourse, use of intravenous drug needles, and medical procedures that involve blood product transfer.

AIDS is most often spread through sexual contact, with the risk increasing with the number of partners. AIDS victims who die of the disease have generally been infected as teenagers and rarely are aware of their illness in the subsequent years, meaning that partners during the intervening years are vulnerable to infection.

Gonorrhea is a disease that has become widespread among teenagers, with about one-quarter of all cases occurring in teens. Teenage girls are frequently not aware of having the disease, since there are often no symptoms, although they may have post-menstrual abdominal pain. Gonorrhea is treatable with antibiotics, although the organism has become resistant to standard treatment, so good medical care is essential.

Genital herpes is caused by a virus similar to the one that causes cold sores on the lips. Blisters appear on a girl's sexual organs, and the infection is spread by contact with the blister. There is no cure for herpes, and there are recurrences throughout life. Genital herpes is related to increased incidence of cervical cancer and can be passed on to a baby during delivery.

Trichomoniasis is an infection characterized by smelly vaginal discharge and itching. There may also be parasites that remain in the urinary tract and continue to cause infection without symptoms. All sexual partners need to be treated, or they will continually reinfect one another after treatment.

Chlamydia is a disease of epidemic proportions in young females and is the major cause of pelvic inflammatory disease. It infects the vagina, cervix, fallopian tubes, and ovaries if untreated, but may show no symptoms. It is a frequent cause of adult sterility and ectopic pregnancy.

Pubic lice are tiny vermin that cling to the skin in the genital area, and lay eggs called nits. The hatching insects cause unbearable itching. A rash often accompanies the discomfort and may be assumed to be the cause of the discomfort, since the insects are too small to see. Sexual contact spreads the infestation.

The following will be helpful:

1. Although parents cannot prevent teen involvement in sexual activity, parental supervision decreases the frequency of sexual activity, and thus the risk of disease. Parents who offer their beach cottage to a girl and her friends for the week can assume far more exposure to sexual activity and disease than parents who join the girl and her friends for a week at the beach cottage.

2. Parents need to stop being afraid of being seen as moralistic and sexually inhibited. However a girl or the larger society interprets the expressed concern of parents about teen sexual activity, the disease risk remains the same. Parents need to give less thought to their own sensitivities and more attention to their daughter's vulnerability to infection. In the same way that she needs protection against crime, a girl needs protection from disease.

3. Communication with a teenage girl begins by showing interest and concern in her life and her choices. Most girls respond to genuine warmth, although family counseling is usually necessary to break down barriers where girls and their parents are in the habit of not communicating.

4. The only sure protection from sexually transmitted disease is abstinence from heavy petting, sexual intercourse, and other activities that involve bodily fluids. Although it is appealing to think of two teenagers exchanging sexual histories and reassuring each other about their health status, there is no way, barring medical examination and testing, that they can be positive of being disease-free even if they were mature enough to discuss fully their sexual attitudes and practices. Nor are they likely to be so socially skilled as to be sexually responsible. Condoms are an effective but not foolproof protection from infection.

5. If a girl is sexually active, insist on medical examination twice yearly for protection and treatment for infection. Do so without moralizing, and tell her you love her. Do not, however, give the impression that you are comfortable with her activity since this may provide a sense of false security that she is not at risk.

6. Explain sexually transmitted diseases, and help her to consider her own cleanliness as a source of safety. Most girls

would hesitate to share a toothbrush or tampon with someone else, and sharing sex introduces far greater risks.

NERVOUS BREAKDOWN

Many of the problems described in this and preceding chapters can be the outward manifestations of serious psychological problems in a teenage girl. Often they appear to be something different, symptoms of a bad or delinquent girl rather than of a seriously troubled girl.

When adults refer to a nervous breakdown, they are usually describing a disintegration of behavior and coping skills that seems to result from emotional sources. Sometimes the true source is a physical condition or illness that has not been diagnosed, for example, thyroid disease.

When a teenage girl has a nervous breakdown or a psychological crisis, she will be unable to proceed with life as usual and will have serious trouble with school, academic work, peer relations, daily self-care, and family routines. Generally parents are aware that something is wrong before it is clear what is happening. There may be a clear source of distress, for example, the death of a friend, from which a girl does not seem to recover, or there may be a minor problem that becomes increasingly severe.

Mental disturbance among adolescents afflicts about one in every fifteen youngsters and may show itself in a variety of ways. A girl may begin to demonstrate unusual behavior or say surprising or disturbing things. She may seem unhappy, tense, or anxious, or she may be apathetic and lethargic, with no energy for activities that used to excite her.

Her routines may become disrupted, and her sleeping and eating patterns may change. She may be irritable, easily angered, or tearful and may have difficulty in making choices or plans. Often these signs appear in healthy teens for brief periods, followed by a return to normal functioning. When they persist for more than two weeks, it is important to help her regain her balance.

Sometimes it is a girl's behavior that sends a message about her internal state. She may suddenly become reckless or confused and show surprisingly poor judgment that she later cannot recall or explain.

There are a number of adult psychological disorders that begin to emerge in adolescence, among them phobias, obsessive-compulsive disorder, and some forms of schizophrenia. Personality disorders usually begin to develop in this period, although they are often hard to distinguish from adolescent excesses and are usually not fully developed until adulthood.

Depressions and anxiety disorders are a problem in adolescence, and they may be overwhelming for a partially developed personality. A girl may become ashamed of her feelings and increasingly isolate herself rather than ask for help. The major concern with depression or anxiety, which are often interlocking, is the risk of suicide.

Often teenage girls suffer from more than one psychological disorder, making a clear diagnosis difficult. It is not uncommon, for example, for a girl to have a problem with anxiety and to be depressed as well.

The following will be helpful:

1. Arrange for a complete physical examination. Accompany a daughter and take a complete list of symptoms and observations that you can give to the physician before the examination.

2. Psychological evaluation by a trained clinician is essential in helping a girl return to normal functioning. Proceed with help even if she seems to regain her balance, since girls often learn to cover symptoms out of shame and a wish to maintain independence. The problems may have only been masked, with continued inner turbulence.

3. Psychotherapy is still the best treatment for emotional problems. It may take many forms, including group, individual, or family therapy, and may utilize techniques such as biofeedback, hypnosis, cognitive analysis, or other approaches. In all approaches, treatment is long-term and change is slow.

4. Some forms of psychological disorder are chronic and do not improve over time. They may be degenerative, in which case the aim of treatment is to slow the deterioration and to limit the damage of the illness. Schizophrenia, manic-depressive illness, and personality disorders are in this category.

5. The use of pharmacological treatments for psychological disorders has gained widespread popularity; clinicians increasingly justify such treatments as necessary to right "chemical imbalances." In a small percentage of cases, medication can

offer relief and help, and dramatic improvement. Far more common is the situation where there are high expectations of medication, followed by small improvement and general disappointment because of another experience of failure and little gain in personal understanding. Second opinions for medication treatments are appropriate.

6. It is most important to keep a teenage girl on track in life preparation through whatever crises befall her, so that her education and personal development continue uninterrupted.

Six

THE PARENT AS
SURVIVOR

TEENAGE GIRLS can have a great impact on the lives of those around them, and it is risky to allow too much to be contingent on the behavior of an adolescent female. Consider, for example, the plight of Henry VIII, king of England, who sought stability for himself and his kingdom in marriage. For his fifth wife he chose Catherine Howard, a pretty fifteen-year-old who had a bit of skill in arts and crafts and a great taste for adventure. Catherine, Henry's "rose without a thorn," had led a largely unsupervised life until she became queen to the irritable, overweight, fifty-year-old monarch. His great passion for her led him to make her grants of land and jewels and to persuade parliament to give her powers and privileges that made her virtually independent of the king, powers that no queen had ever possessed. A teenage girl unused to controls, Catherine's penchant for adventure led to amorous exchanges with several young courtiers at the palace, which made her the pawn of court intrigues. A brokenhearted Henry executed her before her seventeenth birthday, casting the kingdom once again into confusion.

Most teenage girls have considerably less impact on their surroundings than the youthful Queen Catherine, but parents can be deeply affected by the course of a girl's development and by the problems that develop. Sometimes the effect of turbulence is much greater for the parents than it is for the girl, and she seems more emotionally resilient in the face of disaster, or perhaps she is merely naive.

How can parents get through a girl's troublesome times without undue wear and tear? The key words here are "limit,"

"limit," and "limit," for in response to the expansiveness of teen girls, their wild behavioral variations and excessive emotional reactions, parents need to adhere to their own course and avoid being pulled into the emotional storms of these years. Restraining one's responses, constricting the intensity of one's feelings, concentrating on moderate approaches that gradually solve problems, all these are parent conservation responses. Adolescents have boundless energy for crises, but adults get used up in the drama of adolescence. When they are truly depleted, there is little energy left for real problem-solving.

Parents who understand that they can't do everything in the parental sphere focus only on a few things and choose priorities wisely. Their expectations of themselves are realistic, and they take a limited approach to what they can offer a teenage girl, without avoiding or denying her needs.

In these years, wise parents avoid becoming obsessed with a teen girl's problems and apportion their energy in a way that balances the focus on the girl with time for others, including themselves.

The following are worth keeping in mind as a way to achieve a healthy balance between oneself and the needs of a teen girl.

Parenthood is a time-limited job

It may not seem so when the going is rough and there are frustrations and continuing problems, but it is still true that the time available to teach a teenage girl is at most about nine years. If we delight in her and enjoy the experience, it is about nine years, and if we find it arduous and draining, it is still about nine years.

After adolescence, all of the concerns and problems do not magically straighten out, and a young woman in her twenties still has many mountains to climb. A parent's period of maximal influence is in the early teen years, and then the influence wanes. This is a relatively brief period, and only so much can be achieved. It is wise to use the time well, but with an understanding, particularly in the difficult moments, that parenting an adolescent is a short-term endeavor.

It is wise to respect the natural limits of the life stage and to avoid prolonging adolescence. When a girl uses higher education to delay adulthood or shares her parents' residence to avoid taking responsibility for herself, then adolescence is taking up space meant for young adulthood. No person can be adult while under a parent's care. To agree with a girl's claim that she cannot manage otherwise confirms her role as adolescent.

Parenthood must end so that a teenage girl can move on through the life sequence and so that parents can move on too. Parenthood is not an identity but is rather a temporary job. The active period of parental work is usually about fifteen years, following which there is only nominal parental activity. If the average adult lives for seventy-five years, this leaves about thirty-five years of adult life without the responsibilities of parenting.

The nonparenting sector of adulthood is a long period and more truly represents life as we know it. There are many ways to fill thirty-five years, and certainly routine daily chores and a job will make time pass quickly. It is worth asking, however, what makes for a good and full life for each of us. As a daughter's adolescence turns into her adulthood, there will seem to be empty spaces and gaps to fill. The experience may be felt as a loss, with hollow internal reverberations, or it may be seen as the opening of vistas and an invitation to new adventures and opportunities, paralleling the experience of a teenage girl.

Parent's memories of adolescence are poor references for decision-making

As we watch our children grow up, there is often a sense of nostalgia for our own youth, and memories and reminiscences are stirred. A mother in particular may feel a sense of familiarity with her daughter's experiences and a sense that they match hers.

Pride of authorship leads us to see the conclusions and deductions that we drew from our youthful experiences as true, and we have lived with them long enough for them to seem trustworthy. If we learned that going steady as a teenager leads to heartbreak and we have held this conclusion without revision for two decades, then it will take on the quality of a sacred truth, encompassing all of the pain and insight of our earlier years.

When we try to share our truths with a teenage daughter, it is unlikely that she will be receptive or even interested. She is busy testing out her own truths, and it is rare that a parent's agenda and a daughter's agenda coincide. Furthermore, most important things in life must be learned first hand, and there are few real vicarious learnings. The thrill of falling in love, the pain of a friend's betrayal, the results of pushing beyond one's limits must all be experienced and assimilated, and we cannot save a daughter from life with our wisdom. Nor should we, for it would deprive her of the richness and depth of a full spread of emotion and cognition and would stunt her growth. If we ask her to live life as a careful observer, relying on our experience for her learning, then we deprive her of the drama of participation and adventure.

It is grandiose to assume that our small learnings are worth casting in bronze and using as the basis for guiding another life. After all, we were her age when we formed our brilliant insights and conclusions, and who is to say that she cannot do better than we did?

We often have far less comprehension than we think ourselves to have, for our memories are edited to fit our beliefs. The surer we are that we understand adolescent experiences, the more likely we are to ignore what we observe, for we become ego-invested in defending our position. It is unlikely that we recall all of adolescence, in particular the confusion, shame, conflict, and self-doubt that go with the period. Instead, we may transfer our adult confusion, shame, conflict, and self-doubt to a daughter and empathize with feelings that she does not have.

Our experience with adolescence is limited to a nine-year period in our lives when we were on the inside of a transition. The teenage years may feel familiar, but this may mislead us and give us false confidence so that we ignore our current observations. Whatever we were in our adolescence, a daughter is a different person in a different age and has only a tangential relation to our memories of the time.

Limit your emotional investment in a teenage daughter

Many parents believe that boundless love for a youngster develops her self-esteem and growth. But love takes many forms, and in adolescence it is important to avoid yoking your sanity to a girl's behavior. When a teenage girl becomes central to an adult's emotional well-being, then love becomes problematical and adults need to protect themselves from frustration and pain by disengaging and avoiding involvement. It is wise for parents to limit their emotional reliance on a girl's behavior. She should be only one part of their life, with many other focal points as well. This allows us to invest our energy where we find it useful and to let the rest go.

This balancing occurs when we limit our exposure to an adolescent daughter. If she marries young and badly, for example, we can avoid listening to the quarrels and complaints and be cheerful and supportive in limited exchanges. We can avoid offering ourselves and our possessions in a way that depends on a girl's response. We may not, for example, let a careless daughter borrow books on our library card, because we foresee the nagging and fights that will ensue.

We can also limit our emotional investment by accepting that a teenage daughter is more or less a child, and that she will therefore often behave childishly. If we are always disappointed or angry because of her behavior, it is because we do not see her clearly. We can hope and believe that she will become a strong and capable woman, but this is quite different from insisting that she do so right now and assuming that she does not do so because of orneriness. Even schizophrenics are capable of periods of lucid thought and reasoning, but they remain psychotic.

If we rage and fume because of a teenage girl's behavior and demand that she be more mature, then we are blaming her for her childishness and rejecting what she is. While teaching helps us learn and move to higher behavior, punishment rarely does. We are also demanding that she behave maturely because we deserve better, and entitlement is always a childish justification.

To tolerate a teenage girl, with all her childishness and immaturity, is not an act of great patience, but is instead an acknowledgment of reality. It saves our energy and strength for those battles in which we can make a difference; it is akin to carrying an umbrella on a rainy day, rather than raging against the weather.

As a daughter grows out of adolescence, a parent who has loved and cared for her through these years may experience powerful feelings. No matter what the experience has been, the distancing that is part of this transition will be felt as a loss. Raising a teenage daughter involves feelings, behavior, and plans that are an important part of an adult's life, and rarely do these taper off without notice.

Reactions to loss include a sense of regret and lost opportunities, guilt for inadequacies, and failure for expectations not met. When we grieve for a friend who has died, there is always an awareness of the things we could have done or said. The ego is diminished and lessened when emotional losses occur, and the breaking of the connection between two people is felt as inadequacy. As a daughter moves into adulthood, there is likely to be a sense of loss as we give up the girl in exchange for the woman.

If we see parenthood as a time-limited venture, this feeling will be lessened somewhat, although we are still likely to search our souls or to defend our parenting defensively when the loss is registered. Our period of tutelage does end, and then a girl may feel far more distant from us and far less emotionally accessible. It is wise to plan for this time and to diversify one's emotional investments.

Avoid perfectionism

In looking at oneself as a parent or at one's daughter, it is wise to avoid thinking of what she or we could be and to use instead the standard of *good enough*.

This may feel like resignation to imperfection, which it certainly is if we are raising human beings. Adults are noticeably imperfect, and we all begin as imperfect teenagers, but imperfection does not necessarily doom us to an unfulfilled life. Rather it is the fear of risk-taking and the resistance to learning that doom us to an unfulfilled life.

But if risk-taking and learning are to proceed and give the

greatest benefit, then it is necessary to avoid the evaluations and judgments of the perfectionistic mind. It is wise to observe our conversation to notice how frequently criticism, ridicule, and negative evaluation creep in, for a judgmental attitude structures our speech habits. To see the world with a fault-finding eye is a habit that is learned and can be unlearned.

A judgmental eye is usually a critical eye, one that takes pleasure in pessimistic observations and predictions. When we need to find fault and see wrong, we are usually reassuring ourselves of our own goodness and power. Usually, this is the relief-giving exercise that is needed to offset the internal criticism which we level against ourselves. Judgmental people are always trying to mollify the internal dragon of a conscience that devours them by casting somebody else in. Sometimes these voices come from a parent's parents, whom that parent could never please as an adolescent.

Perfectionism in parenting suggests that there is a measure of success or failure in raising children, yet how do we judge the success of an individual life? At the very least, we wait until many years of adulthood have elapsed before judging whether a life has been well spent, and we certainly don't judge at the beginning if we are wise. If we are truly wise, we don't judge at all.

Many lives that begin with messy teen years reach a surprisingly successful adult peak, and many young lives that begin with great promise disintegrate. It might be best simply to offer kindness and guidance and to attribute the outcome of parenting to a youngster's abilities, proclivities, and deficits.

Much of the pressure parents feel to raise perfect children comes from peers, in this case, other parents raising teens who seem to have achieved high standards of success. In fear of peer criticism parents often pressure their own children to achieve in various ways. It takes a great deal of courage to be ourselves and to raise our children as we see fit, even though the popular wisdom may demand other than what we would choose.

To resist peer pressure in middle age, it is wise to cultivate an honest appreciation of ourselves and to notice our good points while forgiving our shortcomings.

It is also helpful to avoid thinking too far into the future and not imagine all the good or bad things that might happen to our daughter because of our choices. The future of the cosmos, after all, does not hinge on the way our daughter turns out. Teens and adults sometimes make unfortunate choices and bad judgments, but life goes on. What's more, life doesn't always give us what we want or what we feel we deserve, and there may be great disappointments in raising children, particularly if we want a great deal. But if there is love and our children are alive, then we have great wealth. We need to avoid greed and the belief that we are entitled to more.

Pay attention to your own adult life

Parents of teenage girls often feel used up, for all of their caring goes to nurture a young person, and there is little left over. If we asked secondary school teachers to work sixteen hours a day, seven days a week, they would quickly run out of steam, but parents often expect themselves to do so. It makes sense to conserve our energy by withdrawing at certain points to save ourselves for other pursuits, for no one can work continuously.

When parents give more than they have, no amount gratitude will restore the sense of balance in the parent-daughter relationship. And to remind ourselves that we were once children who received endlessly and gave little will not soothe an exploited parent.

Sometimes exhausted parents look to a daughter to restore their emotional reserves, forgetting that she is an immature organism barely able to care for herself. The nature of the parent-child relationship is one-way, the strong caring for the needy, and a reversal cannot occur for many years and after much maturing, if at all. A teenage girl's feelings are far too raw and youthful to deal with the seasoned and complex needs of adults.

Teenage girls need to learn good manners and caring habits, but they cannot be expected to act as mothers for a beleaguered parent. A girl's unfinished and unintegrated self demands her constant attention, and she will be able to give to others only briefly.

While parents serve as the foil against which a girl grows up, parents can begin to have their turn as a girl reaches maturity when they can consider their own needs more attentively.

As parents, adults are limited in who they can be, for their efforts often must focus on parenting. As the job ends, parents can begin to examine themselves to establish a broader identity. Like the layers of an onion, we can explore which parts of ourselves are temporary and optional and which are central to our image of ourselves as people. Parenting is one of these layers, but there are many others.

As we pay attention to adult life, one day at a time, parents can set goals, problem-solve, and develop skills that have no relation to parenting. This is living in the present rather than parenting, which always has an eye on the future. When we think about mortality and the need to use whatever time we have wisely, we begin to identify priorities in our lives and to act on them. In taking care of adult life, we insulate ourselves from the random emotional fluctuations of a teenage girl's life.

Plan for retirement

Just as living in the present insulates us from the fluctuations in a girl's life, planning for our retirement as parents helps us to separate our future from hers. For even if everything ends poorly and her adulthood is the worst imaginable, our lives can be what we make them and do not depend on her for fulfillment. We cannot wait to retire until a girl has turned out as we hoped, for then we are hostage to the pace of her growth and make her responsible for our life satisfaction.

Just as a teenage girl is on the brink of a new stage in her life, so also is a middle-aged parent about to deal with the departure of a youngster. A girl may have great self-doubt, little experience, limited judgment, and many deficiencies, and so does an adult on the brink of the second half of life. But to both of them comes the requirement for risk-taking and a graceful moving ahead.

Parent and daughter are not totally linked to each other, and a parent may do poorly in moving on while a daughter does well, or vice versa. The best that they offer each other is to make their own transition as successful as possible and to find a way to be eager about the future, without reference to each other. Neither human being has any greater intrinsic right to a happy life than the other. Even though a girl is younger, she should not absorb all of the adult's energy, for she is not that important.

Adults may be able to generate some of this eagerness by recalling the period when they first began to see life, in their own early adolescence, and to identify those stirring and energizing experiences that motivated them. The wildest dreams, the drive to jump out of bed on a Saturday morning, contain the unique images that form each person's perspective of the satisfying life.

The experience of being a parent serves as basic training for the rest of life. It teaches, generally through trial and error, all of the skills and cognitive habits that make for a satisfying lifespan. Wisdom, patience, planning, tolerance are all the result of many years of looking at what is best for younger, dependent ones.

Have a limited view of your own importance

When children are small, adults have enormous control over their behavior, which can make parents feel omnipotent and powerful enough to shape a youngster's future. As children become adolescents, the limits of adult power are clear, so that by the age of sixteen, when teens are often gone with friends in cars to places unknown for lengthy periods, it can feel as though a parent has no control whatsoever.

Children are always somewhat disappointing when they become adolescents, for the potential they had as children, when anything seemed possible, has now had a chance to manifest itself, and it becomes clear that they will be more ordinary than exceptional and that they will not achieve our wildest dreams.

Sigmund Freud believed that parents, and in particular mothers, were the major source of influence on psychological development, which might have been true in his case but has limited applicability in an age of mass communications. The effects of nation, neighborhood, siblings, innate talents and limitations, peers, and random events are at least as powerful as a parent's influence.

As a girl moves along in adolescence it is wise to see ourselves more as observers and less as directors and to allow her to take center stage in directing her behavior, with parents as loving consultants. The model of the driving instructor is most useful here: a girl learns to drive by having the instructor next to her and not in the driver's seat.

Sometimes a parent can offer little to a girl but compassion and caring, and this may feel truly inadequate if the situation is demanding. In the long term, compassion is a powerful teacher, forcing the focus onto the best interests of a girl and helping her to see herself clearly and without shame. Girls remember those who love them and internalize the voices to guide them.

Indeed, the most powerful control we have over a daughter is our love for her and our concern for her welfare, for these are rare and unique gifts. It may seem as though we have little influence, but this may be because we fail to use our most powerful influence, our love and concern.

At times modern psychology gives the impression that the complete technology for raising perfect children is readily available, but there is still great debate over what constitutes the best parenting practices. Even if one raises a healthy youngster, a great deal of what passes for mentally healthy behavior is unattractive. In any case, although psychology can offer help in childrearing, it cannot change the basics of personality or physiology.

In the same vein, it is wise to accept our own inadequacy in parenting. A girl wants the adventure and exhilaration of life, along with complete security, a package far beyond the power of any mortal to bestow. These needs drive a girl out into womanhood and, if she is lucky, will energize her all her life.

In one area, however, we have enormous power: the control of our own behavior. We cannot make others do anything, but we can shape our own behavior and direct it in ways we see fit. In directing our own behavior, we can have a great influence on a girl's vision of life and of herself.

Humility can seem like a surrender to a teenage girl, but it offers a parent enormous strength. By being humble we give up the need to prove that all of our rules are perfect or that our decisions are always best, for we become nothing more than fallible human beings.

We can insist on healthy choices for a girl, not because we deserve them or are entitled to them, but because we are committed to her welfare as we understand it. As parents our integrity demands that we do the best that we can, with no promise of reward, for parenting is not a bargain we strike with a child, stipulating that we will be good parents if she is a good daughter. We are entitled to nothing in raising children, although we may get a great deal from the experience. If we develop the habit of enjoying the pleasure and tolerating the difficulties, we can be much happier. Far more difficult is the road where false pride leads us to demand that we deserve such and such or that we shouldn't have to put up with such and such. We can set and enforce rules that are good for everyone without basing them on our rights as parents.

Much of a teenage girl's behavior is not contingent upon adults and, contrary to what parents sometimes think, is not done to spite or anger them. For most teenage girls, parents are about as important as plumbing, which is to say, they are usually invisible to her and of concern only when inadequate.

To keep a teenage daughter, let her go

There is always a degree of alienation as a girl experiences adolescence since she becomes a stranger to parents who have known her as a child, and she is now something else. What's more, most middle-aged parents have very few teenage friends. The concerns of the two ages are quite different, so that teenagers as a group may seem alien to parents. As she grows into adulthood there is likely to be more common ground with a daughter, but in the teen years adults will feel that their daughter has gone where they cannot go.

Even though there may be a great sense of familiarity, a teenage daughter is truly a stranger, for on the inside she thinks very differently from the way she did in the old relationship with her parents. It helps to notice this distinction and comment upon it, or a girl may have to make a point of setting herself apart from parents. Human personality is robust and asserts itself subtly or dramatically.

It is also useful to treat a teenage girl as a new acquaintance and find ways to share pleasures with her that can last over the decades of adulthood. Help her to convert herself to an adult in your life, one who can be happy and productive.